GW00758837

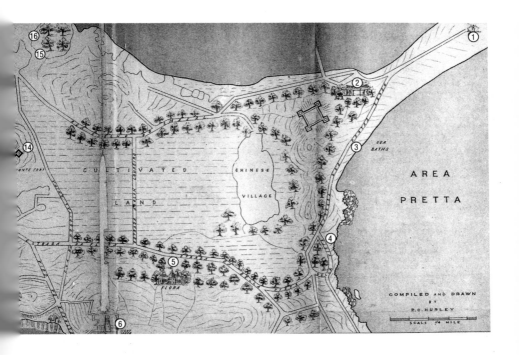

M A C A O :
MYSTERIOUS DECAY AND ROMANCE

MACAO:
Mysterious Decay and Romance

AN ANTHOLOGY
SELECTED AND EDITED BY

Donald Pittis and Susan J. Henders

HONG KONG
OXFORD UNIVERSITY PRESS
OXFORD   NEW YORK
1997

Oxford University Press
Oxford New York
Athens Auckland Bangkok Bogota Bombay
Buenos Aires Calcutta Cape Town Dar es Salaam
Delhi Florence Hong Kong Istanbul Karachi
Kuala Lumpur Madras Madrid Melbourne
Mexico City Nairobi Paris Singapore
Taipei Tokyo Toronto Warsaw
and associated companies in
Berlin Ibadan

Oxford is a trade mark of Oxford University Press

First published 1997
This impression (lowest digit)
1 3 5 7 9 10 8 6 4 2

Published in the United States
by Oxford University Press, New York

British Library Cataloguing in Publication Data
available

Library of Congress Cataloging-in-Publication Data
available

ISBN 0-19-590569-5

Printed in Hong Kong
Published by Oxford University Press (China) Ltd
18/F Warwick House, Taikoo Place, 979 King's Road,
Quarry Bay, Hong Kong

In memory of

Austin Coates (1922–1997)

That night the wind freshened; we made the land at early light, took a wild Chinese half naked pilot, passed the Lema and Ladrone Islands, and were requited at last for all the idle hours in the China Sea, by being obliged to shorten sail, and thus, with stretching canvas, we went flying into Macao Roads, and into anchorage.

OSMOND TIFFANY, Jr., 1849

ACKNOWLEDGEMENTS

This anthology would not have come about without the help of many people. We extend our special thanks to Renata Britton for her wise editorial advice; to Richard E. Strassberg for his new translation of Kong Shangren, 'Trying on Glasses'; to Professor C. R. Boxer for his translation of Fujiwara Tadazumi, 'The Worm-like Barbarians of Macao'; to Malcolm Watson for his translation of Zhang Rulin, 'Anchored off Ilha Verde: Arriving at Macao after the Morning Rice'; to Naomi Azrieli, François Blanc, Ken Chan, Elisabeth Köll, Rui Ramos, and Steve Tsang for their collaboration on other translations; and to Chan Cheung Wai, Gerald Lamoureux, Joanne Pawluk, François Soulard, and Adrienne Mong for their photographs.

We would like to thank the following people for giving generously of their time and expertise in other ways: Nigel Cameron, Filipe Nunes de Carvalho, Mary Child, the late Austin Coates, J. S. Cummins, Jens Meydam, David Faure, César Guillén Nuñez, Horatio F. Ozorio, Daniel Pires, Steve Tsang, and Barbara-Sue White.

We are grateful to the following institutions: the Bodleian Library, University of Oxford; the Hakluyt Society; the Instituto Cultural de Macau; the Instituto Português do Oriente; the School of Oriental and African Studies Library; and the Sociedade Portuguesa de Autores.

The publisher extends its thanks to the following individuals and institutions for their permission to reproduce or translate material protected by copyright: 'Macao' from W. H. Auden, *Collected Poems*, by W. H. Auden, copyright © 1945 and renewed 1973 by W. H. Auden, reproduced by permission of Faber and Faber Ltd. and Random House Inc.; 'Betty', 'Intercepted Letters', from 'Betty', *Intercepted Letters: A Mild Satire on Hongkong Society*, published by Kelly and Walsh, reproduced by permission of Kelly and Walsh; C. R. Boxer, 'The Worm-like Barbarians of Macao', from C. R. Boxer, *The Great Ship from Amacon*, published by Centro de Estudos Históricos Ultramarinos, and 'The Nine-year-old Heiress' and 'The Dutch Attack', from C. R. Boxer, *Fidalgos in the Far East, 1550–1770*, published by Martinus Nijhoff, all reproduced by permission of C. R. Boxer; Austin Coates, 'The Pensioner', from Austin Coates, *City of Broken Promises*, published by Oxford University Press, reproduced by permission of Austin Coates; C. H. Drage, 'One Murder, Four Deaths', from *Servants of the Dragon Throne, Being the Lives of Edward and Cecil Bowra*, published by Peter Dawnay, reproduced with permission of C. L. Drage and the other executors of the will of the late Comdr. C. H. Drage; Ian Fleming, 'Macao' from Ian Fleming, *Thrilling Cities*, published by Jonathan Cape, © Glidrose Productions Ltd. 1963, US copyright renewed 1992, reproduced by permission of Glidrose Publications Ltd.; quote from Ian Fleming in 'Introduction' from John Pearson, *A Life of Ian Fleming, Creator of James Bond*, published by Coronet Books and Hodder and Stoughton, reproduced by permission of John Pearson; Leila Hadley, 'The Wickedest City of the Far East', from Leila Hadley, *Give Me the World*, published by The Travel Book Club, reproduced by permission of Leila Hadley Luce; Gerald Locklin, 'phil lays down his saturday for his new friend' and 'he would've doubled the tip', from Gerald Locklin, *The Macao/Hong Kong Trip*, published by Tears in the Fence, reproduced by permission of Gerald Locklin; extract from Macao entry in Oxford English Dictionary (Second Edition) on Compact Disk, published by Oxford University Press, reproduced by permission of Oxford University Press; Camilo Pessanha, 'Desejos', from *Clepsidra e Outras Poemas de Camilo Pessanha*, João de Castro Osório, ed., published by Ediçoes Ática, translation by permission of Ediçoes Ática; Robert Shaplen, 'A Corner of the World', from Robert Shaplen, *A Corner of the World*, published by the Cresset Press, reproduced by permission of Peter Shaplen and the other executors of the estate of Robert Shaplen, with thanks to *The New Yorker Magazine*, the original publisher of the story; Frederic A. Silva, 'Macao is Roots', from Frederic A. Silva, *All Our Yesterdays*, published by Uniao Macaense Americana, reproduced by permission of Frederic A. Silva and Livros do Oriente; Manuel Teixeira, 'Bonnie and Clyde of Macao', from Manuel Teixeira, *Macau Durante A Guerra*, translation by permission of Manuel Teixeira.

ACKNOWLEDGEMENTS

The publisher would like to thank the following individuals and institutions for their permission to reproduce illustrations: endpapers map of Macao, reproduced by permission of the British Library; the photograph on page 241 reproduced by permission of Joanne Pawluk and Gerald Lamoureux; the photographs on pages 16, 88, 98, and 211 reproduced by permission of François Soulard; the photograph on page 108 reproduced by permission of Adrienne Mong; the illustrations on pages 169, 180, 205, and 206 reproduced by permission of the School of Oriental and African Studies Library; and the illustrations on pages 184 and 186 reproduced by permission of Sociedade de Geografia de Lisboa.

In some cases it has not been possible, despite every effort, to locate those with rights to material possibly still in copyright. The publisher would be glad to hear from anyone who holds such rights, in order that appropriate acknowledgement can be made in any future editions.

A NOTE ON SPELLING & PUNCTUATION

In almost all extracts that we discovered in the English language, we have been faithful to the original version, only occasionally altering spelling and punctuation to make an excerpt easier to understand. The subject of the anthology appears variously as 'Maccao', 'Macau', 'Hauo-king-gao', 'Ama ko', and so on, as in the originals. In introductions and our own translations, however, we have used the traditional English spelling of 'Macao' or, where appropriate, 'Aomen', the Chinese name for the city. Similarly, we have opted for the Portuguese spelling of 'Camões' except where the traditional English 'Camoens' was used in the original texts. We have used *pinyin* romanizations for most Chinese words in our introductions and translations.

CONTENTS

CONTENTS

xiii

CONTENTS

CONTENTS

CONTENTS

INTRODUCTION

In 1959, the British novelist Ian Fleming is said to have sat on a Macao balcony overlooking the Pearl River estuary and mused: 'I suppose a man could be happier here than anywhere else in the world.' He paused, sipped his drink, and gazed at the boats tacking up-river. 'For about a fortnight.'

Given that Fleming was a writer of thrillers, evidently prone to ennui, perhaps his comments could be taken as a compliment. Certainly others have found in Macau fascinations to last a lifetime. The oldest continuous European settlement on the China coast, it was once the greatest trading emporium in Asia and the staging post of the missions to Christianize China and Japan. A magnet to opulent merchants, it has been a haven for ruthless pirates, tormented poets, and legendary gangsters. A city where East and West met and mingled, it has its restless ghosts and sacred places. This anthology brings together a few of their stories.

Our first encounter with Macao was during the cold Chinese New Year of 1988. The persistent rattle of exploding firecrackers outside our hotel window made for sleepless nights, and the old city's maze of cobbled alleys, veiled and crumbling houses, and Lunar New Year crowds for hectic, but enchanting days. We have returned to the enclave many times since, each trip rewarding us with new discoveries of Macao's historical and cultural richness.

However, like all those who love the place, we have become increasingly concerned that the architectural remnants and other less tangible elements of that heritage are threatened. Today, Macao's cityscape is very much part of that massive construction site otherwise known as the Pearl River Delta. In 1999, the enclave reverts to the administration of the People's Republic of China. The end of four and a half centuries of Portuguese government and European settlement brings with it many changes, some long overdue, others deeply worrying.

This anthology is our contribution to efforts being made to preserve the enclave's past and share it with those who wish to look beyond Macao's overrun casinos and tourist sites. The book is by no means a documentary history and is far from comprehensive.

Rather, it provides a taste of what, to us, are the most interesting, riveting, and delicious tales of Macao and its people.

A settlement that has been the focus of interchange between Europe and China for so long necessarily accumulates an extensive written record in many languages found in books and papers strewn about the world's libraries, archives, and attics. Reading through some of the published legacy, we found some truly original writing, among it the poetry, travelogues, historical accounts, diaries, letters, short stories, novels, official papers, and journalism extracted on the pages of this book. A good many of the excerpts are several hundred years old, virtually all are from sources long out-of-print, and some of them are published in English for the first time.

Our selection is skewed. Pirates, gangsters, romantic heroes and heroines, gamblers, business tycoons, and opium smokers figure more prominently in its pages than the enclave's quieter residents. Bloody wars, police swoops, saintly miracles, and ghostly encounters dominate the tamer, but admittedly more typical, activities of everyday life. The voices of men are heard more than those of women. The views of opinionated outsiders—especially British and American writers with their own particular views—are more numerous than those of Macao's long-term residents, although we have also included selections translated from Chinese, Portuguese, French, Japanese, Dutch, and Spanish.

From today's vantage point, many of the opinions the writers express are unacceptably intolerant of those of other religions, cultures, races, sex, or station. We do not condone their ingrained bigotry any more than we excuse the bloodthirsty savagery that occurs in some of these tales, but both accurately reflect the life and times of those who passed through Macao—the first and last European territory on the China coast.

PART 1

THE DARK DAYS

A man sick of the world, worn out and disgusted with himself and every one else, would find Macao a home more suited to his palled tastes and jaded spirit than any other spot that I could name.

OSMOND TIFFANY, JR., 1849

Many writers have portrayed Macao as a quaint, mostly harmless backwater living quietly off the avails of petty human weakness. But for others, the enclave has been far from oblivious to the larger moral and political questions of the age. At no time was this more so than during the tragic years of World War II and its immediate aftermath. The fight against European Fascism and Japanese militarism, the struggle between Communists and anti-Communists, and the contest to define the parameters of the post-war order all spilled into Macao.

Before the conflict, Portugal had come under the autocratic control of António Salazar, whose repressive police state was friendly to Nazi Germany and Fascist Italy. When war broke out Portugal declared itself neutral. Macao became the only place in the Far East where a European flag still flew, however tenuously, as the Japanese army swept through China, capturing Hong Kong in December 1941 and virtually surrounding the enclave.

Macao was overwhelmed with refugees. Several countries had spies resident there. Gangsters, often under Japanese military protection, took advantage of the chaos and the desperate hunger of so many. There was disease, starvation, and rumours of a black market in human flesh. And, after Japan's surrender, war continued between Chinese Communists and Nationalists.

1

MACAO

W. H. AUDEN

The poet, W. H. Auden, travelled to Macao in 1938 only a few months after Shanghai had fallen to the Japanese. One suspects that Auden heard the ghostly rattle of those distant guns as he walked the streets of Macao, a city that to him seemed unconnected with the anguish of war. Yet the horrific battles already raging in Northern China would soon engulf the south and seep into the enclave itself.

A weed from Catholic Europe, it took root
Between the yellow mountains and the sea,
And bore these gay stone houses like a fruit
And grew on China imperceptibly.

Rococo images of Saint and Saviour
Promise her gamblers fortunes when they die;
Churches beside the brothels testify
That faith can pardon natural behaviour.

This city of indulgence need not fear
The major sins by which the heart is killed,
And governments and men are torn to pieces:

Religious clocks will strike; the childish vices
Will safeguard the low virtues of the child
And nothing serious can happen here.

2

THE BONNIE AND CLYDE OF MACAO

MANUEL TEIXEIRA

Father Manuel Teixeira might disagree with Auden's impressions. A well-known Macao historian and Jesuit priest, Teixeira lived in the enclave throughout the war. While acknowledging that Macao escaped the worst of the calamity, his memory is haunted by the starving refugee children who begged in the streets and the criminals who preyed on a population hostage to Japanese goodwill. Some of the worst of these were the rice racketeers, Wong Kong Kit and his spouse.

Wong Kong Kit was the real 'Clyde' of Macao during the Second World War. He had a sidekick in his wife and Madam 'Bonnie', an illustrious seamstress whose cruel hands gripped two revolvers instead of embroidery needles. She could shoot as well with her left hand as her right.

These two oriental gangsters appeared as if by magic at our border. They established their 'Bonnie and Clyde' firm under the superintendency of the Japanese gendarmerie on Avenida do Coronel Mesquita, where Chü Tak Kei lives today. And what a firm, Holy God! Two lunatic types, schizophrenics with hereditary defects. There were sandbags on the veranda, a terrace with mounted machine guns, and a uniformed sentinel at the garden gate.

Their business was espionage, pressuring the Portuguese government, and, above all, controlling all the rice imported from China so as to levy a 'tax' on it. And what methods those racketeers used! Wong travelled through the street in two cars with eight men armed with Mauser pistols and revolvers of no less than .38

3

calibre. And he had the support of the commander of the Japanese gendarmerie, Colonel Sarva, and his assistant Yamaguchi. . . .

The Japanese controlled Southern China, although Chinese Nationalist guerrillas managed to annoy the occupiers here and there. The department in control of rice was in the southern city of Canton. The department's branch in Macao was under the control of the Japanese gendarmerie and had Wong Kong Kit at its head. This *imperium in imperio* naturally caused friction, which occurred almost daily.

I remember how many times, upon leaving the house, I had to turn back because the streets were blocked with sandbags and barbwire. There would be a rattle of machine guns and a victim would fall dead in a pool of blood, knocked down by an agent of Wong Kong Kit.

The police were soon on the scene . . . but they were in a difficult situation. Macao had become a refuge for the wildest people. They all brought their political loyalties and even changed their colours when convenient. There were Japanese, Germans, English, Americans, pro-Chiang Kai-shek Chinese, and Chinese who were pro-Wong Kong Kit, the puppet of the Japanese.

The game had rules. Every time a member of one faction was killed, a member of the same rank of the other faction would have to be killed. So, if a Chinese Colonel was assassinated, a Japanese Colonel had to be assassinated too. In the face of this, the independence of Macao was endangered at various times, threatened by the fury of the Japanese, who had Asia under their thumb. . . .

The Assassination of a Smuggler

Rice is the basic foodstuff among the Chinese. The Macao government had to feed 500,000 mouths, so it tried to secure the precious cereal by any and all methods. It bought the grain at more than $100.00 per pico and sold it through the Import Regulatory Commission for only $70.00. Some private shops sold it for as much as $300.00 to $400.00 per pico.

Macao's police commander, Captain Ribeiro da Cunha, planned an original system for importing rice from China and getting around Wong's racket. In essence, he co-operated with the

4

smugglers, assuring them that the government would buy all their rice so that they did not have to pay Wong Kong Kit. Putting this plan into execution, he started to protect three smuggler brothers by the name of Wong Cheong, Wong K'an, and Wong Sam, of whom only the last is still alive.

Besides his headquarters on Avenida Horta e Costa, Wong Kong Kit had a branch in the Grand Hotel Kuok Chai in room number 410. It was there that he imprisoned and interrogated the rice importers, forcing them to pay up. As the three Wong brothers did not, they went onto Wong Kong Kit's black list along with Dr Pedro José Lobo, who was the Governor's assistant, Captain Ribeiro da Cunha, Commissioner Pinto de Morais, and others.

Times were bad for everyone, including the government, whose own money only circulated in Macao and which obviously had neither Chinese or Japanese currency. Therefore, it paid the importers in a very original form, only justified by the wickedness of the times.

The three Wongs worked intimately together. In exchange for their rice, the Macao government gave them arms for the guerrillas who fought the Japanese in the Nam-tau-van and Pak-chiu regions. They got a rifle for each 34 picos of polished rice. All the old rifles and pieces of the gunboat *Pátria* gradually went in this way. Gasoline, the cannons of Macao's old forts, and even the contents of the forts were also carried off to Japan to pay for favours granted to Macao. Only extreme necessity can justify this, and Macao was in such a predicament.

Wong Kong Kit did not tolerate for long that trio that paid him nothing. One fine day when Wong K'an carried a cargo of rice in his boat, he was assaulted near Macao, barbarously slaughtered with all of his crew. Not even the infirm were spared. This was the price he paid for his dedication to Macao.

The Assassination of Fernando Rodrigues

Ribeiro da Cunha scored a great triumph by seducing the secretary of Wong Kong Kit into becoming a double agent. From that time, the secretary regularly passed information to the police concerning the day and hour when rice was due to arrive at the various quays in Macao. As a result, the police would invariably be there a half hour before the agents of Wong Kong Kit, depriving him of his opportunity to levy the tariff.

One of the rice merchants was Fernando de Senna Fernandes Rodrigues. He imported the grain from Chinese territory, using smugglers to get it to Macao. Wong Kong Kit sent the merchant a warning to stop his business. Fernando Rodrigues disregarded the warning. The police had information that something was being plotted against Fernando Rodrigues and offered him a bodyguard. However, Fernando Rodrigues never showed fear and was something of a celebrity for the brawling and shooting that had almost landed him a sentence of banishment to Timor. He refused the help of the police, only ordering that the door of his house (the current Pousada) on Praia Grande be grated with iron bars. He continued with his rice trade.

Three months later there was a great brawl over some rice on the quays in front of the current Palace of Distribution. Fernando Rodrigues was attending to the unloading of some of the grain when two agents of Wong Kong Kit presented themselves to claim it.

'The rice is ours,' one of them said.

'It is mine and very much mine,' bellowed Fernando. The agent went away with his face punched in and a bloody nose.

Two months later, on 9 July 1945, Fernando Rodrigues went with his daughters Alina and Norma to the funeral of Dr Wong. Afterwards, they were going down Rua do Cemitério when, arriving at the corner of the high school (today the Delegation of Health in Tap-Seac), they were fired at by an assassin. On seeing her father bleeding, Alina threw herself in front of him. Several bullets perforated her intestines, leaving her hanging between life and death. Norma, the stronger daughter, grabbed the collar of the assassin's coat. He fired the last bullets from his revolver into her.

Some high school students chased after the gunman, who ran breathlessly towards the headquarters of Wong Kong Kit. He hurled his revolver into the garden of a private building on Estrada Adolfo Loureiro, making it easier for him to run. . . .

I was visiting at the S. Rafael Hospital at that time and, from the window of a top-floor room, saw a trail of blood on the esplanade. I ran to the ground floor and found Fernando Rodrigues already dead. I administered the extreme unction (under condition), then attended to Norma, who immediately made her last confession. From there, I ran to the S. Janário Hospital, where Alina had been taken. She also made her last confession and asked me insistently to attend to her father and not abandon him. Alina hung between life and death for several days. She only knew of her father's death once she was out of danger. . . .

Meanwhile, Wong Kong Kit had his uniformed guard at the door of his house, but Captain Cunha posted a permanent guard in front of the same house and installed a telephone in a tree. It was this guard—no. 38, a Portuguese refugee from Shanghai—who caught Fernando Rodrigues's assassin when he tried to enter the lair. . . .

The Assassination of the Japanese Consul

Macao should be grateful to the memory of Fukui, who was Japanese consul here during the war. An elegant diplomat, he was intelligent and good-hearted. Fukui immediately perceived that Wong's firm, under the black wing of Colonel Sarva, resorted to criminal expedients to run its dirty, vile business. He not only frustrated the evil intrigues of Wong and Sarva, but resolved many cases in Macao's favour by appealing directly to Japan. Sarva's orders came from there, so he had to submit. But he wanted to get rid of this hindrance once and for all.

The consul lived on Calçada do Gaio and left the house on foot every day. One fine day, upon arriving at the Entrada da Vitória a little below his house he fell, pierced by the bullets of a hit man in Sarva's pay.

I perfectly remember the anxiety that we felt at that time! 'The consul assassinated? By whom?' we all wondered. Naturally, by Chinese nationalists, many assumed. 'It is the end of Macao,' everyone said. We lived anxious days, but nothing happened. Sarva let out that it was agents of Chiang Kai-shek, but he took no action against them. In the end, the Japanese resolved the case quietly amongst themselves, and we came out safe and sound from one more squall. . . .

A Visit to the Hospital

Wong Kong Kit and his wife were the greatest criminals in Macao. The terror they inspired and the protection of the Japanese military they enjoyed made them untouchable. But Ribeiro da Cunha feared no one. He resolved to confront the tiger.

Cunha used to make police swoops in various parts of Macao, during which he would block the prohibited zones with barbwire and machine guns. One fine day he set out to capture the chief gangsters—the illusive Wong and his consort in marriage and crime. The two frequently went to China in a car, armed to the teeth and followed by another car with well-equipped bodyguards. Cunha knew they usually returned between 10 o'clock and midday. He declared the area extending from the Porta do Cerco to the city a prohibited zone precisely when the two tigers were due to return to Macao.

This is what happened.

The police ordered them to stop. The gangsters, who judged themselves untouchable and never took notice of the police, drove on unperturbed. The police opened fire. Their Excellencies did not stop. Cunha ordered his officers to shoot to kill. The driver of Wong Kong Kit's car fell dead, Wong's arm and leg were grazed by bullets, and the calf of his consort's leg was torn apart. The eight bodyguards abandoned their car and ran away, although the police managed to capture two or three of them.

Wong Kong Kit looked like a little lamb bleating. His wife, to the contrary, growled like a tiger, she was so upset by her husband's crying. Both ended up in the hospital, where some agents of Colonel Sarva's appeared, demanding that the gangsters be taken to China for treatment by Japanese doctors.

Then it was the turn of the police. Pedro Lobo is the man of the hour. He is the guy who knows oriental psychology better than anyone (he was oriental, after all), the one who resolves all situations. Lobo had no arms nor men, but he held trump cards superior to all: an oriental patience, fine diplomacy, convincing words, gold, and port. The offer of some dozens of bottles of this precious liquid, some little slaps on the back when his guests were drunk enough, and all barriers fell. Lobo said 'Yes', the governor responded 'Amen,' and off went the wounded and their wounds to China with no reprisals against their firm. They returned to Macao cured.

The war was nearing its end. The police received orders not to let that assassin leave Macao again. . . .

Save Yourself if You Can

The first atomic bomb fell on Hiroshima, marking the beginning of the end. The world was stupefied, Japan trembled, and Emperor Hirohito took steps towards peace. In Macao, we heard muffled rumours here and there.

The second atomic bomb fell. It was every man for himself. Confusion reigned in the general headquarters of Colonel Sarva and Wong Kong Kit. They burnt papers. There were movements of baggage and people as each one tried to escape. Their consciences accused them of countless barbarities: they were only concerned with saving their own skin. There was a coming and going of cars through the Porta do Cerco. . . .

The police were alerted and ordered to stop the departure of the protagonist of the tragedy, the infamous Wong. Suitcases and packing cases were searched, as were the passengers of cars. But in the confusion some big packing cases passed through without inspection. Within one of these was the macabre Wong, reduced to a simple piece of unidentified luggage. That was how he saved himself. But this baggage, this dead weight, this encased mummy was going to make the news again.

9

In fact, the scoundrel soon appeared in Lapa, where he robbed five big fishing boats, three of them carrying polished rice. He put his people on board and all their possessions, which were numerous. Among these were ten cases of empty beer bottles stuffed with Hong Kong currency and 47 catties of gold. He was no fool that clever rogue! . . . There he was chief of Lapa, dominating all of the island up to the Porta do Cerco. His reign will be very ephemeral.

It was 15 August 1945. With the unconditional surrender of Japan, humanity could breath once again. Ever since the Sino-Japanese War erupted in 1937, Macao had been a vast concentration camp from which no one could leave without falling into the hands of the Japanese, the soldiers of Wang Jingwei [head of the Japanese puppet government in Nanjing] or the anti-Japanese guerrillas. I had such an experience myself. I was on a fluvial excursion to Ilha Verde and, passing near a big lorcha, saw that it had a lifeboat and asked the crew whether they wanted to sell it. It was wartime and one sold everything. They asked for only 15 patacas, which I immediately paid and took the little boat away with me. I took it on various excursions to Lapa and Ilha Verde, inviting colleagues to come along. The last trip was to Lapa. We were four priests: one Chinese Jesuit, one American priest, another Macanese, and me.

We had stopped by a pool of crystal water to eat oranges when, suddenly, three Wang Jingwei supporters descended the mountain. They had no uniforms and were shabbily dressed. Their faces were evil. They greeted us amiably: 'These foreign devils came here to poison the water. Take them prisoner and confiscate their boat.'

The Chinese Jesuit argued with them, saying that we came in peace, only intended well towards the Chinese, and ran the Chinese College of S. José.

After much parley they finally said, 'Fine. They can go, but confiscate the boat.'

We pointed out that we could not return to Macao without a boat. The Macanese priest, getting impatient, said to me, 'Father Teixeira, let's go kill them and bury them in the sand, and that's it!' I had already burst out laughing when those three ragamuffins had given us permission to go back to Macao without a boat. Now I laughed even louder at the bragging of this swashbuckling Macanese.

In the end, they let us go, boat and all. It was the last time that I was served by my poor little boat. When the Japanese bombarded and invaded Lapa, thousands of refugees escaped to Macao. I surrendered my little boat for the evacuation of refugees and never heard tell of it again.

The Tragic End of an Assassin

The police had to get their hands on Wong Kong Kit, the terror of Macao and murderer of so many people. But no one knew where he was. Pinto Morais was charged with finding out. From September to December 1945, he inquired all over Hong Kong for information about the bandit's whereabouts.

He finally discovered that Wong was on the island of Sá-Ü-Chong west of Hong Kong with 100 armed men. Morais knew that that particular zone was under the control of the Communist General Chang Sang, whose soldiers were guerrillas. Moreover, he learned that Wong, having nowhere else to go, planned to link up with the general and his men. Wong's secretary, the double agent, told them that his boss had built a cement tank on the island and hidden his fortune inside.

The general was informed of everything. In particular, he was told that Macao was only interested in the criminal—and that he could keep Wong's fortune. This awoke the general's greed. He promised to help the Macao police capture the bandit.

The plan was as follows. The general would visit the island on a predetermined day and hold a big banquet to celebrate his alliance with Wong. Wine would flow copiously. Then when Wong's men were intoxicated, the general's guerrillas would take their weapons.

Sometime during Morais' travels between Hong Kong and Macao . . . Major Hall-Caine of British military intelligence had learned what was up. Therefore, when Morais arrived in Hong Kong, Hall-Caine was waiting for him at the dock. As the British were also interested in Wong's capture, Morais asked Y. C. Leung to provide him with facilities in Hong Kong. Leung had worked for British intelligence in Macao and now served the British in Hong Kong. It was not difficult for him to arrange a launch and crew for Morais to go out to the island to capture Wong. The

11

British planned to seize the gangster when the launch returned to Hong Kong and to try him as a war criminal.

Morais had already patrolled the island in a fishing boat to observe Wong's position. The gangster lived on a hillside in a thatched hut partly constructed with the walls of a ruined house. His men lived at the base of the hill.

As there was no coal in Macao, the police had to fuel the launch with firewood. It went so slowly it took twelve hours to get to Hong Kong and another twelve to reach Sá-Ü-Chong. Morais took eight agents, disguised and equipped with light weapons and three machine guns. One was Cortiço Pais, another Artur dos Santos (Cascais), and the rest energetic Chinese. They took on firewood and water in Hong Kong. Hall-Caine once again told them to deliver Wong to Hong Kong afterwards.

When Morais arrived at the island on 4 December 1945 he did not know whether the general had fulfilled his promise to get the men drunk. However, he decided to attack at 6 a.m. Locating the thatched hut, they opened fire and ordered Wong and his men to surrender as they were surrounded. Wong thought he was encircled by British troops and gave himself up with his eight companions. Confusion reigned at the base of the hill below. Wong's men looked for their weapons, but could not find them. After taking the gang to the launch, Morais sailed for Hong Kong. But before arriving, he made a square enclosure out of firewood. He put the men, who had already been tied up, inside and covered them with the wood.

When Hall-Caine met the launch at the quay, Morais told him he had arranged for Wong to hand himself over at the Kowloon frontier the following week. With that, Hall-Caine invited Morais for lunch, and Morais asked him for men to guard the launch against intruders. The British major agreed. Thus, although unaware of it, the chief of intelligence was to guard the man that he had made so much effort to hunt. He had the fish in his hands, but let it slip away.

Morais asked Hall-Caine to accompany him to the telegraph office before going to lunch. There Morais telegraphed Captain Cunha: 'I did not get anything.' According to prior arrangement, this meant that the operation had succeeded and Wong taken prisoner. On seeing the telegram, Hall-Caine—who knew Portuguese—rubbed his hands with glee, anticipating nabbing

Wong at the Kowloon frontier and making the necessary preparations.

Morais came back to Macao with his rich catch. On the outward journey as on the return, the antediluvian launch, so senile and decrepit with its hull covered in patches, had frequently refused to budge. It was a burst pipe here, a loose patch there, a thousand and one accidents. New patches and new rags were brought to tamp the holes and staunch the liquid seeping from the boat's pustules.

In Macao, a police van waited to take the illustrious guests to Police Command on Rua Central. Six of the prisoners were handed over to China, who treated them as they deserved. The double-agent secretary—who had provided all of the information about the island and the treasure—was compensated and freed.

On being questioned, Wong said that he would forego interrogation and instead presented an account of all he had done in Macao. But, rather than the normal sort of account, he composed a novel based on his life ending with a song set to music of his own composition and entitled, 'Farewell to Life'. Captain Cunha took this novel away with him. It is a pity that he has never published it. Someone who saw the song and played it on the piano told me that it was really sad.

A week later, Morais went to Hong Kong and Hall-Caine was on the quay. 'You played a trick on me,' he said with a smile. Morais told Hall-Caine that Wong had to be taken to Macao first. However, if the British wanted him, they could ask for his extradition. As Wong belonged to the Japanese secret service, the British and Americans were naturally interested in the criminal. Hall-Caine warned that Wong's friends and backers might try to abduct him, so urged Morais to guard him well.

It was thought best to transfer him from Porta do Cerco to Police Station No. 4. But would he arrive there or be lost en route? Wong's destiny was decided. He himself had already sung his *adeus* to life.

Wong was put into a police van with four armed agents. Upon arriving at Estrada Adolfo Loureiro an agent opened the van and invited him out. Wong alighted and was cut down by Morais and Cascais.

The curtain fell. A report on the affair was drawn up and then shelved: 'Ah! The scoundrel. He tried to escape!'

3

A CORNER OF THE WORLD

ROBERT SHAPLEN

With the surrender of Japan, the peninsula became a tiny theatre in the emerging Cold War, with sympathizers of both the Chinese Communists and the Nationalist Generalissimo Chiang Kai-shek jostling for influence. For the local Portuguese establishment, the anti-communist struggle was part of an ongoing crusade against godlessness and social disorder. This ominous portrayal of the moral dilemmas of post-war Macao is taken from a short story by the American writer Robert Shaplen. The story first appeared as articles in The New Yorker Magazine, *where Shaplen was a staff author for more than thirty years.*

Shaplen covered the Pacific theatre of the war for Newsweek, *staying on in the region afterward. His own introduction to the story explains something of the real-life events that inspired this disturbing fictional tale.*

Wherever you went in the East, people talked about Macao as a place of sin and revelry, but you didn't really start hearing the facts until you reached Hong Kong. They were fabulous, all right, the stories you heard. During the war one way to escape to Free China was to get smuggled to Macao first, and then make arrangements with the local pirates for the rest of the trip. The pirates figured heavily in most of the tales. But it wasn't until you got to Macao yourself and the initial impact of its old European charm wore off that you realized what it was. I

14

remember the Governor's secretary in the marble house used both as an office and a residence. He was very cordial and took great pains to emphasize the sense of order in the colony. When I spoke about the press he was full of patience for my lack of comprehension. 'You have the Anglo-Saxon conception of such freedoms,' was what he said. 'We have our own conception, and we find it more successful. Who can say which one of us is right?' . . .

When after the end of the war Dr Georg Richter took the steamer from Hong Kong to Macao, he told himself he would never leave. There was no place he wanted to go or that would, for that matter, welcome him. America, perhaps—but he was not inclined to line up with thousands of fellow refugees, to wait for limitless months for the promised visa, to have the visa become his life and being, the terrible talisman of more flight and escape.

For ten years Dr Richter had been escaping. He had escaped first from Germany, and then, gradually and painfully, from his memories of Germany. In Shanghai, one cold dreadful winter of the early war, he had escaped death from pneumonia. Later, in Canton, and then in Hong Kong, he had narrowly escaped hanging when the Japanese discovered he was both a Jew and an Allied spy; at the war's end he was hiding in the Kwantung [Guangdong] village hut of a loyal 'Chungking' family. In all his time in China Dr Richter had seldom escaped poverty, and frequently he had faced its end-product, starvation. His wife was dead, he was weak from wandering and sickness, he felt unable to minister for himself, let alone for others. With what little he had left he had come to Macao because there, he thought, he would not be bothered. He was fifty-two and he had been living in the Portuguese colony for more than a year.

From the first he had been strangely pacified, and, mocking himself, he called it age and decay. For many weeks he had refrained from looking even at the censored Portuguese newspaper, which he could scarcely comprehend anyway, or at the English-language papers the ships brought over from Hong Kong. He was done with it—with all of it. Too often, and for too long, he had sacrificed medicine for politics, and his own health and safety for dreams that had betrayed him. From Vienna and Berlin to

15

Shanghai and Canton, it had been the same—and then it had brought him to the Chinese peasant's hut, fleeing once more, squatting at midnight in a mud field with dysentery, his guts drained and aching and the whole long war's despair in his fever-clouded eyes; he crawled back to Hong Kong, a stranger.

As the months in Macao passed he regained his strength. The enthusiasm, he insisted, he had laid aside for good. But he did not mind listening; it was amusing sometimes to engage the outworn ideas of the colony's main citizens who called on him as a German man of science (they did not know he was a Jew) when they were ill. In the filigreed homes on the waterfront or high on the hill beyond it, Dr Richter sipped their mellow port and let them talk. 'We are a sensible people,' they would tell him. 'Premier Salazar has found the true way. We are the world's last remaining democratic aristocracy.' And Dr Richter smiled as he drank their toasts. When he walked home at night through the cobblestoned streets, past the ancient churches and the iron-railed houses

mirroring a dead Europe, he could hear the faint clatter from the gambling parlours below, off the Avenida Almeida Ribeiro. Perhaps, if it were not too late, he would meet a quiet pair of nuns at dusk, on their way back from the Chinese mission, their shrouded figures gliding softly past the cracked yellow walls, and he would bid them good-evening, still smiling, and receive in return their reflected vision of God. This, then, was what he was finally to have—a petty fascist's benevolent wine, the cold, pale smile of a nun, and his own belated nirvana.

It was, all of it, a lovely anachronism, and Dr Georg Richter whispered to himself that it was all he wanted.

On mornings such as this, when the weather was fine, he liked to stroll along the docks and the inner harbour and into the sections for the Chinese poor. From here he could look across the peninsula head to the Chinese mainland. It gave him a certain satisfaction to gaze upon what he had escaped. . . .

He was walking back through the near-noon heat when he came to the small street that led to the electric works. He remembered hearing about the strike the afternoon before, at the home of one of his Portuguese patients, a match manufacturer. The man had said, so matter-of-factly that it had passed Dr Richter by (the words came back to him now), that 'we've told the police not to hold off any more.'

There was a crowd in front of the iron gate of the company. As he approached, Dr Richter heard a collective shout and then a mass sigh. The crowd split and, all in a moment, as if it were done purposely for him, the doctor saw a man run out, his arms raised supplicatingly, and then the downstroke of the club, the white contorted grimace of the Portuguese policeman, and the look of puzzled vacancy on the man's face as he went down, his arms dead and his body a heap before it struck the ground. The policeman straightened, aware of what he had done, and a naked glimmer of fright danced across his eyes. Then he looked out at the mob, walked a few steps and waved his stick as if to disperse it. It was a matter of seconds before the crowd came to life. The men surged forward, there was a whistle blown, shrill, then muffled, and as he stood a few yards away, Dr Richter felt his own eyes blur and his brain whirl back. As a witness in a court he would have been useless; he would only have remembered what he had seen long years ago.

He heard a voice at his side. Half-mesmerized, Dr Richter slowly turned his head. There was a young American in khaki beside him, an officer—he glimpsed the silver flash on one shirt lapel. In response to Dr Richter's uncomprehending stare, the man spoke again.

'What is it—a walkout?' he asked, but Dr Richter was already looking beyond him, to the corner, where more dark-uniformed figures were running. The whistles had begun again and they seemed to be exploding out of swollen cheeks in otherwise featureless faces, while from inside the gate came the deeper wail of the company's stack. This time Dr Richter closed his eyes. He heard the flat brutal snap of blows, and the shouts, and above them—or was it below?—the slow words of the lieutenant; 'This must be the electrical company. They told me there might be a strike.'

17

The young man's voice sounded like those of other young Americans Dr Richter had heard, almost toneless, without inflection. 'Yes,' the doctor finally answered, his eyes still shut. 'They want more money. The inflation gets worse.'

The fighting had stopped. A car drew up and, quickly, three of the Chinese workers were thrown in. The crowd moved away, disintegrating before the whirling clubs of the police reinforcements. The company whistle gave a last sonorous blast and its wisp of white steam dribbled off into the blue sky. The street was quiet. Inside the gate the door of a small brick house opened and a Portuguese in white trousers and shirt walked slowly across the yard. He stood by the gate and nervously drummed his fingers against the bars. A few feet in front, curved and limp on the curb, lay the strike leader who had tried to placate the policeman and had been the first hit. The Portuguese drew a cigarette from his shirt pocket.

Across the street, in the shade of a high wall, Dr Richter hesitated. He felt peculiarly trapped. The young American officer was looking over at the factory compound, as if appraising it. The doctor gently braced himself against the wall and then moved forward. He went across the road and bent down on one knee where the man was lying. Carefully, he turned him over and wiped the blood from his face with a handkerchief he drew from his jacket pocket. The man was a half-caste, part Portuguese, part Chinese. His shirt was torn and his breast was bare and smeared with blood. There was a crooked gash on his forehead from which the blood still ran. Dr Richter felt his pulse; it was slow but firm. He looked up for the first time at the Portuguese inside the gate.

'He is hurt,' the doctor said.

'Obviously,' the Portuguese replied, without removing the cigarette from between his thin lips.

'Perhaps we could bring him inside?' the doctor said. 'There must be water inside to wash him with.'

The Portuguese said nothing. The doctor paused a moment, stood up, bent down again and observed the man's half-open eyes. Then he looked back through the bars of the gate.

'I am Dr Richter,' he said. 'Dr Georg Richter, a physician, you see.'

The man in the yard shrugged. He flicked the cigarette out past Dr Richter's head. The American officer walked over to where the doctor was kneeling and stared down at the unconscious figure.

'Is he badly hurt?' the American asked.

'He has a concussion perhaps,' the doctor said. 'There is also some shock. It is to be expected, of course. In such affairs. . . .' He left the sentence unfinished.

The Portuguese rattled the lock of the gate as he examined it and then turned toward the brick house. As he went up the steps he looked back into the street. Dr Richter lifted his head at the same moment and the two men regarded each other through the shimmer of sun as through a sheet of yellow gauze. Then the Portuguese opened the door and went inside. Dr Richter could still see him moving about, a dark shadow; without knowing, he felt certain the man would go directly to a telephone.

The American was also looking. His mouth had acquired a sudden firmness. 'Some bastard,' he said.

In the gutter the eyelids of the half-caste flickered, and in his own body, still kneeling in the heat, Dr Richter felt a nervous quiver. A queer sense of frustration rose from the base of his stomach; with it, even worse, was a feeling he recognised but tried not to identify. But he knew what it was: it was fear, a very special kind of fear that had to do with old reprisals.

He stood up again, briefly dizzy, and with his sleeve wiped the perspiration from his face. The American was still standing beside him.

'What can you do with him?' the American asked, glancing down.

'We must get him out of the sun,' the doctor said.

'Where?' inquired the officer, and he bent down to take the man's feet.

Dr Richter looked around. The Chinese hospital was half a mile away.

'We can take him to my house,' he declared at length.

They managed the bottom of the street, the wounded man sack-heavy and still not conscious, although he had begun softly to moan through his oblivion. Below, in the shade, the doctor motioned to set the body down. There was a public pump nearby and the doctor rinsed his face and hands and washed the handkerchief with which he had wiped away the man's blood. Then he cleaned the man's face, removing the blood where it had dried. He thought it strange the area was so deserted. The police had done their job well. The few people who passed in the dust hardly looked at them. Dr Richter wondered if the other strikers realized that one of them had been left behind in the gutter. Probably not; it had all happened so fast. Yet there was something macabre about the way men regarded life and death in the East, as if they were never really to be considered apart. In religion, it was the same as in violence.

The lieutenant had lit a cigarette and offered Dr Richter one. The doctor shook his head and then changed his mind.

'It's a tough load,' the American said. 'Might as well. Is it far to go?'

The doctor looked up toward the old Monte Fortress and the ruins of St. Paul. He pointed. 'My house is there below,' he said. 'Only another three hundred yards.'

'I could get a ricksha.'

Dr Richter considered for a moment and then he said, 'No, that would not be good. Under the circumstances, I do not think so.' The circumstances, of course, concerned himself as much as the man on the ground. So much had changed in the last hour that Dr Richter was only beginning to comprehend the significance of his morning's walk; but he was certain that something had come to an end. It had begun when he had moved from the wall to the gutter by the company gate, and when he had looked into the eyes of the Portuguese in the white shirt he had known it for sure (he remembered now that he had seen the man before, at some party on the hill). The rush of fright and fugitive helplessness he had felt while kneeling by the curb had been no positive physical thing, spelling out impending danger. But Dr Richter knew it was already more than that: another dream was about to betray him; the rest hardly mattered.

The wounded man stirred and for the first time his eyes opened to cloudy awareness. The doctor bathed his face and wrists again, and presently, with the help of the American, he got the man to sit up and then to stand supported between them. In this fashion, with the man's arms around their shoulders and his feet dragging, they reached the doctor's house.

The doctor put the patient in the bedroom. There was, he thought, a mild concussion. He determined to let the man rest, and he administered a sedative. He would have to decide later what to do with him, but for the present sleep was essential. He changed his clothes and went back inside. The lieutenant lay on the couch, a drink on the floor alongside.

'Ah, I am glad you are resting,' the doctor said. 'You would like a shower?' The lieutenant declined.

The doctor poured himself a drink and set it down. 'I must thank you for your help,' he said. 'Alone it would have been impossible.'

For a moment the lieutenant said nothing. Then he took a fresh cigarette and sat up as he lit it. He looked at Dr Richter through the smoke, squinted and tilted his head in the peculiar way Dr Richter remembered in other Americans, with a certain loose jauntiness.

'You sort of stuck your neck out, didn't you?' the lieutenant said.

Dr Richter laughed. 'I do not understand,' he said.

'Look,' the lieutenant said, 'I wouldn't have helped if I hadn't known that much.'

'Yes,' the doctor replied. 'I suppose I should have realized. That is also very American.'

'What are you, a German?'

Dr Richter introduced himself. The lieutenant's name was Robert Gordon. He had come to Macao the night before. 'They gave me a few days' rest,' he said. 'I always wanted to see the place before going home.'

In the time immediately after the war the British had sent men over from Hong Kong for recuperative leave in Macao, and at that time the Americans had come also, on their own. But in recent months there had been no Americans at all, at least none that Dr Richter had noticed, although he supposed there were civilians by now, who came to visit the gambling parlours.

'Will you have lunch?' he asked. Lieutenant Gordon said yes and the doctor went to tell the houseboy. When he came back he filled the two glasses. 'Everyone drinks too much,' he said, 'myself as well.'

'It's a solution,' Gordon said. 'Why do you do it?'

'I am a refugee in more ways than one,' Dr Richter replied. 'But I exaggerate, it is really not so bad.'

'Does it happen often, the way it did this morning?' the lieutenant asked.

'No, not so often. The Portuguese are—very careful. They do not allow it. It is a sin, you see, to strike. It is a democratic weakness, a cultural *faux pas.*'

'Would you say it was spontaneous? I mean—well, justified?'

'I do not understand your point,' Dr Richter said.

'I mean do you think there are Communists responsible?'

Dr Richter coughed. It was difficult, sometimes, to talk to these people, to anticipate their unappeased directness. And yet, he supposed, from the standpoint of Lieutenant Gordon—and from his own as well, perhaps—it was a sensible enough question. But it was primarily this bluntness that set him off. For a moment Dr Richter's mind went back again, far back to the days before Hitler, when there had been time to be both bohemian and doctrinaire, or when he and his friends had at least thought there was time.

'It is hard to talk about, without knowing the facts,' he finally replied. 'Of course, what you say, what you imply, may well be true. This is a very hard place, here, to understand. There is Chinese intrigue, and Portuguese intrigue as well. It is a place of conflicts inside conflicts, and treacheries inside treacheries. But the strike of course must be justified.' He paused to catch his own words and thoughts.

The lieutenant's voice was strangely soft. 'Yes,' he said. 'The poor bastards must be having it tough. Either way, they're apt to get it in the neck.'

The Chinese came in from the kitchen with sandwiches and a bottle of wine. Dr Richter motioned his guest to the table. They were silent as the doctor drew the cork.

'Tell me about yourself,' the lieutenant said, as he started to eat. 'What brought you here?'

'It is a long story,' Dr Richter laughed. 'It is not worth telling, you know.' But he was glad the lieutenant had asked. 'I have a divided allegiance, you see,' he said. 'I have gone two different directions and I have made a total circle.'

'It starts with Hitler?' Gordon said.

'No,' said the doctor. 'Hitler only drew the circle.'

The lieutenant went on eating sandwiches and drinking wine while the doctor talked. Not since he had first come to China had Dr Richter engaged in such a conscious process of recall. He spoke as if his time were running out and the man across the table held some invisible cosmic stopwatch against him. He spoke tenderly and dramatically of his early days in Germany when he had been an active Socialist, of the easy commingling of *gemütlichkeit* and parliamentary debate, even during the after-war bitterness, of the creeping fear that had come into their lives as the doctor and his Social Democratic friends were pulled under by the twin waves of red and black.

'We were fools, I suppose,' the doctor said. 'We should have realized sooner. . . . So, because I am a Jew, I came away almost at once—to China. Eventually, of course, it would have been the same if I had been only an intellectual, or a doctor only, without a religion.'

'And in Shanghai?' Gordon said.

'Shanghai was full of such foreign pilgrims as myself,' Dr Richter said. 'We were pilgrims in reality, searching for our own souls. If we had had something beyond our despair and defeat to bring, we might at least have been tributaries, as long before, but even that compensation was taken away. We lived all together, in a heap, in a place called Hongkew—but, of course, you must know it—and it was bad enough before the Japanese came, before 1937. Afterwards, it was an Oriental ghetto.'

'Your divided allegiance,' the lieutenant asked, 'how did that develop?'

The doctor smiled as he put his wineglass down.

'A man does many things he never dreams of,' he said, 'especially when it is a matter of starvation or death. In one way, there was a brilliant cynicism, a wonderful trick, to what happened in my own case. You see, in Germany I had been a doctor dissatisfied with being a doctor alone. So I took part in politics. In China, where to be an intellectual is enough, traditionally above politics or medicine, I found myself prostituting my scientific knowledge for the aid of the jungle-fascists. In running away, I had only put my head further into the jaws of the beast.'

'But you became a fighter again?'

'Yes, eventually, out of shame perhaps, or as in a forced fever, to escape a new illness. When you have been condemned at the point of an Oriental sword, to commit an abortion on a Japanese general's German mistress, your illness becomes a madness. There is nothing left but flight from such nightmare, at any risk, death, dismemberment, anything at all. I was fortunate. I managed to escape. . . .'

23

'If you had the sort of experience with the Chinese that I did,' said the lieutenant, 'there must have been moments, even then, that made it seem pretty futile.'

'There were many such moments,' Dr Richter said. 'Yet, if I may be permitted, if you will pardon my saying it, your American soldier has much yet to learn about the world, about this part of the world in particular.'

Lieutenant Gordon looked up and his eyes met the doctor's. For a moment, neither of them said anything more. Then, unexpectedly for Dr Richter, the lieutenant laughed.

'Okay,' he said, 'I guess I know what you mean. I suppose it takes a guy like you who's had it from both ends to come up with sympathy. I didn't mean it that way—the way maybe you've heard it, about the "wogs" and the "slopes" and all that.'

'You meant it from the standpoint of your American efficiency?' It was Dr Richter's turn to smile. 'Ah, there it was difficult, I am aware. I was not ever in Chungking, or with the armies in the provinces. I was with peasants in villages here and there, and sometimes in Hong Kong or Canton. Even the British agents, when I met them, they were not "British". They were "wogs".'

'So then you came to Macao?'

'That has been my latest escape,' the doctor said. 'It has been successful, you know, up to now.'

'How about these people here?' Lieutenant Gordon asked. He liked the doctor but the remark about Americans, he felt, gave him licence. 'Do you actually like following the bastards of the world around?'

Dr Richter got up from the table and went to the window which looked out on the crooked cobblestones that sloped off into the main part of the colony. It was quiet in the street and in the house, so quiet he thought he could hear the beating of his heart through the oppressiveness of the heat. And, once again, he was conscious of having arrived at another ending.

'I know,' he said, 'I know, I have no answer, except—I was tired, and sick as well. It is a difficult thing, when you have been committed to wandering, to know where to stop. The alternatives are not always many.'

Behind him, in the room, he heard Lieutenant Gordon get up and then the sound of a match being lit. There was a painful emptiness now, a void. Dr Richter did not want to move; he felt a burning in his eyes, and he did not want to see the expression on Lieutenant Gordon's face. He knew why the lieutenant had asked the question, and he believed the lieutenant now wished he hadn't. But he did not actually mind, for he was already involved in the new net of his own introspection. The lieutenant had meant no harm, and had he not, besides, helped with the half-caste?

He saw a girl come along the street, searching out house numbers, and at once he knew who she must be. She looked more Portuguese than Chinese and she wore a faded print dress. Ten yards away she glanced up and saw the doctor just as he was about to call her. He waved instead and pointed to the door. A few moments later she was with them in the room.

'Is he here? How is he?' she asked, and she almost whispered. 'You are Dr Richter?' She had looked first at the lieutenant, noticing his uniform, and then at the doctor. The uniform had frightened her, before she recognized it.

'Yes, your—he is your father?—is inside.' Dr Richter replied. 'You need not be afraid.' He motioned his hand at Gordon. 'You see, there is a friend of liberty with us.'

The girl remained standing in the centre of the floor. Her expression had none of the brooding passivity or frequent hostility of pure Chinese in the presence of foreigners.

'They told me,' she said, and she spoke a little louder than before. 'They saw you take him away.'

'Who was that?' the doctor asked.

'When the police came we went away, but there were some who saw what you did. They came to tell me at my house. My mother is worried. She is crying still.'

The doctor got up and beckoned to the girl. Together they went into the other room. The man lay asleep, breathing deeply. But his face was reposed and, laying a hand on his forehead, Dr Richter noted the fever had gone down. The girl moved forward as if to touch her father, but the doctor waved her back. They went out again.

'We must let him sleep,' he said. 'He will be all right, but I think we will keep him here tonight. Tomorrow we can bring him home.'

She was silent for a moment as she summoned her words. 'You are very good,' she said at length. 'It is very kind of you. I do not see why you have wanted. . . .' She let the sentence drift off.

'I am a doctor,' he said. 'It is as simple as that. There was nobody

25

to bring water even.'

'We were frightened,' the girl said. 'The police forced us to run. We did not realize. We would have soon come back.'

'Of course,' the doctor answered.

The girl moved toward the door as Lieutenant Gordon asked, 'How's it going? The strike, I mean?'

She hesitated before replying. 'It is the first strike since the war,' she said. 'They are strong. They do not give us permission. But if we do nothing, it will be the same always. There is not enough to live on today.'

Now the doctor spoke softly, as if only to himself, as if that particular idea had just reached him. 'That is so,' he said, 'there is not enough.'

'How long has it lasted?' Gordon asked.

'About one week already,' the girl said.

'Tomorrow in the morning we will bring your father home,' Dr Richter interposed. 'If you will come early perhaps—with a cart or a truck?'

'We have a small cart,' the girl replied. 'We will come, my brother and myself.'

'You must tell your mother to stop weeping,' the doctor said. 'Tell her he is all right, it is only a bad headache. Tell her you have seen him sleeping peacefully.'

'I will tell her,' said the girl.

'If there is something you need, some money perhaps, I will be glad,' the doctor said. 'I will give it to you as a loan, if you wish?'

The girl seemed flustered and the two men saw her eyes grow moist and bright. She rushed across the room and took the doctor's hands in hers. Then she lifted her face and looked at him. 'Thank you,' she said. 'The committee has money for the families. My father is one of them.' She walked to the door and went out. Lieutenant Gordon went to the window and watched as she went up the street and around the wall at the corner.

'She's lovely,' he said. 'I wonder how old she is.'

'She is probably older than she looks, or than you think,' the doctor answered from the back of the room.

'Perhaps about twenty-five. It is hard to tell with those of mixed blood, with the Portuguese especially.'

'We didn't even ask her name.'

26

'It is a trifle.' The doctor laughed. 'It is easily repaired.'

The lieutenant laughed too. 'You misunderstand,' he said.

'But of course!' said the doctor, and both of them laughed together.

The lieutenant reached for his cap on the polished table. 'I must go,' he said.

Dr Richter arose and walked with the lieutenant to the door. 'This evening I have been asked to the house of a Portuguese on the hill. It is an informal visit. He has been ill but he is now better. I would be glad to have you accompany me. You will come?'

Lieutenant Gordon paused, holding open the door. 'If you're sure it will be okay,' he said. . . .

Gordon debated what to do. All in one morning he had been thrown into things he had come to Macao to get away from; and yet it had amounted to something entirely different. When he had left to catch the boat at Hong Kong, the major, his commanding officer, had told him, in that easy post-war fashion that fell just short of an order, 'Get a good rest, but keep your eyes open. That's a hot little place down there.' And instead of letting it go and just saying, 'Sure,' he had made the mistake of asking a question. 'How do you mean?' he had said as if he hadn't known. And the major, who liked to talk, had leaned back from the desk. 'Well,' he had said, 'during the war you know what it was, they used it for everything, all of 'em, the Nips, the Portos, and the rest of us. If it weren't for the war up north the Gimo [Generalissimo Chiang Kai-shek] right now would be hollering holy hell to get it back, like Hong Kong. But now he's not so sure he wants it. So it's a fight, and the last report we got was that the Commies are getting the jump, in the unions and so on, like in Hong Kong too. Just look about, and see what you hear.' That was a favourite phrase of the major's, to 'see what you hear'. Sometimes he turned it around, suggesting listening with the eyes. The major could be very annoying. Somewhere along the line he had picked up a phony British accent and a pair of paratroop boots.

Lieutenant Gordon had said he would do what he could and had left, regretting his stupidity. Actually, he knew, it made little difference. He could tell the major anything and, besides, he was going home in a month to be discharged. He had given up, some time ago, the idea of staying in service, in intelligence; the major had been one of the main reasons.

And now, in his first morning, he had run into just the sort of thing the major had meant. Under ordinary circumstances the thing to do would be to visit the British consul and to talk to some of the Portuguese. But Lieutenant Gordon dismissed these alternatives from his mind. He thought, instead, as he walked over the uneven stones down to the Avenida Almeida Ribeiro, of Dr Georg Richter and of the daughter of the half-caste striker. When he got to the entrance of the hotel he turned in and went up to his room, where he switched on the fan and fell asleep.

There was a vestige of dusk in the sky when the doctor and the lieutenant left the doctor's house together. They went up past Loo Lim Yok's Garden and the monument that commemorated the repulse of the Dutch, until they reached the reservoir and the outer port. They had not talked much on the way. The doctor was filled with a private sadness that sprang from his earlier reflection; he had sat for the greater part of the afternoon by the window of his living room with the presence of the injured half-caste inside a kind of divining rod that served to stir up more and more of his past. The lieutenant was vaguely troubled by his inability to get his superior officer, the major, out of his mind; he wondered if, even only for his own edification, he should not make further inquiries in the colony as to the undercover nature of the Kuomintang–Communist rivalry.

At the entrance to the terraced path Gordon asked Dr Richter, 'This patient, he is also a friend of yours?'

The doctor smiled his soft smile that seemed sometimes to be as much in mockery of himself as filled with forbearance toward others. 'I must be honest,' he said. 'Senhor Perez has good wine, but his wine is no older than the ideas in his head. He is a curiosity, more than a friend. I have had too much of friends, perhaps. . . . He might have been an enemy once.'

The linen-robed servant let them in and led them to the porch where Senhor Perez sat ensconced in a suit of white as though in a suit of soft armour. He arose and extended his hand to the doctor and then to Lieutenant Gordon.

'I have brought an American,' Dr Richter said, with purposeful effect. 'He is lonely, like all Americans abroad.'

'But that is excellent,' Senhor Perez asserted. 'The Americans now come only seldom to Macao. It is a pity.' He motioned them

28

to chairs and shouted for the servant to bring drinks. Senhor Perez looked to be about fifty, Gordon thought. He was thin, with a face that was sharply featured and full of nervous expression. In one moment it seemed both in affinity with his hidden demons and charged with vengeance against them.

Lieutenant Gordon decided that a formal reply was called for. 'It is a beautiful place, Macao,' he said. 'You have a fine home.'

'It is nice of you to say so,' Senhor Perez replied.

'The colony is no longer the same, unfortunately. The war has left its mark.'

'How so?' the lieutenant asked. He felt, in asking the question, a virtuous atonement for having slept all afternoon.

'It is difficult, in a world of no law, to maintain a standard of order,' the Portuguese replied. 'You have heard, perhaps, of the new disturbances at the electric plant?'

Dr Richter coughed and sipped his drink. Senhor Perez looked first at the lieutenant and then at the doctor.

The lieutenant finally broke the silence. 'I happened to be passing by,' he said, 'just when—'

Senhor Perez interrupted. 'And Dr Richter also, I have heard.'

'I have never approved of police brutality,' the doctor said, with sudden sharpness.

'But my dear friend, you misunderstand,' Perez declared. 'There are none of us here who enjoy the method of force.'

'Then why do you use it?' asked the doctor.

Senhor Perez shrugged. It was the same sort of shrug the man behind the gate at the factory had given Dr Richter that morning. 'What are we to do?' he asked. 'We are involved here in a contest with men of no principle. You are aware of the nature of the war in China, of the contest for power. There is nothing we can do except to stand for the order and peace we have created. It is your fight as well, Lieutenant.' And he nodded his head at Gordon.

Lieutenant Robert Gordon, in the seconds that followed, thought of several strange and disparate things. He remembered the day the war ended, in Chungking, when he had weaved down the perilous mud steps of the city, laughing and shouting '*Ding hao*' as the coolies grinned back at him; he remembered the Chinese civilian he had had a fight with earlier, in Kunming, who he had struck in a drunken rage over inefficiency and waste (the major had said to 'forget it'); he had a vision of Japanese planes overhead in the night, when he had lain half-immersed in mud and water at the bottom of a trench; and, finally, he thought of how Dr Georg Richter had released himself from the sheltering wall that morning in Macao and had slowly moved across the street toward the man in the gutter. All this, for Robert Gordon, seemed in sudden delicate counterpoise to the dark omniscient face of the Portuguese across the porch, as if this were some quick moment of reckoning that had caught up with him.

He set down his glass and drew on his cigarette. 'You are mistaken, Senhor Perez,' he said. 'We have never been involved in the same fight. And we have intended a different peace.'

Once again the Portuguese shrugged. 'You may be right, of course,' he said. 'You Americans are forever dreamers. You believe in your dreams, in your silver ribbons of words, and then you come to us to learn the methods of realism. You will pardon me, Lieutenant, but for us—you have the manner of hypocrites.'

He smiled at Gordon, as if to show he meant no harm, that his remark was the thrust of a friendly fencer, delivering an historical riposte. Lieutenant Gordon raised his glass to his host and they drank in silence.

'But Dr Richter,' Senhor Perez continued, 'our friend the doctor, you see, is not so fortunate. He has no home at all. He is a man without a state. Once he was a German but he was ashamed of it. Now he has no country—it is no longer his fault of course, but he is unable to represent any creative difference of opinion, even such as yours and mine. It is a matter of interpretation— democracy; there are many answers. But first—you must at least have something positive to believe in.'

Dr Richter wore his softest smile. 'I have no home, you are quite right,' he said. 'Belief? Perhaps, too, I no longer have belief. But I have a memory, you see, and unhappily then a conscience. The one follows from the other.'

'We must be careful how we demonstrate the relationship,' the Portuguese smiled back. 'This is something that creates misunderstanding, particularly during a period of emotion, such as after a war.'

'Your informants are most active,' the doctor said flatly. His voice was suddenly hollow, as if he spoke out of the depths of an empty hall.

'I speak as a friend,' Senhor Perez said. 'You have nothing to gain.'

'And what,' asked Dr Richter, 'have I then to lose?' And now he spoke with painful self-mockery, as if he were playing the tragic clown.

'A resting place,' Senhor Perez said softly and with no apparent sentiment. 'A place where you might also have a cross placed over your grave.'

'I want no crosses,' the doctor said angrily. 'I have no use for crosses, and I want no forgiveness. I want nothing—only the opportunity to forget.'

'Whatever it is you wish to forget,' said the Portuguese, 'what you are doing is instead the way of remembrance. If it is contentment you seek, my friend, I should advise the method of non-interference.' He smiled at the doctor, who looked away. 'Like myself, you have reached the age of the philosopher,' Senhor Perez added. 'We should withdraw then, you and I, to reflect upon our sins, to anoint our souls for our God.'

Dr Richter gave a long, loud sigh. His whole frame seemed momentarily to shake, and he looked old. 'I thank you for your advice,' he said. 'With regard to salvation, it is something to consider.' He rose and, staring at the lieutenant across the porch, waited. Gordon finished his drink and put out his cigarette. Perez was still smiling. He came with them to the door.

'Please understand,' he said, as he took the doctor's arm. 'We have grown fond of you here. There are so few people with intelligence. I would like to believe you will be careful in this time of wrong events. These affairs are nothing that demand involvement, yours or mine, or that of our friend here, the lieutenant.'

At the gate the doctor paused. 'You have managed to find out much in a short time,' he said, 'but it does not surprise me. I should have remembered that too. It is not only news that travels fast; it is fear that moves even faster. This morning—you have heard it correctly—I gave aid to an injured labourer in the demonstration. But this evening it is you, and not myself, who is afraid. Of what are you afraid then, Senhor Perez?'

The Portuguese did not answer. He stood instead on the edge of the steps and gazed out across the city. The lights of the

31

gambling parlours flickered below, and far off along the Chinese shore the glimmering bulbs of nocturnal fishermen hovered above the water. 'It is a lovely sight, don't you think?' he said, dreamily. 'The East at night is beautiful.' There was no need for him to say anything more. He bade them good-night.

PART II

TEMPTATIONS

She gambles, reeks of opium fumes, and encourages all the other sins usually thrown in with a thoroughly bad life.

ALEKO E. LILIUS, 1930

Macao's association with temptations, legal and otherwise, is no recent phenomenon. In the 1740s, a Franciscan monk described the colony as infected with 'lechery, robbery, treachery, gambling, drunkenness and other vices.' The colony's international reputation for gambling dates at least from 1778, by which time, the Oxford English Dictionary records, a 'gambling game at cards' called Macao and described as 'a kind of vingt-et-un' was all the rage in fashionable European salons.

However, it was only in the 1850s that the Portuguese government began licensing the Chinese gambling houses that had long existed in the settlement. It was a desperate measure. Macao was losing trade—and the accompanying tax revenue—to the new British free port of Hong Kong and the other Chinese treaty ports forcibly opened to Europeans after the first Anglo-Chinese or Opium War. Today, Macao's casinos pour money into the government treasury. Feeding and housing the tourists they attract helps drive the city's economy. In recent decades, as in the past, gambling and its associated vices, opium, and prostitution have fascinated and repelled those who have written about the territory.

THE WICKEDEST CITY OF THE FAR EAST

LEILA HADLEY

In 1954, 25-year-old Leila Hadley set out on a sea journey through the Far East with her six-year-old son, Kippy. A disillusioned New York public relations executive and disenchanted divorcée, Hadley sought 'to be a stranger in a world where everything I saw, heard, touched, and tasted, would be fresh and new.' Her impulsive sense of adventure landed mother and son in Manila and then Hong Kong. From there, she and a journalist friend, John Chiu, boarded a ferry to the 'iniquities of little Portugal', leaving Kippy safely behind in the capable hands of his amah, Ah Ling.

John had another attractive suggestion to put forward. Later in the week he was going to Macao. Did I want to come along? I did. The idea of going to this Portuguese island colony of vice and opium intrigued me, but the getting there had been problematic. If Macao was, as it was acclaimed, the wickedest city in the Far East, it was hardly the place to take Kippy and, thinking ahead to lonely, embarrassingly suspect meals in restaurants, I hadn't particularly wanted to go there on my own. John, who made frequent pilgrimages to Macao to see a Eurasian dance hostess with whom he had a comfortable and convenient arrangement, was just the escort I had in mind—a pleasant male, helpful, unobtrusive and preoccupied. . . .

Leaving Kippy in Ah Ling's lap listening to a story about the Mo, an animal that eats up bad dreams, I set out with John for the iniquities of Little Portugal.

The coastal ferry that was to take us there, the motor vessel *Tai Loy*, was scheduled to leave at ten in the morning. Time being the flexible matter it is in the Orient, we left closer to noon. The *Tai Loy* was small, painted a dazzling white, and armed against pirates with guns and an iron net spread around and across the top deck. To my dismay, she was also equipped with a public address system that was blasting forth 'You Are My Sunshine' when we first climbed aboard.

A tally man was collecting number sticks from a procession of coolies working to unload bottle-necked baskets filled with dried fish from the junk on our left. A group of women with babies tied to their backs had formed a human chain to pass along trays of cucumbers and red peppers from another junk to a truck waiting farther on down the line. On either side of us, fishing and cargo junks huddled to the quay side, clapping slowly against the water, showing bleached gray hulls and a tangle of tall masts and archaic rigging.

The deck of the junk to our right was heaped with iron-bound crates, burlap sacks, gasoline drums and plaited bamboo hampers; a pig was tethered to the mainmast; squawking chickens were caged on the stern, and the single clear space on deck had been spread with newspapers and set aside as the field of operations for a mah-jongg game. The players crouched over the rectangular ivory pieces, apparently unconcerned that they were plunk in the middle of the traffic. A young girl stepped as delicately as a cat around them, moving back and forth with dirty clothes which she attached to a hooked bamboo pole and swished about in the water; the clothes were hauled in, looking miraculously clean, and hung on the rigging.

Four children, none over a yard high, and one barely walkable, frisked and tumbled about the crates and hampers, and for one dreadful moment the baby looked as though he would topple from a gasoline drum and fall into the circle of mah-jongg players. The players remained imperturbable, just as if they knew he would be rescued by one of the other children, grabbed around his naked bottom and lugged off in the nick of time.

The game was interrupted when one of the players got up to make use of an open privy jutting over the gunwale. Anticipating his purpose, he rolled up the leg of his wrap-around black trousers as he left the game to cross the deck. I was still new enough in the East to be mildly startled by these deviations from Western conventions of privacy. I had been more startled to discover that for all their exquisite civilization the Chinese had none of our evasive refinements of conversation, none of our reticences, none of our unmentionables. That morning, for example, I had asked John how he was.

'Not too good,' he said. 'I've a hemorrhoid that's been acting up.' And then, lapsing into his pre-Westernized character, eager as only an Oriental can be to discuss a physical liability, he had gone on to give me an intimate medical account of the cause and cure of his ailment. Afterwards, it had taken an effort on my part to think of him in any but this context, and at a loss for nonclinical conversation, I had turned my attention to the mah-jongg players on the neighboring junk.

The game had been finished, the pieces shuffled rattlesomely and another game begun when 'Anchors Aweigh' blared from the public-address system, and at the same time the *Tai Loy* hooted and began to back off from the quay. The tall masts of the junks merged together, saw-toothed rudders blurred beneath patterned sterns, and almost without knowing it, we were out in the harbor. We sailed due west into the South China Sea, slipping between Cheung Chau Island and the headlands of twin-humped Lantao, and then we were outside the Bocca Tigris, the wide lower mouth of the Pearl River, for centuries the crossroads of a rich river and sea traffic in silk and tea and opium.

A few wooded islands appeared. A portly comprador in a white drill suit, who had been silently sipping a gimlet and studying the *South China Morning Post* folded back to the shipping pages, looked up and pointed them out to me. They were piratical strongholds, he said, as well as the sites for Communist gun emplacements. So far, the Communists had fired upon only three ships for sailing too close to the islands, but the pirates attacked frequently. Only the day before, a ferry bound for Hong Kong had been looted and several passengers killed. The few other passengers about received the information with the indifference of good Taoists. I seemed to be the only person who was not a fatalist, and I was certainly the only one who showed relief—I could feel the muscles in my face relaxing—when there were no signs of forthcoming aggression.

We put into the Porto Interior of Macao in the middle of the afternoon and moored between two black-canopied brothel boats from Canton that appeared to be deserted. For a town which profits hugely from the smuggling of gold, opium, arms and ammunition, a town famous as a sink of iniquity, Macao seemed curiously innocent, a little, fair Mediterranean-looking town with villas of flaking pink, white, blue and yellow plaster shaded by the wavy boughs of big, dark trees. Back from the quilted blue silk of the harbor, the ruins of old chapels and the moldering culverins of crumbling forts were peaceful and sun-warmed, the basking places for velvety geckos with eyes that never closed. There was a garden with black-crested bulbuls and sparrows flying through it, where Camoëns was supposed to have written the *Lusiad* sixty years after Vasco da Gama, besting the Adamastor, the dreadful phantom of the Cape of Good Hope, had discovered a new route to India.

In the town, cobbled alleys and wide *avenidas* centered with the diamond spray of fountains were named for Portuguese saints and heroes. But the blood that coursed through these arteries, the blood that gave life to the island and to the town, was pure Chinese.

Along the *avenidas*, coolies pedaled bicycle rickshaws around the marble pomp of statues of Portugal's great men, and the Sacred Heart College, conducted by Canossian nuns, was flanked by a Chinese bazaar. The squalor of a refugee squatter's camp encroached upon the ground of a Dog's Home; and there was a confusing propinquity of firecracker factories and monasteries, incense-stick factories and orphanages, churches and joss houses. Where the business-like Chinese had converted villas into stores, bamboo awnings painted with vermilion ideographs hung from the wrought-iron complicacies of early nineteenth-century balconies, and the bright-colored splash of these cryptic signs was giddily incongruous against a backdrop of fading rose and amber façades.

This was the operative incongruity of Macao, the commingling of the European old with the Oriental new, decrepitude and vitality fusing together as pleasantly as the tinkling shrill of bicycle-rickshaw bells and the sound of clocks chiming in broken church towers. In the drowsing afternoon, Macao was believably what the guidebook said—an island of peculiar charm, and the ideal place for a quietly entertaining holiday. Then the darkness, so quick to come in the East, leaped down.

I returned to the hotel, where I had left my suitcase, had a bath, dressed, and went down to the lobby, where a few dapper Chinese were fanning themselves with bamboo fans, not so much to keep cool but as a practical measure against swarms of flies and mosquitoes. I waited for John and his dance-hostess friend to show up.

They came at last, John leading the way, followed by a sulky-looking girl in green satin whom he introduced as Miss Fereira. She gazed at me appraisingly. My jewelry was not as sumptuous as hers, my nails not as long or so brilliantly painted, my dress of a duller color and a less extravagant cut. Miss Fereira permitted herself a thin little smile. And then the three of us went outside into the dusty night-glitter of the street.

'Where shall we go?' John asked. 'A Portuguese place?'

'Oh, no,' Miss Fereira protested. 'Why don't you take us to Fat Siu Lan's? The food's so different there.'

'All right,' John said, hailing two bicycle-rickshaws. 'All right, Fat Siu Lan's.'

From her tone and from his, I presumed that Fat Siu Lan's was expensive and wrongly supposed that it would turn out to be a clip joint with nothing to recommend it but the cachet of expensiveness.

Bicycle bells shrilling, our rickshaws joined the company of other rickshaws rattling along the principal thoroughfare of the Avenida Almeida Ribeiro. At a corner, solemnly regarded by a plaster bust of an unsmiling saint, we turned and headed down another avenue. The faces of pedestrians were ghastly in the whitish glare of the street lamps, the banyans lining the way frenzied by the wind blowing from the sea, and all at once the town seemed strangely malignant. We turned from the broad *avenida* into a narrower street, and from the street into a lane, and from the lane into Rua da Felicidade, an alleyway between cavernous stone shelters, a hellish little Street of Happiness inhabited by prostitutes costing two patacas (about thirty cents) an hour.

Soliciting for them were foul old women who set up a maniacal shrieking the moment our rickshaws came in sight. As there was only a flapping curtain before each entrance hole, the coupling taking place inside the shelters was carried on unhidden from passers-by. To be certain that I should miss nothing of this dreadful show, the rickshaw boy stopped pedaling, pointed to a cavern where the cotton curtain had been blown completely aside, and roared with laughter from the sheer prurient amusement of it all.

Mercifully, Rua da Felicidade branched off into a cobbled lane, and it was here that the establishment of Fat Siu Lan was located, a dilapidated three-storied wooden house given the appearance of a pet shop by the piled-up cages and tanks outside containing lobsters, turtles, mice, monkeys, poultry, fish, and snakes. Three shaven-headed children, scarcely bigger than dolls, were poking a straw through the interstices of a cobra's cage. After having told them not to—much to their delight—I stepped around buckets of excreta and a barrelful of garbage placed for collection, and followed John and Miss Fereira inside.

To the left of the first landing of a steep and shaking flight of stairs was the kitchen, a square room with a mammoth coal stove built of brick and tile. Two cookboys in blood-stained aprons stood side by side at a center table and slivered frog meat and bean sprouts into matching shreds, while another helper, with the same painstaking accuracy, measured a smidgin of ginger against a candareen weight resting on the pane of a brass scale.

Unaware of the gastronomic surprises in store, I continued up the stairs to the private dining rooms (the Chinese shun the barbarous custom of eating before strangers) and found myself in the midst of a great brouhaha. John had run into a friend of his, the kingpin of the local firecracker industry. The kingpin had already ordered a slap-up dinner for himself and eight friends, and he insisted that we join him.

The eight friends, all shouting jovially, swarmed into the corridor and swept us through a beaded curtain into a room festooned for the occasion with ropes of multicolored paper flowers. The room was hot and smoky. A naked light bulb and a push-button bell dangled on two long wires twisted together from the center of the ceiling and, as I came in, someone rang the bell, pushing it in a way that caused it and its companion light bulb to swing back and forth, the penduluming bulb filling the room with rocking shadows.

A covey of attractive singsong girls floated forward with trays of melon seeds and almonds. Other singsong girls materialized with butterfly pianos which they hammered with drumsticks to produce a gonging con brio, a form of music so unfamiliar that it didn't appeal to me in the least.

A small boy with a face as flat as a kitten's wandered from guest to guest rattling a begging-box. Around his neck was a placard which said, 'Ladies and gentlemen and soldiers and sailors, through no fault of mine I am an orphan. Please give me money. Thank you.'

I helped myself to some melon seeds, and then wished I hadn't because the husks were as much of a problem to get rid of as olive pits. There were spittoons provided just for this exigency—large brass affairs embossed with dragons and peonies—but I couldn't bring myself to use them. Somewhat self-consciously, I balled the wet husks in my hand and dropped them from the window.

Glasses were briskly filled and emptied and the finger game was played to determine who should pay for the next round. The finger game is more or less like the nursery sport of wood-paper-scissors-stone done to the count of ten in Mandarin and ending with a lot of mysterious finger waggling by the participants. The chorus bears no trace of the unmeasured rhythms and the intonational vagaries associated with Eastern music. On the whole, I thought it sounded like what you find yourself, or at least I find myself shouting at a football game.

Since no one spoke to me, I stood by one of the singsong girls and stared with mindless fascination at the flexible drumsticks whirring against the wires of the zitherlike butterfly piano. The drumsticks were tipped with triangular pads and looked as if they would make perfectly functional shoe trees.

A man on my left offered me a gimlet and a card that identified him as Li Fook Wo, a director of the Au Pit Seng Trading Company and the vice-president of the Hang Tai Match Factory. 'What brings your husband to the East?' he asked. I said that I had no husband, that I was just traveling about with my young son.

'Ah,' he said thoughtfully, fingering a gold Parker pen clipped to his breast pocket. 'Do you want to sell your passport?'

No, I didn't, I said, pleased as Punch to have been mistaken for an adventuress and quite unconcerned with his suggestion, which was too disconnected from reality even to bother thinking about.

'Well, if you change your mind, let me know,' Mr Wo said—or perhaps his name was Mr Li: the Chinese have a baffling practice of reversing the customary order of given names and surnames.

'You're sensible not to sell your passport in Macao,' said the gentleman on his left. 'You can get double for it in Bangkok. Permit me to give you the name of a friend of mine.'

'Please don't bother,' I said quickly. I was sorry to give up my short-lived role as an adventuress, but it was beginning to make me feel uncomfortable. 'I really don't want to sell my passport at all.' Was it my fancy, or did Mr Wo wink at me? 'I'm sure that we can more than meet any Bangkok offers,' he murmured.

I saw a wolfish old man, fat and mincing, like a doll on an elastic string, walk over to Miss Fereira and pat her on the bottom. He was a *ham sup lo*, she told me later—a Cantonese slang word which, literally translated means a wet and salty one.

We sat down finally at a large round table spread with a plastic cover on which had been placed ivory chopsticks, porcelain soup spoons, small dishes of soy sauce and at each place a rice bowl, a soup bowl and a shallow bowl for bones. The singsong girls laid aside their butterfly pianos and, stationing themselves behind us in demure and smiling complaisance, wiped our hands and brows with steaming almond-scented towels.

Tea was served, brewed in individual lided cups, pale green Iron Goddess tea from Fukien. Everyone agreed that it was excellent, perfectly cured and with a fragrance far superior to that of Dragon Well and chrysanthemum varieties. Presumably for my benefit, some talk about the weather in English followed, and then the conversation was resumed in Cantonese.

Snake soup was served next, and since it would have been disgracefully rude to have refused it, I sipped at the verbena-perfumed broth and tried to overlook the parings of yellow-striped snakeskin swimming about my spoon. The broth had an odd, almost pleasant taste. Although the snakeskin strips undulating in the bowl killed any enjoyment I might have had from it, I managed to keep up the pretense of eating until the waiter came to take the bowls away.

The guests, murmuring approval, picked judiciously at subsequent dishes of fried shrimp and glistening coral-colored lima beans. In deference to me as the only foreigner present, the choicest morsels were pinced together with chopsticks and courteously deposited in my bowl. Until I had almost eaten the last of them, I didn't realize that the lima beans were newborn mice coated with honey.

Then in came a blue and white rice-patterned platter heaped with transparent globules resembling giant Vitamin A capsules. With the suppressed pride of one offering a soup tureen of caviar, the Firecracker Kingpin identified these as brandied snakes' eggs. Marvelous for one's glands. 'The best you can buy,' John sang out fulsomely to me from the other end of the table. 'They're imported from Singapore.'

I shall throw up, I thought, I shall certainly throw up if I eat one, but I ate two, swallowing them whole, and nothing happened except that for the rest of the evening I was haunted by the idea that they were going to hatch inside me.

There were successive courses of roast pigeon, ricebirds and abalones, and the excellence of these, combined with a taste of the hot rice wine everyone was drinking, gave me, for the first time in the evening, a momentary sense of well-being. After each course tea was rebrewed, and the handmaidens performed their swabbing operations.

I comforted myself with the thought that the worst was over and helped myself to some more chopped abalones. The beaded curtains were pushed aside, and a waiter padded in carrying before him a monkey in a basket. The monkey, wedged so tightly in the oval-shaped basket that only its wrinkled, rather querulous little face was showing, was passed about the table for our inspection. I surmised that we were in for some sort of entertainment, although I hadn't expected to see a performing monkey. When the subtle intelligence of the Chinese is expended upon amusement, a trick animal is just not the sort of thing you expect.

I waited for the monkey to dance or whatever it was going to do, but instead the waiter sliced off the top of its head with a meat cleaver. The monkey gave a dying scream, twitched for a few seconds, and its basket was then set in the middle of the table. Everyone stood to scoop a teaspoon of steaming brains from its grisly half-head.

5

FOR A MESS OF POTTAGE

C. A. MONTALTO DE JESUS

Although born and educated in Hong Kong, the writer and historian Carlos Augusto Montalto de Jesus regarded himself as a son of Macao. As such, it pained and disgusted him to see a city once glorious within Portugal's extensive commercial and religious empire become ever more dependent on the profits of gambling. He wrote this lament for the once holy city in 1902.

For many years after suppressing the customs revenue Macao laboured under great financial stress. Loans were obtained from Macanese citizens, funds drawn from the government's financial agency in London. And taxation yielding but little, revenues were created by licensing Chinese gambling houses, though in contravention of the penal code of Portugal. The degradation of a historical emporium into the Monte Carlo of China with the attendant social demoralization and dependence upon a source of revenue which China then held as tainted—such was one of the most deplorable penalties entailed upon Macao by the freeport policy of Hongkong. There gambling licences were also resorted to but overruled, though advocated as a preventive of rank corruption in the police force.

Crowds of Hongkong gamblers usually resorted to Macao for *fantan*—so patronized by them that the dens display flaring signboards as 'first class gambling houses', to the holy horror of Hongkong pietists and pharisees. At the Hongkong share market, however, extensive 'jobbing' and 'rigging' went on freely, openly, as if they involved no gambling at all, howsoever ruinous such business orgies might be to many people.

On the other hand, a viceroy of Canton was dismissed for countenancing the *weising*, a lottery on the issues of literary examinations in China. But the inefficacy of prohibitive measures eventually led to their repeal on economic grounds, whereby Macao's *weising* monopoly and revenue decreased considerably previous to their substitution by other popular lotteries. Thus, from Macao the Chinese government learnt to legalize not only *weising* but eventually *fantan* too; and from Hongkong, the nation-poisoning opium traffic, despite Emperor Tao Kuang's vow that nothing would induce him to profit by the vice and misery of his people. . . .

Yet, there is the grim paradox of China being perverted by Christian traders and overrun by missionaries preaching the altruism, the purity of Christian morals, so badly needed in Hongkong and Macao. Bygone, alas, were the days when Macao deserved the appellation of Holy City, and when her greatest shortcoming lay in subserving the rapacity of mandarindom. Now, also, by legalizing Chinese depravities for a mess of pottage the erstwhile august city could only vegetate in a degradation far worse than the Chinese domination of yore, expiating thus the ill-starred struggle for freedom, with a deserted freeport turned into an Ichabod recalling the bitterest plaints of Jeremiah over Jerusalem's disgrace.

6

A MOST INGENIOUS SYSTEM

CARLOS JOSÉ CALDEIRA

For Carlos José Caldeira, a Portuguese journalist who lived in the city from 1850 to 1851, a confusing mixture of specie was only a small part of the exotic complexity of Macao's early system of licensed gambling. Although clinical, Caldeira's description is valuable as one of the few accounts of the two forms of gambling that first filled Macau's public coffers: the Chinese lottery and latão, *from the Portuguese word for brass and now known as* fantan. Sapecas *were small brass coins of Chinese origin. A tael was a Chinese unit for measuring silver. Patacas refer to the Spanish (or Mexican) silver dollars used widely in the China trade at that time, not to Macao's present-day currency, while* reis *were Portuguese money.*

Since the abolition of the customs house, which had been the only source of income since the founding of the settlement, public revenue has been derived from taxes and duties; from rents, licences, and other small sums; and from monopolies on the sale of pork, beef, fish and salt on Taipa Island, cooked opium, oyster fishing, the game of *latão*, and the Chinese lottery. Public revenues must total around 34,000 taels. The two last monopolies contribute the most important sums and are worthy of some explanation because of their nature.

Latão is a game of chance often played by the Chinese. Similar to the Portuguese game of *banca*, it involves separating a random portion of *sapecas* from a mountain of these coins. After the players put bets on numbers one, two, three, or four, the *sapecas* remaining in the pile are counted four by four at the will of the croupier. This occurs until one last portion remains, which has to be of one, two, three, or four sapecas. The players who have previously chosen that number win two or three times the amount wagered. The bets on the three remaining numbers are lost to the house. There are certain conditions and variations in the ways of distributing the *sapecas* that bear some analogy with those of Portuguese *banca*.

The privilege of running this game is settled by public auction. The highest bidder, ordinarily an agent of a partnership, establishes various houses where the Chinese—who generally have a passion for gambling—gather. Because hawkers offer delicacies and sweets in dice games in all the squares and streets of Macao, young boys end up risking the *sapecas* they have managed to acquire instead of immediately buying what they desire. In this way, they insensibly acquire such a prejudicial inclination for gambling.

The proceeds of the monopoly were once more important, yet they still account for 8,640 taels in the budgets of Macao in 1852 and 1853. Besides these sums, and various inherent expenses, the franchisee secretly pays money to the Chinese mandarins neighbouring the settlement. These officials extract money by threats and all possible methods even from the Chinese who live under our laws and protection.

The Chinese lottery occurs daily and is conducted in a most singular method. Each day a drawing is sold. It consists of 80 Chinese letters printed on a small piece of paper, which also serves as a ticket that the buyer takes for his preferred value from a scale of prices whose minimum is 5 *sapecas* (approximately three *reis*). The price is also stipulated in relation to the number of letters that the buyer wants to play. These are chosen in the act of buying and noted with red marks.

Of the 80 letters, the lottery directors choose a determined number and form a sentence or thought from each daily extraction. This is displayed to the public. The luck of the player is in this sentence including some or all of the letters noted on the ticket. The prize is proportional to the number of letters that he ascertained and to the cost of the ticket. All of this is regulated by calculations of very intricate progression, revealing the great majority of probabilities to be in the lottery's favour. So much so that the grand prize, or the most favourable combination for the ticket buyer (amounting to some thousand *patacas*), can go years and years without being realized. It also happens, although rarely, that one wins a good number of *patacas* with a ticket of only five *sapecas*.

It is a most ingenious system, but incredibly complicated and very difficult to explain in its detail. Nevertheless, that which I have said will give a general idea.

One is amazed by the agility and activity of the Chinese employed in the accounting and service of this enterprise. Each night the accounts are closed, the prizes paid, and the services of the day completed with admirable promptness and regularity.

Many Macao people play the lottery. The impresario pays the government, according to the cited budget, 4,320 taels, spends a great deal on employees, houses, etc, and also gives secret money to the mandarins, just as happens with *latão*.

The revenue of the *latão*, like that of the lottery, has successively diminished with the gradual decay of Macao, the absence of visits by Chinese from the interior and the lack of traffic from ships. Nevertheless, it still produces 18,000 *patacas*.

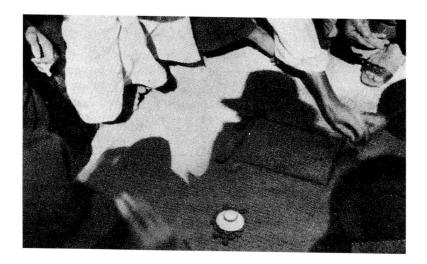

7

THE MONTE CARLO OF THE EAST

FREDERIC COURTLAND PENFIELD

From the late nineteenth century, a description of Macao's iniquitous
gambling parlours was virtually obligatory in travel books about the
Far East. The cocky turn of phrase and sly innuendo in this particular
account, published in 1907 by the American writer Frederic Courtland
Penfield, are typical of many in the genre.

For a place whose commerce is notoriously in eclipse, you are
curious to learn whence springs the golden shower giving
the appearance of prosperity to Macao, for the general
air of the colony suggests an easy affluence. To keep the
governor's palace and the judiciary buildings covered with paint
costs something, you know, while the paved streets and bridges
and viaducts give support to the surmise of an exchequer not
permanently depleted. Portugal, nowadays almost robbing Peter to
pay Paul, is in no condition to succor an impecunious colony
situated in another hemisphere, you are aware, and you appeal for
elucidation of the fiscal problem. 'Very easy, dear sir,' your
cicerone promptly rejoins, 'this is the Monte Carlo of the Far East.
Gambling is here a business—all the business there is, and the
concessions for the *fan-tan* and lottery monopolies pay for
everything, practically making taxation unnecessary.'

The statement would cause something of a shock to a guileless
stranger, especially to one who had believed he had perceived
a natural likeness between the little principality on the
Mediterranean and this beauty spot of the Orient. But China is
rather too far to the eastward of Suez for simon-pure guile, and
the globe-trotter decides to thoroughly explore local conditions by
way of adding to his worldly knowledge. If you go to the post-office

to mail a letter, you recognize perforce how backward a colony of Portugal may be in supplying the trifling requirements of life, for you stand minutes in a nondescript line before your stamp is sheared from a sheet by a functionary having a capacity for activity possibly rivaled by an Alpine glacier—then you wait at the communal mucilage pot to secure in turn the required adhesive substance. A good correspondent in Macao would pass half his time at the post-office, you conclude. . . .

The official bigwigs who administer Macao know that it is as necessary for the Chinaman to gamble as to have food—and the colony accordingly legalizes *fan-tan* and semi-daily lotteries, supplies the requisite machinery for carrying on the games, and reaps a *benefice* for its enterprise that runs the community without further ado. That is all there is to Macao's fiscal policy. Hong Kong, only forty miles across the estuary, bristles with commercial prosperity. The British government permits Hong Kongers to bet on horse-races, buy and sell stocks, and promote devious companies, but forbids *fan-tan* and lotteries. There is, consequently, a daily flow of men, women, and dollars between Hong Kong and Macao. Besides, no traveler not actively engaged in uplifting his fellow-man, feels that he has seen the Orient unless he passes a few hours or days in endeavoring to lure fortune at the gambling tables. . . .

Macao licenses twenty *fan-tan* places, and these run all day and all night, and are graded in their patrons from tourists and natives of fortune and position down to joints admitting 'rickshaw coolies, sailors, and harbor riffraff. The gilded establishment claiming attention from travelers is conducted by a couple of Chinese worthies, by name Ung Hang and Hung Vo, according to the business card deferentially handed you at your hotel, and the signs in front of it and the legends painted on great lanterns proclaim it as a first-chop *Casa de Jogo*, and a gambling-house that is 'No. 1' in all respects. The gamesters whose garments proclaim them to be middle-class Chinamen pack themselves like sardines into the room where the table is situated, for they obviously believe in watching their interests at close hand. The floor above, by reason of the rail-protected opening in the center, is little more than a spacious gallery; but it is there that the big gamblers congregate, natives in costly fabrics, and whose rotund bodies tell of lives not spent in toil. They loll on black-wood divans and smoke opium and send their bank-notes and commands to the gambling table by servant, until yielding to the exalted dreams induced by the poppy fumes. They are polite fellows, every man of them, and make it apparent that they would like to do something for the entertainment of each man and woman tourist in the room.

In this strange establishment globe-trotting novices sit around the railed opening and make their bets on the game below through an interpreter attendant. This obliging man lowers your coins to the croupier in a basket, and draws up any 'bet' you may have had the luck to win. And what a medley of coins you are paid in! There are coins of China and Japan obsolete years ago in those countries, money of the Philippine Islands, even nickels and dimes whose worth has been stamped by Uncle Sam. It is said that half the pocket-pieces of Asia find their way on to the gambling boards of

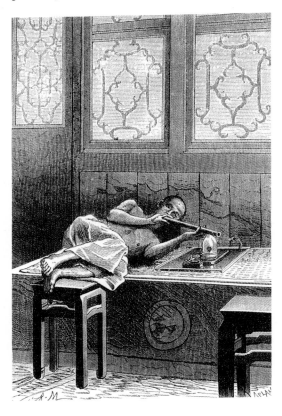

Macao, and that a thrifty croupier seeks to pay them out to the tourist who will remove them from circulation. The linguistic representative of the management endeavors to play the bountiful host to most visitors. He takes one through the building, permits you to peep within a chamber filled with oleaginous Chinamen in brocade petticoats, sleeping off the effects of the opium pipe, explains painted fans and other attempts at decoration on the walls, and indicates a retiring room where you may rest or even pass the night, all without charge.

Then he orders refreshments brought, and with the manner of a veteran courtier proffers a tray heaped with oranges, an egg-shell cup filled with tea that is almost without color, and dried watermelon seeds that you might munch after the manner of the neck-or-nothing gamblers on the lower floor. When you politely decline these, the courtly one most likely says, 'You no likee tea and seeds—then have whiskysoda.' Chinese courtezans, with feet bound to a smallness making locomotion difficult and obviously painful, wearing what in the Western World would be called 'trousers,' and invariably bedecked with earrings or bracelets of exquisite jade, edge their way to the gambling table, and put their money down in handfuls as long as it lasts. To spend an evening in the liberally conducted establishment of Messrs. Ung Hang and Hung Vo is enlightening in various ways.

8

THE FATHER OF THE STRAIGHT WAY

PAUL LINEBARGER

The family of Sun Yat-sen (1866–1925), renowned father of the Chinese republic, had close but uncomfortable ties with Macao and its temptations. Sun was born in the town of Choy Hung in Guangdong (Kwantung) province near the Portuguese colony. Later, he tried to set up a medical practice in Macao, but left after the authorities refused to recognize his medical qualifications, acquired in Hong Kong and Canton. Sun's father had also tried to make his fortune in Macao, but was thwarted by his 'straight way' in the face of its multifarious wickedness. This version of the elder Sun's stay in Macao, published in 1925, is based on interviews with Sun Yat-sen himself. The author, the American Paul Linebarger, was a propagandist and lawyer for Sun's Nationalist Party as well as Sun's authorized—and startlingly puritanical—biographer.

Sun Yat Sen's father once had the wanderlust, and early in his youth had gone to Macao—the 'Goddess Bight'—thirty miles away, as an apprentice, to learn the tailoring trade.

When a Choy Hung lad obtained a job in Macao he rarely returned to remain permanently in the hamlet of the Blue Valley, for the Portuguese, by their close affiliation with the Chinese, adapted their Western civilization to accommodate all the pleasures and vices known to the Chinese; and even a 'makie learnie pidgin' boy had his share in the round of pleasures that the Lusitanians played to the allurement of the Chinese, for they wanted the poor Chinese for labor, and the rich Chinese for their capital. The struggling, adventurous early Lusitanians had brought from the Tagus little save the caravels in which they traveled to the land of spice and silk and jade. For the most part, they came to China empty-handed as beggars, and thus, from the beginning, realized their dependence upon the bounty of Chinese labor, and the prodigality of the Chinese capitalists.

To allure this bounty and prodigality, the Portuguese went to great pains to make Macao the Mecca of the Chinese pleasure-seeker, be he rich or poor, and well might the Chinese of all classes declare, as they made the round of Macao's pleasures,

If e're there was a Heaven of bliss—
It is this! It is this! It is this!

Yes, they made Macao a town of wild and extravagant pleasures, and from the very beginning seemed to have had this end in view. Selecting a site on the meandering tropical coast (noted for its beauty among the Chinese from its earliest days), they raised those walls of yellow, pink, and blue that shone in the glory of Kwantung's sun, like gems half hidden in the green of the Praya Grande, where the skirt of the sea showed the deepest purple of its edge. They established, on a grand and extravagant scale, that master lure to the Chinese sybarite, the gambling-place, and to its wild allurements added wholesale a choice of Bacchanalian dissipations, rivaling, in their ensemble, the orgies of a Pompeian festival. Wickedness throve because it had the support of piety, throve because it was a passive part of the prayers of the church, which depended largely for its living upon the profits of those vices against which it preached.

It was wicked, but it was beautiful. Ah! those blue and pink and yellow walls! A color for each of the master vices, opium, lewd women, and gambling; those master vices that mean to the Chinese, in the unrestraint of his ancient life, a natural pleasure, that he who has the means buys as easily as plucking a flower, and as naturally as the bee sucking honey from the heart of an orchid.

Yes, blue and pink and yellow walls, with flowers and singing birds upon them, and yet, eventually, a noisome prison for so many of those peasant lads from the hamlets like Choy Hung, who had finally come down to the dregs of the cup of pleasure they sought at any price; and, beyond those walls of color, the songs from the flower-boats; the laughter of the pleasure-seekers in the balmy air; the rich and merry festivals, all making a picture in which Macao— swung from the ever summer sky of the Southern Cross like a gaudy lantern, garish by day but tauntingly beautiful as it gleamed out through the midnight hours—had its background in those villages of the Blue Valleys, those hamlets of lowly yet honest toil, of precarious privations and sacrifice, and yet with a compensation for every hour of labor.

When Sun Yat Sen told me about his father's journey and sojourn in Macao, I forecast the usual acceptance of the snares of Macao. For the elder Sun, like all Chinese, loved pleasure, and as he was assured of a position as a tailor's apprentice, it seemed inevitable to me that he should remain in that city of seduction like the great majority that passed that way.

'And your father, how long did he remain in Macao?' I asked.

'Not very long, as I remember; for he became homesick and yearned for his Choy Hung. He was homesick because his duty was at home.'

'Homesick? Duty?' thought I. 'What Chinese lad could be homesick in such a town as Macao?'

' "Homesick" and "duty". Yes,' I reflected, 'here was another foundation-stone in the character of the Reformer. His father preferred the duty of family associations rather than the pleasures of Macao, and with such sense of duty and decency, can we wonder when the boy turns from the colored lights of Macao and follows down the sorghum brakes that line the waters beyond Macao, and lead back to the rude and hard simplicity of his hamlet life, dearer to him than all the pleasures that he had left behind!'

The elder Sun did not come back from the City of Pleasure like the Prodigal Son. He had done well in Macao. He had performed his duty there, and came back to Blue Valley with something of saved money and a knowledge of the tailor trade, which, if need be, he could use to advantage in supplementing his work in the rice-paddies, the bean and cotton fields.

To one who knows the looseness of Chinese morals, this clean home-coming was commendable and remarkable. The red pleasure lights showing out on the moon-lit waters of the Praya Grande were as tiny fireflies in their influence on this youth who was to become the father of one of the greatest reformers of all time. He was made of a stuff that made pure home life a model of duty and ambition. Not for this duty-loving youth were the lascivious passion-songs of the flower-boats, the gilded blandishments of the gaming-houses, and the thick, sweet vapor of the opium couch. With no God, and with no background of morality for a conscience, from his sheer personal respect he had turned away from that midst of smiling, black-haired sirens, the lewd flower-girls, and the unctuous entertainers, and had come back to the bosom of his rude home, clean and wholesome, with his brow held high, to become the progenitor of a family in which, through one single member, the leadership of a great part of this world would eventually be involved.

'I think that your father was wonderful,' I declared.

'Wonderful? Well, he was good. He had the respect of his family and of his fellow-men.'

With this remark a vision flashed before me . . . Macao as I last saw it, with its purple hills, its gay edge of water, and a dozen colors—of man's making—to mingle with the deeper tones of God's own nature.

Then, in the vision, I saw the night fall, and only the red lights of the flower-boats showing, and in the darkness came the wail of the singsong girls as they were driven out into the gloom, emblematic of the decay of beautiful Macao—a fair city, but going down with the cancer of vice to a certain doom. A city—and a youth—and of the two the youth had proved stronger than the whole city, for from his flesh and conscience came the mastery of a self-control that eventually, through his issue, would bring a leadership—a leadership for the better things of life for a whole race.

I think that much of Sun Yat Sen's great moral force came to him as an inheritance from that father who, without knowledge of the precepts of the true God, from the decent sense of his own, fine nature, gave up his easy task of making garments for pleasure-seekers to return to the rude, hard labor in the stony fields of Blue Valley.

9

AN IDYLLIC SCENE FOR A HELL ON EARTH

CROSBIE GARSTIN

After stints as a horse breeder, threshing-gang worker, lumber-camp sawyer, and miner in North America, not to mention a ranger in Matabeleland, Crosbie Garstin found Macao unexpectedly tame. The British novelist, travel writer, and adventurer visited the settlement in the 1920s.

Macao's three centuries of remunerative isolation ended with the settlement of Hongkong. Never scrupulous, from thence on she was to live by any means that presented itself, no matter how disreputable, as an asylum for criminals, a thieves' mart, by smuggling, opium, the coolie traffic, gambling hells and official lotteries. The coolie trade was put a stop to in 1874, but the other activities continue as merrily as ever. It battens on vice, mentionable and unmentionable, and is, in short, a little hell on earth.

There was a book of short stories published lately which had a great vogue in England and the States. The author wrote with an air of intimate knowledge of the world's shady holes and ends. One of the stories concerned Macao. There was a wealthy Englishman in it, a gambling-dive, a naughty Portuguese, a half-cast singsong girl, knives, murder—in fact, as much fireworks as a chap could crowd into three thousand words without setting the paper alight. This story in mind, combined with some foreknowledge of Macao, its history, industries and ideals, I landed in the place with the highest expectations. 'Here,' said I, 'we shall assuredly see some fun.'

I saw as much fun—that is, of the sort I expected—as is evident in a Bedfordshire village on a wet Sunday afternoon in Lent. I went into the gambling-dives, and so far from being robbed, made money. I went into a dark foul little den and bought a gilded idol (stolen, of course) dirt cheap. I hung about dark alleys waiting to see somebody sand-bagged. I had but one encounter. An unwashed half-cast person, who had been watching my peregrinations, accosted me and asked me if I had lost myself? If so, might he show me home? Seeing through his offer, I said he might. But instead of steering me into some noisome dive he faithfully landed me on my doorstep. Very disappointing! I did all I could, but short of batting a policeman under the eye, or setting fire to the bishop, I saw no way of getting myself into trouble. One of my most vivid recollections of Macao is a parade of charming little girls in white, coming demurely out of Sunday School, shepherded by a benign old coloured gentleman in a bowler hat and frock-coat; dear little creatures with large mobile black eyes and the most winning smiles. One fancied the little angels would take wings all of a sudden and go fluttering round one's head, twittering like birds and scattering roses. An idyllic scene for a hell on earth!

For Macao is a hell on earth, let there be no mistake about it. It is a place that thrives on the financial, physical and moral ruin of thousands, luring the feeble-minded to such excesses that in the end they sell their children into slavery or commit suicide, but had I thought about it I should have expected nothing but what I did find, perfect peace—on the surface. To make a resort of that kind succeed it must be made as attractive as possible, and people are not attracted to a place where they get systematically knocked on the head. I feel sure that, when we get there, we shall find Hades itself admirably conducted—on the outside—but it'll be Hell for all that.

The Chinese gambling-house proprietors pay the Portuguese millions of dollars yearly for their privileges and in return demand absolute security for their clients. They want all the money that comes into Macao to pass through their hands and not be side-tracked into the pockets of thugs and thieves. I am told

that, besides the efficient police force, they maintain a secret service of their own. A ruffian flying from mainland justice may abide on the peninsula and no questions asked, but woe betide him if he try any of his tricks on the community.

A resident told me that his sister-in-law came home from a dance to find that her house had been burgled and her very valuable jewels stolen. She notified the police and went to bed. Next morning when her house-boy brought in the coffee he mentioned casually that there was a Chinaman in the kitchen with the *senhora's* jewels. He had been sitting there for some hours, not wishing to disturb the *senhora*. He returned the jewels with no more comment than a grunt and went quietly away. How he caught the burglar and what he did to him was not mentioned. There was no court-case, nothing more said—but probably the gulls saw something, a cord drawn tight about its throat, floating seawards through the Ladrones.

The gambling-houses are mainly situated in the Street of Happiness and are dingy affairs with no pretensions towards decoration except a cheap print or two and notices requesting you to spit in non-existent spittoons. *Fan-tan* is played. . . .

The table is on the ground floor and a certain number of gamblers can be accommodated about it, but others ascend to the first and second stories and get a bird's-eye view of the table down a well cut through the two floors, so that looking upward you see two circles of faces peering down upon you. Bets are taken up above by attendants who convey the money to and from the table in little baskets swinging on the ends of strings.

At a gambling-house every comfort is provided, according to celestial taste. There is no reason why one should ever leave it, as long as the money lasts. The table is open for play day and night, meals are provided for the hungry, opium for the depressed, beds for the weary, singsong damsels for the—let us say—musically inclined. All on the premises.

I was in a gambling-house one evening when there were several excursion boats in from Canton and things were humming in the 'City of the Sacred Name of God'. The little baskets went flying from floor to floor like financial carrier-pigeons, stuffed with coin and notes. The gamesters were mainly Chinese, but my immediate neighbours were a Hindu, a Danish merchant captain, and two little Japanese filles de joie. At the back of the room, oblivious to all else, three opium smokers lay stretched on couches. One, an emaciated European degenerate, lay with his thin knees drawn almost up to his chin, his wide brown eyes glowing blankly into immeasurable distances. He looked like a man who had died leaving in his eyes the first far vision of some unholy paradise. Down below, shorn of head, cigarette-ends trailing from the corners of their mouths, yellow bodies stripped to the waist, stood the croupiers, in strong sartorial contrast to their shirt-fronted Monte Carlo *confrères*—but every bit as efficient, dealing smoothly, swiftly, almost listlessly, with five different currencies and fifty separate transactions at once. To me, with whom any calculation above ten involves the removal of my boots and the calling of my toes to the aid of my fingers, the spectacle appeared little short of miraculous.

The Chinaman is a born gambler, and a good one. Win or lose, there is no sign. Coolies entered, dripping from their labours, risked their pitiable earnings and saw them vanish without a murmur. Rich merchants—having made innumerable calculations, consulted oracles, etc.—staked several thousand dollars at a plunge, and watched them disappear without the twitch of a lip. So it went on, hour after hour, the crowd changing, the little baskets bobbing up and down, the naked croupiers sucking their cigarette-stubs, listlessly handling five different currencies. Men hawked and spat, smoke hung about the lamps, the place stank with the reek of crowded yellow humanity. And all the time, amid the comings and goings, the outcast at the back of the room lay still as death, knees drawn up as in some last rigour, fixed eyes smitten with ungodly visions.

PART III

THE PURSUIT OF GOLD

'Massive houses, with immense verandahs running all round them, and spacious and cool interior recesses, attest to this day the ancient glory of Macao.'

ALEXANDER MICHIE, 1900

Throughout its existence Macao has been a relative oasis of European comfort on the China coast, but the city remained a primitive outpost, far from family, polite society, and political favour. Until recent times the journey was perilous. Still they came. Some were inspired by religion. But whether explorers seeking precious spices, Portuguese accumulating bullion in the Japan trade, British and Americans trading opium for tea, or Chinese attracted by Macao's free-for-all economy, most came dreaming of riches.

10

THE ENIGMATIC DOCTOR LOBO

IAN FLEMING

Like his most famous character, James Bond, the novelist Ian Fleming
was fascinated with wealth, tycoons, gambling, women, and gold.
Fleming indulged all of these passions when he visited Macao in 1959,
collecting material for a series of articles on the world's 'thrilling cities'
for the Sunday Times. *Fleming's travelling companion in Macao was*
the Australian, Richard Hughes, a veteran news correspondent in the
Far East. This tale of their luncheon with the gold king of Macao blends
Bond flamboyance with more straight-laced journalism. In the person
of Dr Lobo's threatening oriental henchman, we see echoes of Oddjob
from Goldfinger, the Bond novel about gold smuggling that Fleming
published the same year.

G old, hand in hand with opium, plays an extraordinary secret role through the Far East, and Hong Kong and Macao, the tiny Portuguese possession only forty miles away, are the hub of the whole underground traffic. . . .

The gold king of the Orient is the enigmatic Doctor Lobo of the Villa Verde in Macao. Irresistibly attracted, I gravitated towards him, the internal Geiger-counter of a writer of thrillers ticking furiously. . . .

So far as its premier citizen, Dr Lobo, is concerned, the most interesting features of Macao are that there is no income tax and no exchange control whatever, and that there is complete freedom of import and export of foreign currencies, and all forms of bullion. To take only the case of gold bullion, it is, therefore, perfectly easy for anyone to arrive by ferry or seaplane or come across from Communist China, only fifty yards away across the river, buy any quantity of gold, from a ton down to a gold coin, and leave Macao quite openly with his booty. It is then up to the purchaser, and of no concern whatsoever to Dr Lobo or the chief of the Macao police, to smuggle his gold back into China, into neighbouring Hong Kong or, if he has a seaplane, fly off with it into the wide world. These considerations make Macao one of the most interesting market-places in the world, and one with many secrets. . . .

We repaired to the Macao Inn on the junction of the waterfront and the Travesso do Padre Narciso. There we met 'Our Man in Macao' and drank warm gins and tonics under a banyan tree while I enlightened myself about the four Mr Bigs—who, with the Portuguese Government in the background control pretty well everything that goes on in this enigmatic territory. In America these four men would be called the Syndicate, but here they are just friendly business partners who co-operate to keep trade running along the right channels. There were at the time, in order of importance, the aforesaid Dr P. J. Lobo, who looks after gold; Mr Foo Tak Yam, who concerns himself with gambling and associate activities, which may be broadly described as 'entertainment', and who owns the Central Hotel, of which more later; Mr C. Y. Leung, a silent partner; and Mr Ho Yin, the chief intermediary for trade with Communist China.

The fortunes of these four gentlemen rose during and after the war—during the war through trade with the Japanese who then occupied the mainland, and, after the war, during the golden days when the harbour of Macao was thronged with ships from Europe smuggling arms to Communist China. Those latter days had turned Macao into a boom town when a single street running half the length of the town, the 'Street of Happiness', had been one great and continuous street of pleasure and when the nine-storey-high Central Hotel, the largest house of gambling and self-indulgence in the world, had been constructed by Mr Foo to siphon off the cream of the pleasure-seekers. Those golden days had now passed. Communist China was manufacturing her own weapons, the Street of Happiness had emptied through lack of roistering sailors, and now pleasure, devoted only to the relaxation of Hong Kong tourists, was confined to the Central Hotel.

Having got all this straight in our minds, it was obvious to Dick and me that only one question remained: where to have dinner before repairing to the Central Hotel? We were advised to choose between the Fat Siu Lau, the 'Loving Buddha', in the Street of Happiness, noted for its Chinese pigeon, or the Long Kee, famous for its fish. We chose the Loving Buddha, dined excellently and repaired to the Central Hotel, whose function and design I recommend most warmly to the attention of those concerned with English morals. . . .

The next morning I was awakened by a European clang of cathedral bells and a thin, distant tucket of military bugles, and we girded ourselves for luncheon with Dr Lobo. Ever since *Life* magazine cast a shining light on Macao in 1949, the Doctor has been very wary of writers and journalists, but the magical name of a friend in Hong Kong had opened even this door for us, and in due course we were picked up by a powerful-looking 'secretary' in a battered brown Austin. We had spent the morning observing a communist co-operative hard at work across the river, admired the awe-inspiring façade of St Paul's Cathedral upon which the Japanese Christian stonemasons had sprinkled plenty of dragons and flying skeletons amongst the angels, and taken note of the hospital founded by Sun Yat-sen in 1906.

Neither the Austin nor the battered Chevrolet in which we later left to catch our ferry, nor the Villa Verde, which belonged to some tropical Wimbledon, suggested that Dr Lobo was worth the five or ten million pounds with which he is credited. At first sight, the Doctor, in his trim blue suit, stiff white collar and rimless glasses, looked like the bank manager or dentist (in fact he started life as an oculist) one would have found in the more benign Wimbledon. Dr Lobo is a small, thin Malayan Chinese with a pursed mouth and blank eyes. He is in his early seventies. He greeted us carefully in a sparsely furnished suburban living-room with a Roman Catholic shrine over the doorway, a large, nineteenth-century oleograph depicting heaven and hell, and a coloured reproduction of a famous picture I could not place—a woman with a bowed head swathed in butter-muslin, who was either Faith, Hope or Charity. A powerfully-built butler, who looked more like a judo black-belt than a butler, offered us Johnny Walker and we launched into careful conversation about the pros and cons of alcohol and cigarettes, neither of which, Dr Lobo said, appealed to him.

A spark of animation came into Dr Lobo's eyes when I said I heard that he was an amateur composer of note. The Doctor said he had been a violinist and had given concerts in Hong Kong. But he was certainly, he vouchsafed, no Menuhin or Heifetz. Nowadays, when he had time, he did indeed try his hand at composing. I asked if we might hear something. Readily Dr Lobo handed us a gramophone record entitled 'Gems of the Orient', privately recorded by His Master's Voice. Meanwhile he busied himself with a large gramophone. The titles of Dr Lobo's compositions were 'Souls in Sorrow', 'Passing Thoughts', 'Waves of the South Seas', 'Lilies of the Mountains' and 'Lasting Memories'.

The Doctor put 'Waves of the South Seas' on the gramophone and turned various knobs, which resulted only in a devastating roar of static from a concealed loudspeaker. More knobs were turned and still the static hooted and screamed. Dr Lobo shouted through the racket that there was something wrong. The secretary was sent off to fetch the house engineer. Dick and I sipped our whisky and avoided each other's eye. The engineer arrived and repeated Dr Lobo's previous motions. Identical hullabaloo. The engineer conjured with the back of the machine while we looked on politely. Dr Lobo adopted the familiar expression of the rich man whose toy is kaput.

In due course the thin, wavering strains of a tune containing vague echoes of 'Tales of the Vienna Woods', 'In a Monastery Garden' and 'Rose Marie' fixed expressions of rapt attention on all our faces. I shifted my posture to the bowed stance with eyes covered which I adopt for concert and opera. There was nothing to do but think of other things until both sides of the longest player I have ever heard had been completed. Dick and I made appreciative grunts as if we had come back to earth, speechless, from some musical paradise. I muttered something about 'remarkable virtuosity' and 'many-sided talent'. And then, blessedly, luncheon was served.

Dr Lobo's dining-room was lined from floor to ceiling with cabinets of cut glass that winked painfully from all sides as if one was sitting in the middle of a giant chandelier. The tepid macaroni and vegetable soup promised an unmemorable meal, so I politely got on to the topic of gold. Yes, indeed, it was an interesting business. Did I know the Bank of England and Messrs Samuel Montague? Such nice, correct people to deal with. No, he hadn't actually got an office in Europe. A manufacturer of baby powder represented him in those parts. The Doctor himself had never been farther abroad than Hong Kong.

I pressed on about gold. As I understood it, I said, Macao had been excluded by Portugal from the Bretton Woods monetary agreement which tied most of the other countries in the world to a gold price of $35 an ounce. Since, for instance, the Chinese price is around $50 an ounce, there was obviously a handsome profit to be made somewhere. Was I correct in thinking that Dr Lobo bought gold from, say, the Bank of England, at $35 an ounce and then sold it at a premium to anyone who cared to buy; how it then left Macao for the outside world being none of his business? Yes, agreed Dr Lobo, that was more or less the position. Nowadays the business was difficult. Before, when the premium over the official gold price had been higher, it had been more interesting. Smuggling? Yes, no doubt such a thing did take place. Dr Lobo smiled indulgently. The people in these parts liked to have a small piece of gold. If they bought gold in Macao, I insisted gently, how did they get it out? Dr Lobo's face went blank. These were matters of which he knew little. He had heard that they sewed single coins into their clothes and hammered thin plates of gold which they could carry in their belts. There had also been a case where some cows had been found to contain gold. The bamboo that is so much a part of sampans, for instance, is conveniently hollow. Was I interested in cut glass? All this glass had been a hobby of his late wife's. It was Stuart glass, the best.

How, I persisted, was the Indian market in gold nowadays? 'I heard it is not so good', said Dr Lobo. Nowadays the Indians were poor. They had no foreign exchange with which to buy gold and nobody wanted the rupee. Previously, he understood, large fortunes had been made from selling gold to India, but nowadays, the eyes twinkled frostily, it was perhaps more profitable to buy newspapers. Yes? This neat reference to the change of ownership of the *Sunday Times* showed that Dr Lobo had his wits about him. . . .

My last sight of the enigmatic Dr Lobo, as we rattled away in the ancient Chevrolet, was of a small, trim figure cutting short the last wave of his hand as he turned and, flanked by the powerful secretary and powerful butler, disappeared back into the villa. What had I learned of Dr Lobo, the gold king whose name is whispered with awe throughout the East? Absolutely nothing at all. What do I think of Dr Lobo? I think that while there may be unexplained corners of his history, as there are in the histories of many a successful millionaire, he is what he appears to be: a careful, astute operator who has chosen an exotic line of business which may have caused a good deal of pain and grief in its retail outlets to the regret, no doubt, of the wholesaler. The respectability of all ageing millionaires is now his, together with the laurels of good citizenship—a doctorate of sciences unspecified and, two weeks after I left him, his appointment as Chairman of the Municipal Council of Macao, a post equivalent to mayor.

11
FAMOUS AND WEALTHY CITY
JOHANNES NIEUHOF

Macao's most prosperous era was its first hundred years when practically all trade between Europe and China passed through the city. The Dutch trader, Johannes Nieuhof, wrote with envy of the city's commercial success after accompanying the Dutch Embassy to the Emperor of China in 1655. The account was translated into English in 1669.

Upon the 14. we came in sight of the Island of Maccoa, and kept us by the heighth of 21 Degrees and 10 Minutes: in the Evening we Anchor'd, and the next morning we set sail. We saw lying upon the Shore several Boats, but not one would come Aboard, notwithstanding all the Signs we made to invite them, so wondrous fearful they are of the Pyrate, cokesing them, who at that times held the Coast in continual Alarm, and whom they undoubtedly took us to be.

Two days we Sail'd under this Island, thence passing by the most famous and wealthy city of Maccoa; and though we came not near it, yet I shall relate what I have understood from others, concerning the Magnificence of this Place, whereof you have a Draught as it was taken at sea.

This seat (which for many Ages has been held for the greatest Trading City in all Asia) lies upon a little hanging Island, fixed to a greater, and is built upon a very high Rock, which rises out of the Water, whose Wall is washed around by the Sea, except on the North-side, where it joins to the Land by a little Slip, so that by the Sea on the one side, and the Mountainous Situation on the other, it is held invincible against the Power and the Strength of any whatsoever. The Sea which surrounds this Place is not very deep, so that there is no harbour near for any great Ships. This City exceeds all others for great Cannon, which are to be had there for a reasonable Rate, and wherewith they drive a considerable Trade, for they are held to be the best of all India, being Cast of Chinese and Japan Copper, and are sent for far and near. On the side of the Land stand only two Castles upon two small Hills, which are however a great defence to the City against any Invasion. This seat has nothing of Trees, or the like, to hinder a fair Prospect toward the Sea. The midst of the old Foundation, ere this City was built, an Idol possessed, called Ama; and because of a safe Harbour there for Shipping, which the Chinese call Gao, these two words being conjoin'd, they nam'd it Amacao, and for brevities sake contracted it to Maccao, or Maccou. This Place (which lay waste and unbuilt) the Portugueses with the consent of the Chineses, did re-edifie and inhabit, which in a short time grew very populous and renowned for Commerce, whither the Portugueses sent great store of Merchandises out of Europe and India by Sea, as also from China. Likewise the Portugueses in Maccao (which doth not a little advance and increase their Trade) have obtain'd that freedom from the Chineses, that they may come twice a year to the chief City Canton, at their annual Marts, and there Barter, Buy, and Sell, and Transport then from thence abundance of several Wares to Maccao: for there is found entred into the Custom-Books (when the Commerce flourish'd in that Place) how much they Imported and Exported; they Exported above three hundred Chests of all sorts of Silks, in each Chest a hundred and fifty Pieces of Velvet or the like: they brought likewise from thence 25 hundred Ingots of Gold each Ingot weighing thirteen Ounces: they likewise commonly Exported eight hundred Pounds of Musk, beside great quantities of Gold Thred, fine Linen, unwrought Silk, Precious Stones, Pearls, &c.

12

VILLAINOUS MERCHANTS

ALEXANDER HAMILTON

By the time the British trader Alexander Hamilton arrived in Macao in 1703, many European nations had established trading links with the Far East and the commercial flowering of the Portuguese city had lost its first blush. Still, Hamilton was evidently impressed with Macao and his description of what he saw is an important record of the period. The trader had come to Macao for urgent repairs, having nearly lost his ship in a violent typhoon. He soon learnt what could befall merchants who lacked the support of Macao's Portuguese officials and, especially, its Chinese mandarins.

Canton or Quantung (as the Chinese express it) is the next maritime Province; and Maccaw, a city built by the Portugueze, was the first Place of Commerce. This City stands on a small island, and is almost surrounded by the Sea. Towards the Land it is defended by three Castles built on the Tops of low Hills. By its Situation and Strength by Nature and Art, it was once thought impregnable. Indeed their beautiful Churches and other Buildings give us a reflecting Idea of its ancient Grandeur, for in the Forepart of the seventeenth Century, according to the Christian Æra, it was the greatest Port for Trade in India or China.

The largest Brass Cannon that ever I saw are mounted in proper Batteries about the City. I measured one (amongst many) out of Curiosity, and found it 23 Foot from the Breech to the Muzzle Ring, nine Inches and a Quarter diameter in the Bore, and it was 12250 Rotullaes or lb. Weight of solid Metal. . . .

The City contains five Churches, but the Jesuits is the best, and is dedicated to St Paul. It has two Convents for married Women to retire to, when their Husbands are absent, and orphan Maidens are educated in them till they can catch an Husband. They have also a Nunnery for devout Ladies, young or old, that are out of Conceit with the Troubles and Cares of the world. And they have a Sancta Casa, or holy House of the Inquisition, that frightens every Catholick into the Belief of every Thing that holy Mother Church tells them is Truth, whether it be really so or no.

The Forts are governed by a Captain-general, and the City by a Burgher, called the Procuradore, but in Reality, both are governed by a Chinese Mandereen, who resides about a League out of the City, at a Place called Casa Branca. The Portugueze Shipping that come there, are admitted into their Harbour, and are under the Protection of the Town; but the Chinese keep the Custom-house, and receive Customs for all Goods imported.

That rich flourishing City has ruined itself by a long War they made with Timore, as I have observed before. They exhausted their Men and Money on that unsuccessful Project of Domination, so that out of a Thousand creditable House-keepers that inhabited the City before that War, there are hardly fifty left; and out of forty Sail of trading Vessels, they have not above five left, so that in the whole City and Forts, there are computed to be about two hundred Laity, and six hundred Priests, and about fifteen hundred Women, and many of them are very prolifick, for they bring forth Children without Husbands to father them. . . .

I went to the City, and applied myself to the Captain General and the Procuradore for Assistance, and they made large Promises. I addressed each of them with a Present of scarlet Cloth, and Surat Atlasses, which they thankfully received, but soon after I found they were in no Condition to assist me. They indeed designed to compliment me with some fresh Provisions, but had not Interest enough with the China Mandereen to get Liberty to send them on board of my Ship.

Nor would he suffer any Body to supply me with Necessaries till he received Orders from the Chontock or Vice-roy of Canton. That Incivility presaged but ill Success to my Affairs there; however, I went and paid him a Visit, and presented him with a Silver Salver and a Piece of Atlas on it, both in Value about 45 *Tayels* or 15 L. Sterl. which he received, and made an Apology for his prohibiting Commerce with my Ship till he had received Advices from the Vice-roy.

He treated me with Tartarian Tea, which I took to be Beans boyled in Milk, with some Salt in it, and it was served in wooden Dishes, as big as Chocolate Cups. When our Regalia was over, I took Leave, and he loaded me with fair Promises, and sent after me a Present of a Hog, two Geese, a Goat and some Wheat Flour, and a small Jar of Samshew, or Rice Arrack. . . .

It was near a Month after my Arrival before the Vice-roy's Order came to settle my Affairs. They had represented to him, that our Ship was a Wrack, and, by the Laws of the Country, she fell to the King; but the Vice-roy distrusting the Report of the Chinese, sent a French Gentleman to bring him true Accounts of our Condition, and what Merchandize we had to dispose of. When the French Man came on board, I entertained him civilly, and gave him a Sight of the Musters of our Goods and their Quality, and we had fished up some small Fir-trees, which we had converted into Masts and Yards.

On the French Man's Return, and giving the Vice-roy an Account of what he had seen, he had seemed amazed at the false Information he had from Maccao, and ordered the *Hapoa* or Custom-master to go and take an Account of our Goods, and take the Emperor's customary Dues, and give me a free Toleration to trade. Accordingly the *Hapoa* came, and brought three Merchants along with him to buy our Goods. When they came on board, they were surprised to see so large a Ship, with so many Guns, having forty mounted, and such a Number of Men, I having above a Hundred and fifty. I saluted the Hapoa with some Guns, and treated him with a Dinner after the European Fashion, and gave him good Store of Wine to wash it down; but he lik'd Canary best, and drank of it till he was well flustred. Then he ordered the Length of the Ship to be measured on the upper Deck, and the Breadth at the Main-mast, and departed.

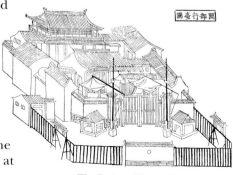

The Customs House, Canton

Next Day I went to visit him, and carried him a Present as customary. In our Discourse he told me, that he had brought a very honest Man along with him, who spake the Portugueze Language, and that he must be my Interpreter at Maccao, and buy all my Provisions spent in the Ship, and on my Table ashore, and that he had also brought three Merchants to agree for my Cargo, all Men of Substance. I answered, as to the buying of Provisions, I had no Occasion for any, and for making a Contract with those Merchants, I had no Mind to it, because I designed to carry my Cargo to Canton in small *Jonks*, and when I arrived in Canton with my Goods, and had enquired into the Market, it would be Time then to make Bargains. He seemed to be angry that I was not directed by him, and told me, that he had taken much Pains to serve me, but that I slighted his service. I answered, that being a Stranger, I might be allowed to walk cautiously till I had informed myself of the current Prices of Goods, and the King's Duties to be paid on them, but I should always have a great Regard to his Friendship. He alledged that there was great Danger in carrying Goods between Maccao and Canton, because there were many Pirate Vessels in the Way, belonging to Quansi, and that neither the Emperor nor the Viceroy could be accountable for what Robberies might be committed by these Pirates. I replied, that I desired none to answer for such Losses, but would be very glad to meet with those Sar-crows, that I might have an Opportunity to make a Present of some of them to the Vice-roy.

When he found that none of his arguments prevailed, he gave Orders to have my Goods put on board of small *Jonks*, and that I might put five Men of my own in each boat for a Guard, and ordered one of his Merchants to accompany me in that which I went in, so that we were twenty-five Europeans well armed, in our little Fleet. We took the inland Passage, which was the nearest, and sailed by several Islands on both Sides of us. I kept in the headmost Jonk, and a good officer in the sternmost; and every Vessel we saw, they told us they were Pirates. I answered them, I wanted to be near them, but I could not perswade them to steer towards them. . . .

When I arrived at Canton the *Hapoa* ordered me Lodgings for myself, my Men and my Cargo in an *Haung* or Inn belonging to one of his Merchants, where none but the French, who had then a Factory there, had Liberty to visit me, and when I went aboard, I had always some Servants belonging to the *Haung* to follow me at a Distance. I had staid about a week, and found no Merchants came near me, which made me suspect, that there were some under-hand Dealings between the *Hapoa* and his Chaps, to my prejudice, but I could not be informed what they designed. At length, one Night I had supp'd in the French Factory, and began to make my Complaint to Mr Petchbertie the Chief, of the strange Method I was treated in, that all Merchants shunned my Company, but for what Reason I knew not. He winkt on me to follow him into his Bed-chamber, and, shutting the Door, told me, that those three Merchants, or rather Villains, Linqua, Anqua, and Hemshaw had paid to the *Hapoa* 4000 *Tayels* for the Monopolization of my Cargo, and that no Merchant durst have any Commerce with me but they, but withal advised me to carry fair with them, and bargain with them on whatsoever Terms they would allow me.

Accordingly I had a Meeting with my Chaps, and, in my Discourse, I told them what the current Price was in Town for every Species of my Goods, and desired to know what they would give. They seemed surprised that I knew the Market, and would fain have known who had informed me of the Prices, but I desired to be excused on that Point, and to proceed to bid for themselves. My cargo consisted in Cotton, Putchock or Radix dulcis [root used in medicine and joss sticks], Rosamalla [hibiscus] or liquid Storax [resin used in medicine] and Surat coarse Chints, which, according to the current Market, would have come to 14000 Tayels, but they would not come within 80 *per cent.* of the Market Price.

I, finding myself insulted, and a Mind to wait on the Vice-king, who resided at a Town called Sachow, about 20 Miles up the River, and, in order to go thither, I applied myself, by the Assistance of the French Linguist, to a Mandereen called the *Chumpin*, for Licence to go to Sachow, and for his Letter of Recommendation to the Vice-roy. The News of my being with the *Chumpin* alarmed the *Hapoa* and my Merchants, who found no Way to impede my going but by seizing any Linguist that should serve me either in Canton or in my Journey, and accordingly as I was going next Day, to receive my Letters, and the French Linguist along with me, he had a small Iron Chain thrown over his Head, (a Custom that is among the Chinese when they arrest a Man) and he was dragged before the *Hapoa*, and was accused of assisting the French in running Goods on board of their Ships, for they had two lying at Whampoa, a Village about 4 Leagues below the City. The poor

Man was kept in Prison as long as I stayed at Canton, and his Imprisonment so terrified the others, that I could get none to serve me but whom those Villains of Merchants recommended to me, and none durst serve me as Linguist.

Finding no Remedy, but Patience, to my disturbed Mind, was forced to comply with the unjust Impositions of the *Hapoa*, and so struck up a Bargain at the villanous Merchants Rates, but to receive silver for my Goods; and after I had delivered them, I desired to settle Accounts, and to have my Money according to Contract. They made up a large Account of Charges, as 3000 *Tayels* for the Measurage of my Ship, 1000 for Liberty to guy Masts, Cordage and Provisions, and 1000 *Tayels* for Presents to some Mandereens, and then they told me, for what remained I should have Goods at the current Price of the Market, tho' I was obliged to take them between 40 and 50 *per cent.* higher. They made me pay 13 *Tayels* per Chest for Japon Copper, which I could have bought for 9 *Tayels*, and for China Copper I was charged ten and an half, which I bought at Maccao for seven, some Fir Masts that I cheapened for 60 *Tayels* they made me pay 250. It was the middle of January 1704. before I had ended my Accounts with them, and I wanted Permission to go to Maccao, but that I could not have. They put me off, from Day to Day, about a Week. At length I visited the French Chief, and he frankly told me, that they would not let me go till I laid out ten thousand *Tayels* of Silver with them, which they were informed I had on Board of my Ship, and that my Merchants had told him so. I answered, that being bound to Amoy, I had bills on Merchants there for near that Sum, which, with my Goods, had been sufficient to have loaded my Ship there for which Reason I had brought no Silver with me; but I found there was no End to their Villany, and therefore I would go without Leave, If I had it not in three Days. He told me of many ill Consequences that would attend violent Courses; but I answered him, that I could no longer bear their Insults, and, if I had not my Permission in three Days, I would run a Muck, (which is a mad Custom among the Mallayas when they become desperate) and that I thought twenty-five Men well armed, were sufficient to go off by Violence, when by fair Means they could not obtain it, that being the last Remedy, what Blood might be spilt in the Action, the *Hapoa* and his Chaps would answer to the Emperor for, who, no Doubt, would enquire into the Cause.

I then bade farewell to all the Gentlemen of the French Factory, and left a Present of 50 *Tayels* for the Linguist that lay in Prison, and came Home to my Inn, and acquainted my Men with my Resolution, who unanimously approved of it, promising to live and die with me, and immediately we new cleaned our Arms, and new loaded them with Powder and Ball, which the Servants of the *Haung* taking Notice of, went and informed my Merchants what we had been doing, and that we lookt brisker than usual. The Merchants went to the French Chief, to see if he knew what Design we had, and he frankly told them all that I had told him. They immediately acquainted the *Hapoa*, who forthwith sent us a Permit for ourselves and Goods, and next Day I departed with twelve of my Crew, and some Goods, leaving the rest to follow with the rest of my Goods and Masts.

In three Days we got to Maccao, and got all Things in Readiness to sail. There were two Portugueze lay in *Tiepe-queberado* [waters near Taipa] waiting for me to accompany them for fear of a French cruiser of 32 Guns, that had been at Manila. One Mr Burno commanded her, who had made his Brags to the Spaniards, that he would bring all the English and Portugueze that were bound from China to the Streights of Malacca, into Manila, and made a Present of our Ships to the Spaniards, which frightened the Portugueze. One was a ship of two and twenty Guns, and the other of sixteen.

However, some China Merchants contracted me to carry them, and about 150 Tuns of Bricks and China Ware, to *Pullo-condore* [islands near the mouth of the Mekong River], and were to pay me 1000 *Tayels*. Three Days after my Arrival came my Masts, and as they were passing through the Harbour of Maccao, towards my Ship, they were stopt by the Procuradore of the City. When Word was brought me, I sent my Purser, who spake good Portugueze, that if my Masts were not delivered the same Day would take the Masts out of their Ships that lay close by me, let the Consequences be what it would. So to avoid Trouble, my Masts were cleared.

Two of my Merchants came to Maccao, under Pretence of clearing Accounts fairly. I invited them on board to dine with me, but they would not do me the Honour. They had heard of the Contract I had made with the China Merchants, to carry them and their Goods to *Pullo-condore*, which Contract they broke, for that strong Reason, that they had bought me of the *Hapoa*, and that

Freight I had no Power to contract for, but they would furnish
them with a Passage for them and their Goods, on the same Terms
that I had agreed on, so I was obliged to lose my Freight.

I received what Goods they were pleased to bring me, but I
found wanting 80 Chests of Japon Copper, and some Toothenague
[zinc] that I had weighed off at Canton, and put the Stocks Mark
on them, I askt the Reason whey they did not deliver those Goods,
since, according to their own Account, there was a Balance due to
me of 1800 *Tayels*. They told me that they would give no more, and
the Balance they would keep, for fear they should lose on my
imported Cargo. I bid them farewell, and promised to let them
hear from me by the first *Jonk* of their's that I met with. Next Day
I sent them my Account, wherein I shewed that they and the *Hapoa*
had cheated me of 12000 *Tayels*, and that I should not fail to make
Reprisals when I met with any Effects of theirs. Accordingly I did
at Jahore, by the King's Permission, seize a *Jonk* of theirs, and
secured their Book of Accounts, having two Portugueze Natives of
Maccao, who could speak and write Chinese, and they found out
what Merchandize belonged to those Villains, which I took on
board my Ship, among which was my 80 Chests of Copper, and 200
Peculs of Toothenague, with my own Mark on them. I drew out a
fair Account, and sent them with a Letter of Advice, that I had
received but a third Part of the Balance due to me, but upon their
fair dealing with the English for the future, I would forgive the rest,
but if they continued to act like Villains, I would prosecute my
Resentment till I had recovered the last Penny of my Balance.

When I gave the King of Johore an Account how they had
used me in China, he wondred that I did not seize all the
other Merchant Goods that were in the *Jonk*, and sell the Men for
Slaves.

13

PEOPLE FOR SALE

RUSSELL H. CONWELL

By the early 1800s, the trade in African slaves was under attack world-wide, but in gold fields, railways, guano pits, and plantations in Latin America, the Caribbean, the west coast of the United States, and Hawaii, the demand for cheap labour was insatiable. One alternative source of workers was the Chinese coolie trade. Ostensibly based on a contract between the workers and their employers, it was really little more than slavery. By the mid-1800s, efforts to stop the worst abuses had led to its banning in Hong Kong, but the traffic continued to flourish until 1874 in China coast ports under non-British flags. Macao remained a notorious centre for the trade during this time. According to Russell H. Conwell, an American publisher and Baptist minister who campaigned against the traffic, it also had the dubious distinction of being the port from which the first coolie ships had embarked with people for sale.

Early in the spring of the year 1847 a square-rigged vessel of eight hundred tons came into the port of Macaow, China, with a cargo of groceries and specie. She was a Portuguese craft named *Don Pedro*, and hailed from the port of Lisbon. It was the intention of the captain to exchange the incoming cargo for tea and silk, which he supposed to be awaiting his arrival. He found, however, that he must wait several weeks for the cargo, as the crop of tea had not begun to come in. This was a little annoying to the impatient skipper, and in expressing himself rather strongly one day in the counting-room of the assignees of his cargo, he was reproved by a senior partner of the firm, and a quarrel with blows ensued. This cost the captain his charter, and he was obliged to look about for some other merchandise. While canvassing for a cargo, he fell in with a Spaniard, fresh from Peru, who had come over to settle some long-standing accounts between himself as a sugar-dealer and a number of the firms in Macaow. The Spaniard was surprised with the cheapness of labor in China and incidentally wished that he had a thousand Chinese in Peru. This led to the discussion of the expediency of taking the Chinese to Peru, and finally to an attempt on their part to load the *Don Pedro* with Coolies. This they did under the pretense of shipping them for Java; but whether any contracts were made with these men is not at present known. They obtained three hundred Coolies, for whose passage the Spaniard became responsible. Near the first day of June the *Don Pedro* sailed out of the port of Macaow with three hundred as happy men as ever trod the planks of a ship. Believing the falsehoods that had been told them, and expecting soon to return to their homes wealthier men, they looked back upon the disappearing shores, sighing only for the time when they should see them again. It is doubtful if any one of them has yet seen their native land, and as doubtful that any of them ever will do so. After one hundred days of storm, exposed to the cold and heat, with half rations and but little water, one hundred and seventy-five were landed at a port near Callao, to be treated even worse on land than they had been on the sea. The Spaniard swore to his own story, and no one could understand the Chinaman's complaint, if he had any to make. They were put on a plantation in the interior where they could not run away, and the experiment of Coolie labor tried for the first time in that state. It was satisfactory to the contractor, and another cargo was sent for. Coming to the ears of planters in Cuba, who knew that in a few months they must part with their slaves, they also sent ships to bring over the Chinese.

The story of the successful Coolie traffic soon spread over the Spanish and Portuguese dominions, and Peru, Australia, Surinam, and the Indian Archipelago vied with Cuba in the traffic of human labor. But it was not to be expected that many cargoes of voluntary emigrants could be procured when it was found that the time for the return of the first shipload had passed, with no news from the husbands and fathers who left in the *Don Pedro*. Besides this, rumors began to be afloat that the Coolies were taken to 'the other side of the world' to be enslaved for a series of years and finally murdered. When the ships which followed the *Don Pedro* on her second visit arrived at Macaow, the Chinese were too much alarmed to be induced by any offers to go on board. Then began that system of kidnapping, purchasing, chaining, starving, and, as it may appropriately be called, murdering, which for twenty years shocked the feelings of all humane persons and cast a dark blot upon the Portuguese and Spanish escutcheons that can never be expunged. Fathers and mothers sold their sons, fugitives bargained away themselves, banditti brought in their male and female prisoners and sold them in lots to the traders, for which sums never exceeding ten dollars per person were thankfully received. The market being ill supplied with purchasable human beings, the traders organized bands of night-thieves, whose business it was to steal into the cabins of the laborers and carry on board the ship the father and sons, and sometimes the whole family. Although the bands were numerous, and Coolies were captured by the thousand, still the demand increased beyond their kidnapping capacity. Then ships called 'Lorchas' were manned and armed as if for war, and sent up the bays and rivers to fall suddenly upon the unsuspecting inhabitants of some rural district. This was a great success. In the face of the navies of the civilized world these pirate vessels carrying

the Portuguese flag would enter some towns unperceived and capture whole cargoes at a single swoop. Old men were seized in the rice fields, boys in the school-room, young men in the shops, and carried by force to the suffocating holds of the vessels at Macaow. The province of Quantung [Guangdong] was filled with orphan children and the mourning white was seen in nearly every household. Soon other ports followed the baleful example, and in the year 1853 Hongkong, Swatow, Canton, Amoy, Whampoa, Cumsing-Moon and several other smaller ports, harbored vessels awaiting cargoes of these slaves. . . .

The present traffic at Macaow consists of prisoners taken in the clan fights, which are of constant occurrence in the western districts of the Province of Quantung, and who are sold by their captors to Chinese or Portuguese man-buyers upon the interior waters,—of villagers or fishermen kidnapped along the coast by the lorchas still kept in the traders' employ,—and of Chinamen who, after having been enticed into the gambling-houses, sell themselves 'as in honor bound' to pay their losses. There are established Coolie-brokers in the city who have a depot or private jail in which they put each Coolie as they get him until they have a full cargo, when they sell them 'in bulk' to the highest bidder. They usually command a price varying from $10 to $27 per man, according to their strength.

During the years 1864 and 1865 there were nine thousand and seven hundred sold to Cuban traders at Macaow, and nearly three thousand at the port of Canton.

14

THE OPIUM CLIPPER

OSMOND TIFFANY, JR.

Macao's economy in the 1800s was heavily dependent on the trade in opium. Ships involved in the business were sleek and well-armed, their crews exhibiting an efficiency previously unique to the British Navy as this dramatic passage published in 1849 describes.

As we anchored in Macao roads, we saw a heavy armed brig going about two knots to our one. She overhauled us, and went past like a flash, dropped her anchor, rounded to, and fired her guns.

She had no name on her stern, and we concluded that she was an American government brig. In an instant her yards were swarming with men, and the sails were furled in man-of-war time and precision. We soon learned that she was an opium clipper, carrying twenty heavy guns, and a crew to match.

Besides the men and officers, the smuggler employs a 'schroff' or assayer, a native whose music has been the jingle of dollars, and whose sight is so keen that he can look further into a lump of sycee silver than any ordinary gazer.

The vessel makes sail with a freight of the 'pernicious drug', and wherever an opportunity presents along the line of coast, she anchors, and a trade is at once begun with the Chinese, who are always ready for the bait.

The chests are brought up on deck, the opium examined, and paid for in the unalloyed metal, the schroff turns over every piece, and hammers into it with an iron spike, and having thoroughly tested and valued it, the bargain is made, the opium sent over the ship's side, and the vessel proceeds on her errand. If the location is a good one, and the flats bite fast, the clipper remains several days dodging about the same spot, and if the government junks are disposed to meddle and look too curiously into her affairs, the ports are thrown wide open just to show her spunk.

Vessels will thus sometimes make very successful voyages, remaining some months on the coast, and returning with a valuable ballast of the best silver.

15

THE CONTRABAND PORT

JULES ITIER

*The Island of Taipa is now closely integrated into the life of the city,
connected by bridges, and home to the university, airport, and
racetrack. This diary entry by the French businessman and traveller,
Jules Itier, commissioned by his government to report on activities in
China, shows that in 1842 the island had a commercial importance of
a different kind.*

Travelled to Taipa. This is the name of a port situated about
four miles from Macao and considered as one of the
dependencies of the settlement. It consists of a group of
sterile islands, inhabited by families of poor fishermen, and offers
an excellent anchorage for ships of 6 to 800 tons. The French
steamer *Archimede* is presently there among a group of European
ships employed in the commerce of opium, since Taipa is one of
the stationing points for contraband trade. We went aboard one of
the vessels which serves as a receiving ship for the drug that had
been run in from India by clippers.

'Who do you aim to sink with that formidable array of cannons?'
I said to the captain, leaping on to the deck. 'Do you intend to
fight off Chinese government inspectors who have the right to
board your ship and confiscate prohibited drugs?'

'If I had nothing to fear but the Chinese government,' he
responded, 'I would keep my cannons down in the hold, for, since
the last war, the law prohibiting opium has been a dead letter.
Today many opium trading areas are spread out along the coast at
the entrance to each port open to European commerce. That of
Kumsing-mun also situated in the Tiger River [Pearl River]
supplies Canton. Floating storehouses are in view of the port of

Amoy. Chusan supplies Ningpo and the ships stationed at the mouth of the Wusung on the Yang-tse-kiang [Yangtze River] openly feed the consumption of Shanghai and Nanking. The Chinese authorities everywhere close their eyes to this contraband and have neither the power, nor the inclination to stop it, because opium has become in the most southern and coastal parts of China, an item of habitual consumption. One no longer smokes in secret or under the threat of the worst form of punishment. It is with the complete knowledge of the authorities that these things happen. This taste, this passion, is widespread in all classes of society, the Mandarins of the lowest rank providing an example, and the trade in opium is forever uncontrolled in China.'

'In that case,' I rejoined, 'why the cannons?'

'It is because,' he said, 'the Chinese pirates who infest this neighbourhood are very fond of our cargo, and because it is necessary to beware of such people. They gather together in large numbers in their boats, and during the night, encircle anchored ships that have no artillery to fight them off. Then they mount a resolute attack, cutting the throats of the crew and pillaging the cargo. Such events are common.'

Others present confirmed the words of the captain, citing a number of recent examples of unequaled audacity acted out in Macao Roads.

I profited from the visit by examining the various qualities of opium offered to the Chinese. Patna and Benares are sold in balls the size of a 32 pound cannonball and weighing about 2 1/2 catties [1.545 kilograms]. Each chest contains 400 balls and weighs one picul [62 1/2 kilograms]. Opium from Malwa comes in irregularly formed rounded lumps quite similar to camel droppings. The individual pieces are sprinkled, within their chest also weighing 1 picul, with poppy seeds with the intention of preserving their proper smell.

The third quality is represented by the opium from Turkey. It has against it, apparently, that it spoils quickly, since it is richer in gummy essence, and thus in morphine, than the opiums of India. Consequently, if care is taken with its preservation, it will necessarily become the preferred type.

PART IV

STRANGE AND GRUESOME TALES

'The statue of St James at the chapel of the Barra fort was reported to be fond of patrolling the beach at night, the boots being found besmeared with mud every morning.'

C. A. MONTALTO DE JESUS, 1926

Severed heads and ghosts have their own certain appeal. Macao tradition is littered with strange stories, most purporting to be true, that spring from a fertile mix of the Roman Catholic celebration of the miraculous and the Chinese infatuation with unquiet spirits. The best of these stories leave you believing their truth, sending a little shiver down your spine. It is certain that many people in the Portuguese city did believe that the supernatural had great powers, including the power of life and death over those who were careless or unlucky. Others, more sceptical, related their stories tongue-in-cheek, or with icy realism. The result is the type of good old tale, told around the fireside or when trapped indoors on a stormy night, that people have always loved to share.

16

HEADLESS VISITORS ABROAD

JOHN THOMSON

There is a widespread belief in ghosts in Chinese folk tradition, a belief sometimes absorbed by westerners who have spent time in Macao. This testimonial supporting the existence of ghosts was recorded by the sceptical pen of John Thomson, the Scottish photographer and traveller who visited Macao in the 1860s.

We pass the gaol, and through the stanchioned windows see a number of wretched native prisoners, who beg of us to befriend them. An American captain with whom I afterward ascended the Yangtsze-kiang, told me the following story connected with this prison, which seemed to him to corroborate his belief in spiritual agency. His father, who had been a skipper too, was one morning about to make sail from Macao, and passed the prison on his way to join his ship. Arrested by the despairing cries of the men within, he turned aside to make enquiries, and learned that three of the captives were condemned to be executed next day. Tossing a quantity of cents inside, he took his departure, and thought nothing more of the incident. But when he reached San Francisco he hastened to his owner's office, and was surprised to find no letters awaiting him from home. He concluded something must be wrong, and the merchant advised him to visit a certain spiritual medium who resided in the town. This he did, and when the séance commenced the medium informed him of the presence of certain spirits around him, reverently bowing before him, and thanking him for some great boon he had conferred on them. They carried their heads beneath their arms, and were declared by the medium to be the spirits of Macao Chinamen beheaded the day after the captain left that port, now come across the ocean to thank him.

17

THE HAUNTED HOUSE ON RUA DO CAMPO

LUÍS GONZAGA GOMES

This grisly local Chinese legend was recorded by Macao journalist and historian Luís Gonzaga Gomes, who first published it in a local newspaper in 1947. Gomes's rendition is ironic and pompous, but he clearly enjoyed conveying the spirit of a tale others found convincing.

The road beginning at the intersection of the streets Praia Grande and Santa Clara e Formosa and ending at Avenida Conselheiro Ferreira de Almeida and Rua Ferreira do Amaral, at the bottom of Calçada do Poço, is commonly known as Rua do Campo for having once been the path leading to the open land outside the city walls.

The Chinese called that street *Sôi-Hâng-Mêi* (End of the Creek), a name perhaps evoking some thread of water that once flowed down the Monte to the coast.

It is said that on this street was a gigantic mansion with a huge garden owned by a wealthy Chinese. But after the era of the *kuâi-tchân-ôk* (demons shake the houses)—that is, the time when Macao experienced a frightening series of seismic tremors, though without grave consequences—no one ever dared live there. Instead, the garden of this vast property was turned into the Jardim de S. Francisco and separated from the house by a lateral street.

The principal entrance of the mansion was in front of S. Raphael Hospital. Its proprietor, who had enriched himself in the salt trade, thought when having the place built that it would house everyone in his family for six generations. Unhappily, in the fourth generation his descendants were obliged to disperse and abandon that mansion without having satisfied the wishes of their illustrious ancestor.

The house possessed five entrances and 31 rooms in total, but no one dared live in it because it had been verified that it was inhabited by 28 tormented souls. As, with time, the number of spirits of the shadows increased, the people entrusted with the care of that useless mansion strew a thousand and one talismans through its rooms and fastened and hung innumerable amulets on its walls to try to end the visits of the dreadful beings to the ill-fated building.

The spirits actually stopped appearing for awhile. However, as soon as they discovered how to annul the effects of the talismans and amulets, they resided in it once again, rendering it uninhabitable for mortals.

The inheritors of that big house, now worthless, spared no expense in inviting the most famous exorcists and bonzes [Buddhist priests] of all the sects to celebrate complicated conjurings and incantations and intone long psalms. It was a wasted effort. The bonzes finally recommended that the discouraged proprietors lay an iron spike eight *braças* long across the main beam of the principal part of the building, leaving six *braças* exposed inside.

This remedy failed as well. Every time the sun set one still heard from every nook and cranny the disquieting music of the phantoms, which surely whispered malevolent plans or arranged sinister devilry. And, in the stillness of the night amid the darkness of the shadows, strange vapours arose and became more dense, gradually forming thick clouds of impenetrable smoke that impeded any daring visitor from entering.

The proprietors of the mansion were not disposed to leave that state of things to continue. They resolved to send an emissary of rank to consult a venerable Taoist *zaco* in the distant retreat of Lo Fau about scaring away such restless spirits of the darkness. The *zaco*, interested in such an intriguing case, but seduced much more by the considerable recompense promised him, personally came to Macao. Having examined the mansion, he recommended that the iron spike be substituted by a dried cadaver.

It was not easy advice to follow. However, acting clandestinely, the proprietors obtained, for a high price, the fresh cadaver of a pirate who had been hung in a nearby village. They eviscerated the dead man, tearing out 'the five entrails and six viscera'. After having pickled him well and dried him in the sun, the Taoist *zaco* undertook to paint the corpse with a series of talismans. What an admirable thing! In both dry and humid weather that shrunken little body remained absolutely unputrefied, without stench or worms.

Nevertheless the expedient did not work, because the demons continued to appear. So a blood-stained rod, the sight of which made mortals tremble in fear, was placed in the fifth entrance so as to restrain the evil invisible beings.

From that point the tormented souls appeared to abandon the mansion. But whoever went there wishing to visit or rent it was received by an old woman dressed in red, saying she had returned to this world to demand reparations for her iniquitous death and would not rest until justice had been done. The people unlucky enough to encounter that old woman were fated to become gravely ill, dying victims of an unknown disease within a few days. Nothing in this world could save them.

The owners of the mansion then decided to hang in the building's interior a gigantic sword weighing some 700 catties and that tradition said had belonged to a victorious general who used to wield it to frighten his enemies. This action was somewhat successful because the tormented souls ceased appearing in the salon reserved for the cult of the ancestors. However, invisible beings continued to inhabit the other rooms.

One day there appeared a group of *auteiros* (the name which in Macao designated the actors in *autos*, that is, Chinese theatrical representations). They offered their services to expunge the haunted mansion of all the spirits that made it uninhabitable.

The owners of the building in question, already disposed to anything that might make their property habitable again, accepted the proposal. The *auteiros* immediately installed themselves in the horrible edifice that no one wanted. Soon after nightfall, one of the actors costumed himself in a Mars-like Kuán-Tái, the god of war. He sat himself in a wide armchair, securing a book of military strategy in one hand and assuming an attitude of reading it, just as the divinity is usually portrayed. At his side, an actor disguised as Kuán-P'eng positioned himself with the appropriate signet in his hands, and, on the other side, another disguised as Tcháu-Tch'óng ferociously grasped a heavy sabre, as if about to slash out.

At midnight, one heard the usual murmur of the souls in malevolent conspiracy. A little later, a woman appeared and prostrated herself on the floor in front of the false Kuán-Tái. Afterwards other souls came, some old, others boys and girls. In total some 30 submitted a petition to the supposed god of war, asking that justice be done for them. The *auteiro* disguised as Kuán-Tái passed the military strategy book into the hands of the one playing Kuán-P'eng, who trembled like an aspen leaf and let out the loud scream that he used to scare his enemies when acting in the theatre. He frightened the souls of the other world, who escaped terrified.

On the following day, however, the three actors had to be taken from the mansion in a wretched state, as they had become completely demented. A Buddhist prior who was consulted about the case explained that it was the work of the victims of an ancestor of the owners of the mansion. The ancestor had been a Taoist wizard who enriched himself through his occult art, robbing the wealth, longevity, spiritual essence, and good luck of his fellow creatures. Therefore, that edifice could only be inhabited by human beings again on the day when the wizard's lineage had become completely extinct. For, only then would the tormented souls stop returning to this world, having no one from whom to ask reparations for the wicked actions of the Taoist sorcerer of whom they had been the victims in life.

It was because of this that the mansion remained abandoned for a long time until the owners decided to sell it. Then it was demolished so that new houses, on a new arrangement of streets, could be constructed on the land where the mansion had once stood.

18

ONE MURDER, FOUR DEATHS

C. H. DRAGE

It is intriguing how, after long years in the Far East, some of the most unbelieving of minds turn to the powers of occult. This story of a deadly curse comes from a biography of Edward and Cecil Bowra. Father and son, the Bowras were both employed in the British-run Chinese customs service. World War I had just come to a close and Cecil, who was a believer in the powers of the occult, was acting as the senior official in the service when these tragic events occurred.

In September . . . Cecil found himself once more officiating as Inspector-General and was immediately involved in one of those sinister oriental mysteries that figure so frequently in smoking-room gossip, but of which one so seldom hears a first hand factual account. The Portuguese colony of Macao consists of a tiny peninsula, less than three miles long and one mile broad, with almost all level land built over, so that the selection of a suitable site for the Commissioner's Residence was a perennial problem that seemed almost impossible of solution. At long last the Bom Jesus property, occupying an exceptionally fine position, encumbered only by the sparse ruins of a long deserted monastery and very reasonably priced, came on the market: Dick, the Engineer-in-Chief, sent a young architect called Arnott, accompanied by a Tidesurveyor on an inspection trip to Macao, where they were joined by the Commissioner, Smollett Campbell, an 'old China hand' of the robust type.

The survey was accomplished by the three Britishers alone, as no single Chinese or Portuguese, whether Customs staff or not, would go near the site. There was a vague and entirely unsubstantiated tradition that, many centuries ago, a bishop had been murdered in the monastery, that Heaven had put a curse on the place and that anyone who had anything to do with it would come to a bad end. Smollett Campbell laughed these superstitions to scorn and was dead within a few weeks, having been admitted to a Hong Kong hospital with typhoid fever, a most unlikely complaint to be contracted by a man of over sixty and who had spent the previous forty years in the Far East.

Soon afterwards the Tidesurveyor died rather suddenly and Cecil, having temporarily deferred all decisions on the Bom Jesus project, thanked whatever gods seemed appropriate that at all events Arnott had left China on long leave and was presumably safe. But the young architect caught influenza (probably an early case of the lethal 'Spanish 'flu' that swept the world at the end of the war) on his homeward journey and died in San Francisco. Nor were the offended spirits yet satisfied, for the next—and last—to die was the Engineer-in-Chief himself.

Four deaths in as many months seems few enough when set against the holocaust of 1918, but they were all men well known to Cecil—in a sense his subordinates—and with his always oversensitive conscience, he felt a measure of responsibility for allowing them to provoke the hostility of occult, esoteric powers, whose existence in the East he had long recognized.

19

THE STRANGE DEATH OF PEDRO VELHO

C. A. MONTALTO DE JESUS

St Francis Xavier died on Shangchuan (Sanchuan) Island near Macao in 1552, his dream of a universal Christian state unfulfilled. To believers, the extraordinary story of the death of one of his Macao contemporaries, Pedro Velho, proves Xavier's prophetic gifts. The events are retold here by the historian C. A. Montalto de Jesus. The tale begins as Pedro Velho, a founder of Macao and one of its leading merchants, unexpectedly says goodbye to his companions.

I t is related that at an entertainment he mysteriously bade his friends farewell, invited them to his funeral, and after settling his worldly concerns he repaired to church, prepared for death, and impersonating the dead, lay on a bier amidst lighted tapers, while priests officiating at a requiem mass chanted for the repose of his soul. When after the ceremony his servants lifted the pall with which he had enshrouded himself, they found him actually dead. It transpired that at the entertainment he received what he deemed a death-warning predicted by St Francis Xavier at Sanchuan.

Among the villagers of that island, there was a pretty girl. To save her from the temptations to which she was exposed, St. Francis appealed to the generosity of Pedro Velho, who, though unbelieving in matters of faith,

never denied pecuniary assistance to the holy man in his charitable doings. In return for a marriage portion to the sweet girl of Sanchuan, St Francis blessed the donor, and that death might not overtake him unprepared, foretold that his last moment would be at hand when he found good wine tasting sour: it was what happened at the entertainment. This prediction served well to attest the saint's gift of prophecy at his canonisation.

20

A TRUE GHOST STORY

WILLIAM C. HUNTER

That this ghost story does not require a belief in ghosts to ring true makes it even more haunting. It involves the final days of one of Macao's best-known bankrupts, Thomas Beale, who lost a huge fortune during a Chinese crackdown on the opium trade. The strange story of his disappearance was recorded by a China trader who lived in Macao at the time and knew him well.

In the *Chinese Repository*, volume xi, occurs the following:— 'The late Thomas Beale left his residence in Macao about 5 o'clock p.m., December 10, 1841. From that time all inquiries for him were fruitless till the 13 inst. January 1842.'

The gentleman to whom allusion is here made was the oldest foreign resident in China, having arrived prior to 1785. He would relate his visit to the ships of Laperouse, which refitted at Macao in 1787. He came from England to join the licenced house of Shank and Beale, of which his brother Daniel was the partner, and who died at Macao, January 4, 1827. Mr Thomas Beale came out at the time when foreigners were not allowed to remain in the Canton Factories after the despatch of their vessels. After many years he had given up business and was preparing to return to England, when, going to Macao for a visit on his way home, circumstances led him to pass there the remainder of his days. I forbear any particular reference to business transactions with a Portuguese gentleman at Macao, which were currently spoken of when I arrived there in 1825, and which ended in the loss of the large fortune that Mr Beale meant to retire with.

When I first made his acquaintance at Canton, where he happened to be on a visit when I landed, I was struck with the first remark he made, when Mr Covert, to whom I was consigned, said to him: 'Here is the youngest arrival from America we have seen yet;' to which Mr. Beale replied: 'So they are beginning to send you children!' Mr Beale was in a comfortable position at Macao. He occupied one of the finest of the old Portuguese houses, enclosed within high walls, on a narrow street know as Beale's Lane, from his brother having lived in it before him. To it was joined a large garden, filled with the choicest and rarest of plants and flowers, a Bombay mango tree in full bearing, lychee and orange trees, and the custard apple, &c. It possessed an aviary also, in which amongst the brilliant peacock and the mandarin duck, with many strange and scarce birds, was a live bird of paradise, at that time the rarest of all. The garden, arranged as Chinese gardens are, with the flowers and plants growing in pots, was one of the sights of the city, and to it its proprietor granted access to his own friends and their friends and the casual visitor to Macao, with all reasonable freedom. He was himself one of the old school in its fullest signification: stately in person, somewhat formal, with distinguished manners. On my short visit to Macao, en route to Singapore and Malacca in April 1825, I presented to him for his aviary two living quails, which had been my companions on board the Citizen on the passage out from New York; the birds thrived and left numerous descendants in the land. Between this time and 1841 the old gentleman had fallen into great difficulties, while a natural pride withheld him from seeking that assistance which all who knew him (and could do so) would willingly have rendered. He, however, sought quietly that of his compradore, an old and faithful servant, and some time before the final catastrophe he had taken refuge (unknown to anyone) in his house at Mong-Ha, a village about a mile beyond the walls of Macao. As events marched on, Mr Beale related to me that the most painful thing to him was the impossibility to make certain payments to some Chinese of Macao for friends who had left the country. One of them calling as usual, on behalf also of several others, was unable to collect the amounts due. Mr Beale explained his inability to pay, and was met with this reply, translated from pigeon English: 'Mr Beale, let it give you no pain. You are old now, and trouble of mind must be avoided. For years, old and young, we have known you; we reverence you, and we beg you not to give way to sorrow on our account. Some of us are well off; we will help one another.' 'This conduct,' said Mr Beale when he related the story to me, 'caused me more grief than anything else; it touched me bitterly. What noble words, what kind-heartedness from those poor people!'

One evening before his final disappearance, he came to my house on the Praya Manduca (the Macao inner harbour). It was about nine o'clock; a visit so late in the day was quite unusual for him—then over seventy. After being seated a few minutes he made known the object of his call. It was with heartfelt satisfaction that I complied with his request for pecuniary aid, planting in his hands an order on Messrs. Russell and Co.'s compradore for 600 dollars. He soon after took leave, with the assurance from me that whenever I could be of further use, he must come frankly and let me know. I did not see him again until the morning of December 10, 1841, when coming from my private residence to the office on the Praya Granda, I met him about ten o'clock on the corner of Beale's Lane and Mr Nye's house. It was one of those glorious Macao mornings. We chatted about the beauty of the weather, the delicious balmy air, and so on; then shook hands and parted. He was going, he said, 'as far as Anderson's' (our Macao physician), who also had a public dispensary. From that day the old gentleman disappeared. We were lost in conjecture as to his whereabouts; he had not been at Mong-Ha, as some of us imagined. At length, on January 13, 1842, his body was found at Cacilha's Bay, embedded in the sand, by some Portuguese boys, while hunting for shells. The discovery created great excitement; everyone rushed to the Campo across which the road led to the bay. I jumped into my sedan, called for Mr Lejee, one of the partners of Wetmore and Co., and together we were borne rapidly out of the city gate. Some Portuguese, who passed us going towards the city, cried out 'Senhor Beale!' the Chinese echoed the name 'Low-pe-tae' ('Old Beale's younger brother'—by which he was universally known by Chinese). As we approached the road leading to the gate of San Antonio we met a great crowd following a brancard, which we followed also, to the mortuary chapel of the Old East India Company. On an appointed day the little chapel was densely crowded with official and other Portuguese, with Spanish, English, and American friends, and many Chinese, who had come to assist at the last offices for the oldest foreign resident at Macao, whose name had been a household word for close upon two generations.

Six months had come and gone after the funeral, when three Chinamen, humbly clad, sounded at the gate of his old residence and asked to see the compradore. On being admitted, one of them explained the object of their visit. They came from Fisherman's

Point, which forms the northern boundary of Cacilha's Bay. It was occupied by these men, who fished and cultivated small patches of paddy ground. One of the men then went on to say: On the evening of the 28 day of the 10 moon (December 10) last year, a foreigner came to our huts. He spoke the native dialect. He told us that on the beach at Cacilha's Bay a dead man was lying; 'if he was not buried, we, being the nearest Chinese to it, the Mandarins would molest us, perhaps hold us responsible for his death, as you know they often do.' We one and all replied that our safety was not to go near it, and then with guiltless words we can confront the officers. The stranger said, 'But the spirit of the dead man, deprived of rest, will hover about you night and day so long as the body is above ground. It will haunt you; think of what I say.' We again, one and all, thrice replied, 'that being without sin in this matter, the gods will chase away the spirit; we will not be haunted.' The stranger said, 'The wretched spirit will bring you other ills. Your paddy will yield no rice. Your nets will catch no fish: you will be reduced to misery and want.' He knew our customs and our prejudices. We understood his words. We consulted together with fear, and decided to go and bury the body that evil might be warded off. We were gathering such implements as we had and were about to start; it was then near the second watch (9 to 11). The stranger stopped us. 'No, not to-night,' he said, 'but at dawn of day; you can then see clearly, and may bury suitably in a deep grave; is it not so?' 'Yes,' we answered, 'it is so.' He then placed in our hands this small packet, which you will notice has never been opened, ascended the hill and disappeared. At early dawn we crossed the hill and descended to the bay. We walked along the sands, when suddenly we came in sight of a dead body, completely clothed, lying on its back. Now, hurrying on, as we approached it we trembled with fear: we saw in it our visitor of the evening. We asked one another, was it the man himself who came to us, or was it his spirit? We know they transform themselves at will. Our limbs shook. Afang said, 'Quick! there is the morning's light; if discovered here we shall have our heads cut off.' We dug a grave in the sand, placed the corpse within it, and filled it up with reverence. When we again reached our huts, we burnt incense and dedicated a 'lob-chok' (a red candle), to the spirit; we burnt fire-crackers, and thus removed all cause for further visits. With time we heard of a Macao foreigner being missed—it was spoken of in the market-place. We said nothing for fear we might be taken and executed on suspicion. Now there is no longer anything said, the event is long past, we have come to return the packet with its contents as we received it. We cannot take a reward for such a work as we performed. On opening the packet, the three men having departed, it was found to contain four dollars! Small gifts or rewards were usually done up in red paper—as this one was. The fisherman's story was taken down in writing by the compradore and read over, a copy of it he gave to me, of which this is the translation.

21

A PLAGUE OF SUICIDES

JOHN HENRY GRAY

This short note from the diary of the Archdeacon of Hong Kong during his travels in the region in the 1880s is gruesome in its hard factual nature rather than the art of its telling.

A t Macao I found a body suspended from the bough of a tree which stretched across the street. Several persons were passing at the same time, but the melancholy spectacle seemed to excite no emotion, scarcely to attract attention. No one seemed to consider it a matter of consequence whether the body was to remain hanging or be taken down.

22

NOT ONE ESCAPED

JUAN GONZALEZ DE MENDOZA

A miracle is in the eye of the beholder. One such marvel was reported by Father Juan Gonzalez de Mendoza during his travels in the late 1500s. It records the fate of the inhabitants of a Chinese town who dared to scorn a neighbour who had converted to Christianity in Macao.

There was a man naturally borne in this kingdome, who for certain occasions went forth of the same, and came and dwelt amongst the Portugals, who, seeing the Christian ceremonies, and being touched with the hand of God, was baptised, and remained certain yeares in the same towne, giving outwarde shewes to bee a good Christian, and one that feared God; at the end thereof he changed his minde, and determined to returne unto his owne countrie, and there to live according unto that which he had learned of the Christians, the which he beleeved to doo with ease, without any gainesaying or contradiction. Whereas when hee came thither, hee did observe all such things as a Christian was bounde to doo: but amongst other signes and tokens of the same, he made a crosse and set it by the door of his house, whereunto he did reverence at all times, when he passed by the same, with great devotion. His neighbours when as they saw that signe, a thing of them never seene before, and howe that the Christian did make particular reverence, they beganne to mocke and scorne him and the crosse, and pulled it downe from the place whereas it was set, and did other things in dispite thereof, and of him that had set it there in that place, whose hatred and discourtesie was so much that they determined in their minds to burne it, and to put the same in execution, who, at the same instance, did all miraculously die; I say those that would have burnt the same, the which was seene of many other, who have given sufficient testimony thereof. And within fewe dayes after, all the whole linage of those dead persons did follow the same way, and not one escaped. This miracle being spread throughout all the kingdome, the naturals thereof set up many crosses in all parts.

PART V

UNLIKELY LOVERS

'Because the dowries are so massive, an excess of gentlemen and nobles go there to provide themselves with wives.'

MANUEL DE FARIA Y SOUSA, 1675

'In the views, the aspect of the whole place, the sense at once of mysterious decay and romance, with which this paradise of the China-Portuguese fills the mind, there is nothing of common-place life or activity.'

OSMOND TIFFANY, JR., 1849

'From the windows or balconies glancing eyes look down behind their fans, and send a thrill through the blood of each admiring devotee below.'

JOHN THOMSON, C. 1868

Macao's labyrinth of winding streets lined with faded pastel residences seems a perfect setting for a haunting romantic tale. In recent times there has been no shortage of fictional romances set in the city. In the 1952 film, *Macao*, Robert Mitchum and Jane Russell fall in love amidst the action of a classic *film noir*. There is a litter of pulp novels, an author who takes the name Marshall Macao, and a small number of better books like Timothy Mo's *An Insular Possession*. But the Macao love story is a far older tradition. Many in the genre are true and feature the most improbable pairs.

23

THE NINE-YEAR-OLD HEIRESS

C. R. BOXER

Nothing inspires passion like a large dowry. That was certainly the view of the Portuguese adventurers who vied for the attentions of a wealthy nine-year-old Macao orphan. This true story, which took place in the early eighteenth century, was published in 1948 by Charles Boxer, the eminent historian of the Portuguese empire. Antonio de Albuquerque, Captain of Marines and the orphan's leading suitor, eventually became Governor and Captain-General, partly on the strength of his new wife's fortune. Related in swashbuckling style, the tale has all the elements of a great romantic adventure.

W̲e have already observed that Macao was then a favourite resort for impecunious suitors from other parts of the Portuguese Asiatic Empire, since many of the local damsels were richly dowered. The greatest catch at the time of Albuquerque's arrival was an orphan heiress named Maria de Moura, whose tender age of nine years did not deter two ardent lovers from pressing their suit. These were respectively the frigate's first lieutenant, and the captain of marines. The latter had the support of his commanding officer and (even more valuable) that of Bishop Casal and the Jesuits. On the other hand Dom Henrique de Noronha had the tacit approval of the grandmother, who felt, perhaps not altogether unreasonably, that the child was too young to know her own mind. Matters came to a head one fine afternoon in June 1709, when Maria de Moura was more or less forcibly abducted from her grandmother's house, and solemnly betrothed to Antonio de Albuquerque by the Vicar General, Lourenço Gomes, at the parish church of Saint Laurence.

A few weeks later Albuquerque whilst riding through the streets to the Franciscan Convent, was shot at by a negro slave of Noronha's armed with a blunderbuss. The shot went wide and Albuquerque, who was nothing if not courageous, attempted to ride his assailant down, but the culprit made good his escape. Returning from his fruitless pursuit through the Rua Formosa (near the modern Riviera Hotel, familiar to all visitors to Macao), Albuquerque was fired at from the window of a house on the street corner by Dom Henrique himself, whose aim was rather better, since the bullet struck him in the right arm above the elbow. Wounded as he was, Albuquerque rode on to the Franciscan convent, where a third attempt on his life was made by another negro slave whose aim was as poor as that of his colleague. The intended victim had to be helped from his horse at the convent gate, where the hospitable friars gave him a welcome sanctuary. The municipal surgeon and the ship's doctor who were called in to heal the wound made light of the effects, but an English surgeon from a passing East-Indiaman, who came to see the patient a fortnight later, diagnosed that gangrene had set in, and advised immediate amputation if his life was to be saved. On hearing this, Albuquerque sent a message to his sweetheart, asking whether she would still be prepared to marry him when mutilated by the loss of his right arm. Maria de Moura made the classic reply that she would marry him even if his two legs were cut off, so long as he was still alive. The old chroniclers naturally extol the mutual faithfulness of this couple who were so readily prepared to sacrifice all for love; and the sensation created by this affair was for many years commemorated by a popular folk song which ran:

Não he tão fermosa
Nem tão bem parecida,
Que, por seu dinheiro
Maria arma tanta briga

which may be rendered into English as:

She is not so beautiful
Nor yet so fair
That for her money
Maria should cause such stir

105

But the lovers, as Shakespeare's Lysander might have told them, were by no means out of the wood yet. At Christmastide that year [1709] the unfriendly grandmother, Maria de Vasconcelos, appealed to the Senate to take charge of her granddaughter, since it was plain that Antonio de Albuquerque intended to kidnap her on board the frigate and carry her off to Goa. The Senate was rather embarrassed by the request since the courtship of Albuquerque was strongly supported by the frigate's captain, who went so far as to land detachments of sailors and marines to protect the lovers from further molestation. Moreover the Senators' previous efforts to interfere on the grandmother's behalf, had been rudely rebuffed by the Bishop and his Vicar-General, nor were they more successful this time. Meanwhile Dom Henrique de Noronha, after the failure of his murderous attempt had sought sanctuary in the Dominican convent. The Governor had this place surrounded by a detachment of soldiers, but the culprit made good his escape during the night and took refuge in the house of Charles Maillard de Tournon, Patriarch of Antioch. Here he not only remained unmolested, but was visited by his friends, and by the other jealous but unsuccessful rivals of Albuquerque for the hand of the fair Maria de Moura. . . .

True Love ran its chequered course for a full year after the attempted assassination of Albuquerque, until finally the devoted pair were safely united in holy wedlock on the night of the 22nd August 1710. Even then the wedding was nearly substituted by a funeral, as another jealous rival, Francisco Leite, laid a murderous ambush for Antonio Albuquerque. Fortunately for himself, the captain of marines had taken the precaution of having the chapel guarded by a company of his men, whilst more fortunately still, the would-be murderer mistook the rendezvous and went to the wrong church by mistake. His staunch friend the frigate's captain, Jeromino de Mello Pereira, was present at the ceremony; but his unsuccessful rival, the First Lieutenant, was presumably amongst the band of Francisco Leite who lay waiting in vain for the appearance of the betrothed outside the Church of Santo Antonio.

The Albuquerques' married life lasted four years and seems to have been ideally happy, if the subsequently bereaved husband's later actions are any guide. His 'very rich and very beautiful' twelve-year old wife presented him with a daughter in 1712, who lived only a week, and two years later with a son. The birth of the latter was a signal for great rejoicing, Albuquerque giving Chinese plays in the street outside his door (another interesting example of Chinese influence on Macaonese social life) and organizing equestrian sports and other displays at his own cost. The infant's christening on the 27th July 1714, was a sumptuous affair, dignified by the presence of the Governor with two companies of soldiers, and celebrated by discharges of cannon from the citadel of São Paulo do Monte. All these rejoicings were cut short by the unexpected death of the mother four days later, which induced a contemporary chronicler sententiously to observe

O que de manhãa foy mimo
He ja lastima de tarde

'What is joy in the morning, turns to sorrow at night'.

24

THE PENSIONER

AUSTIN COATES

Martha Merop was a self-made businesswoman who, by the early 1800s, was one of the richest people on the China coast. In the 1950s, Austin Coates became fascinated with her story and used historical documents and oral tradition to bring her to life in the book City of Broken Promises, *still in print and one of the most captivating tales of the city's past. This extract recounts the first meeting between Martha and the man who would later become her husband, the newly arrived Thomas van Mierop of the British East India Company.*

Though it was past the siesta, the shutters of the high, narrow Portuguese windows of the Rua do Hospital remained shut; but as Abraham Biddle, key in hand, mounted two paved steps to a tall double front door, Thomas observed by the slight movement of an upper-floor shutter that though Macao houses sometimes wore an air of somnolence it should not be inferred from this that the people inside them were asleep. Just as small as the world of the foreign traders in China— though more settled, in that its inhabitants came and went only by birth and death—was Macao itself, a world in which it was prudent to keep shutters closed.

Before they were fully inside the hall

two Chinese servants in white tunics hurried down from the upper floor, noiseless in neat black cloth slippers, the shape of which stood out markedly in the dim light against the white stockings and puttees in which their baggy black silk trousers were gathered. Without waiting for orders they began flinging open the shutters in the ground-floor rooms, although in fact there was little to see in them—being level with the street, they were conspicuously empty of possessions.

Upstairs other servants were opening shutters on all sides, filling the house with light, bringing its quiet old dignity to life.

'I needn't labour the fact, Mr van Mierop, that these are premises fittin' for a gentleman.'

They were standing in what William Urquhart had used as his living room. It was in complete contrast with the arid lower rooms, the life of a Macao house being conducted (with the exception of cooking) entirely on the upper floor. Persian carpets of appropriate sizes covered nearly every foot of floor space, out across the landings and into other rooms beyond. There were some good pieces of English furniture, but the larger cabinets and almeiras were Portuguese, ornately carved with pilaster and acanthus, with which were blended peonies and other Chinese motifs, masterpieces of the cabinet-maker's art. The room was large, stretching from the front of the house to the back, divided centrally by an arch decorated with some Chinese craftsman's painstaking imitation of Portuguese manueline. The arch, giving the room two distinct parts, enhanced it with a subtle intimacy. Urquhart, it appeared, when not tippling, occupied himself sketching local scenes. A sketch of the broad sweep of the Praia Grande, 'the more spacious harbour', hung between two of the tall, fanlighted windows, the little panes of which were made of transparent seashells permitting a soft grey-green light to penetrate. There were pipes on a small round Spanish piperack table, and a finely carved cheroot box which, as Biddle casually opened it, Thomas saw was still half full of Manila cigars.

But it was someone else's house—not Abraham Biddle's to rent or to sell, nor yet the property of the second generation of Gonçalves Sequeira. It was William Urquhart's house. His character rested on it with quiet endurance, even from so distant a place as the cemetery on St. Helena, and from the life beyond.

109

'It's not every gentleman, even from the Honourable Company, that I'd bring to this 'ouse, Mr van Mierop.'

'I appreciate your sentiments,' Thomas replied. 'But I would not be able to occupy it as it is.'

Biddle assumed an expression of innocent astonishment.

'Is there somethin' yer object to, Mr van Mierop?'

'Object? No. But these are the late Mr Urquhart's effects. They will be wanted by his relatives. I—'

'Set yer mind at ease on that score, Mr. van Mierop,' Biddle interrupted in a sterner tone. 'When I say that once the will is proved yer may purchase from me whatever furniture yer wish, I mean just that.' He mollified his voice. 'May I be permitted to explain, Mr van Mierop, that this too is China fashion. It's the custom for a new officer in China to in'erit—if I may use the word in a not very correct sense—the possessions of the officer 'e's replacin'.'

But Thomas had made up his mind. The house was preeminently a home, and with fifteen years or so to consider, this was what mattered.

'At the same rental?' he inquired.

'With somethin' additional for the 'ire of the furniture,' said Biddle softly.

'Agreed.'

'Yer've made a wise choice, Mr van Mierop. May I congratulate yer. I think I may prophesy yer'll find this 'ouse satisfactory in every way,' he said with the same implication of sin that entered his voice whenever he was being polite; and as he smiled, with the rumour of a chuckle in it, he closed the shutters of one of the windows facing the street, thus depriving of a view two sallow-faced Macao Portuguese women whom Thomas had not noticed, but whom Biddle, even without apparently looking in their direction, had detected as they gazed, with the fixed Asian expressions, through a partly open shutter on the other side of the street.

Thereupon Biddle, obsequiously looking his client straight in the eye, handed him the key and took his leave. A moment later a deferential intake of breath at the doors to the front staircase indicated the compradore's arrival.

The compradore was a small wizened man with greying hair beginning to go thin. He had cadaverous cheeks, a few teeth missing, and wore a dark brown Chinese longcoat, with the same cloth slippers as the servants. He looked more like an ancient sage than a purveyor of fruit and vegetables. He bowed and grinned.

'Morning, Master,' he began, despite the fact that it was afternoon. 'My velly solly, Master, you good flen Uk Hak Master him die. Velly bad joss pidgin.'

It was Thomas' first encounter with business English, as it was uncritically called, and spoken at speed it was somewhat breathtaking. He furthermore found that unless he too spoke in the same way the compradore had difficulty in understanding him. He made a somewhat uncertain *début* in this new art, after which the compradore snapped his fingers and the servants, waiting just out of sight, came in to be presented.

'Number One, Number Two, Number T'ree, Number Four,' announced the compradore, who did not trouble himself with names.

A series of pale, ivory-skinned faces, with foreheads shaven, giving their heads an unrealistically dome-like appearance, came in and bowed. Last to be presented was a short, dark-skinned lad with grey eyes.

'Him velly fool boy,' explained the compradore benevolently.

'What does he do?' asked Thomas, appreciating that the house was monstrously overstaffed.

'Him open door when Master come back nightee time. But him velly fool. No talk talk.'

The compradore smiled significantly. The fool boy grinned. At another snap of the compradore's fingers all withdrew.

In solitude Thomas took in the strangeness of it. It was as if, in taking the house, he was taking on the life of another person where that other life left off. He felt he was prying into the secrets of that other man, as if within these walls he himself were little more than an eavesdropper.

The light was failing, and a wind was rising from the sea. A servant quietly set down a silver tray on which were a decanter of port, a glass, and a covered silver dish which on inspection Thomas found contained shortcake. The intrusion drew his thoughts back to practical matters. There was still one more person he had to interview. He asked to see the compradore again.

'I understand Mr Urquhart had a pensioner, whom I'm responsible for. I should also see him.'

111

The compradore looked blank

'No savvy.'

'Pensioner,' Thomas repeated. 'Mr Urquhart's pensioner.' At the corners of the compradore's eyes intelligence awakened. His mouth, half open in perplexity, opened a little more.

'My savvy. Master like him come?'

'If it's convenient.'

The compradore waddled away.

Thomas glanced casually at the view from the rear french windows. Immediately behind the house a granite rock rose exactly to the level of the upper floor. On the rock's flattened top was the garden, consisting solely of potted plants. A wrought-iron bridge connected it with the rear balcony, and beyond the rock, on rising land, were the grey, double-tiled roofs of a number of low Chinese houses—no walls or windows were visible—beyond which grass and rocks rose, filling the view, to the central hilltop fort, the Monte, which he had earlier seen from the sea. Observed at closer range the fort was less imposing. Despite its cannons nosed seaward over the roofs, an air of dereliction invested it, as though not having been used for a century or so, the cannons might emit only birds' nests.

Drawn by the lonely sadness of the view, he moved nearer the window, and as he did so became aware that in the fading daylight a figure was standing in one of the inner doorways. That it was a girl—one of the servants, evidently—he saw at once, and equally dismissed further thought about it. He had already seen below the french windows that the servants had their wives and children staying in the compound, their quarters occupying the lower parts of the hill like a small village.

From the front staircase a servant entered bearing a globe lamp with a candle in it, which he placed near the polished but empty fireplace. In the new brightness as the lamp was brought in—the candle was placed before a polished reflector—Thomas took a second look at the girl. She was younger than he had imagined. She stood to one side of the doorway, her body held in an attitude neither bold nor timid. She seemed to have come up neither to transmit a message nor to make a request. Having neither of these motives, her presence assumed the nature of a statement of fact— a statement, he judged from the way she avoided the centre of the door, of unwilling fact.

Her eyes, up-tilted and almond-shaped, and her pale, exceptionally smooth skin suggested that she was Chinese; yet the way she wore her fine black hair, and her black dress, short and shapeless, was more European than Chinese. Still no more than a child, could she have been one of the servants' daughters, influenced in some way by the Portuguese?

'Yes?' he said, expecting to give her the confidence to speak, and moved a pace toward her.

Something in the ivory stillness of her face altered. Across her temples he noticed the pulsating of two slender veins close to the surface of her limpid, youthful skin. He went no nearer. Despite his inability to read the meaning of an oriental expression he sensed, more than saw, that her look was of fear. Aware of something moving on his left, he glanced towards the street where, in a window of the house opposite, a lamp was passing. In the concealment of darkness those sombre Asian eyes were still watching him over there. They were excited about something.

He turned back to the girl, and as he did so, feeling suddenly hot under the collar, understood the China fashion meaning of the word pensioner.

25

A CURIOUS INSTANCE OF FIDELITY

GEORGE BENNETT

The fabulous profits of the opium trade bought many an extravagance for Macao's European residents, but none so renowned as the aviary and gardens of Thomas Beale, once one of the wealthiest of the country traders. Mr Beale's collection of East Asian flora and fauna contained 2,500 plant species alone, cuttings from which found their way to many European collectors. When the naturalist George Bennett visited the aviary and gardens in 1833, Beale had already lost much of his fortune, but still devoted himself to the natural history of the Far East. An aviary seems an unlikely setting for a love story—unless the lovers are of the feathered sort.

The great object of attraction at Macao, (together with the agreeable society of the English and American ladies, and the beautiful specimens of the fine arts to be seen in the painting room of the celebrated Chinnery,) is the splendid aviary and gardens of T. Beale, Esq. How pleasant it is to see this gentleman (now resident for upwards of forty years in China) devote his leisure moments to the care and delight of the elegant and brilliant productions of nature, both in the animal as well as in the vegetable kingdom. On entering the large doors, which open from a narrow lane, the ear is saluted by various noises proceeding from a number of caged birds, inhabiting the verandah of the dwelling. The peculiar notes of the Minas, the different screams of Loris, parrots, and parroquets, the twitting of the smaller birds, are variously heard vying with each other in loudness; the occasional caw of the aethereal Paradise Bird, or its resounding note of *whock, whock, whock*, is also heard. . . .

The Mandarin Teal, or *Een-yêong* of the Chinese, is also much and justly admired. The plumage of the drake is remarkably elegant, that of the female plain and undecorated. . . . These little creatures are regarded by the Chinese as emblems of conjugal fidelity, and are usually carried about in their marriage processions.

The following curious instance of fidelity was mentioned to me, as having occurred in the instance of two birds of this species:— A drake was stolen one night, with some other birds, from Mr Beale's aviary; the beautiful male was alone taken; the poor duck, in spite of her quacks during the distressing scene, was left behind. The morning following the loss of her husband the female was seen in a most disconsolate condition; brooding in secret sorrow, she remained in a retired part of the aviary, pondering over the severe loss she had just sustained.

Whilst she was thus delivering her soul to grief, a gay, prim drake, who had not long before lost his dear duck, which had been accidentally killed, trimmed his beautiful feathers, and, appearing quite handsome, pitying the forlorn condition of the bereaved, waddled towards her; and, after devoting much of his time and all his attention to the unfortunate female, he offered her his protection, and made a thousand promises to treat her with more kindness and attention than her dear, dear, lost drake; she, however, refused all his offers, having made, in audible quacks, a solemn vow to live and die a widow, if her mate did not return. From the day she met with her loss, she neglected her usual avocations; her plumage became ragged and dirty; she was regardless of her appearance; forsook her food, and usual scenes of delight, where she loved to roam with him, now absent, and to excite his brave spirit to drive away all the rivals that might attempt even to approach them. But those fleeting hours of enjoyment had passed, perhaps never to return; and no consolation that could be offered by any of her tribe had the least effect. Every endeavour was made to recover the lost bird, as it was not expected that the beautiful creature would be killed.

Some time had elapsed after the loss, when a person, accidentally passing a hut, overheard some Chinese of the lower class conversing together; he understood sufficient of their language to find out that they said, 'It would be a pity to kill so handsome a bird.'—'How, then,' said another, 'can we dispose of it?' The hut was noted, as it was immediately suspected that the lost Mandarin drake was the subject of the conversation. A servant was sent, and, after some trouble, recovered the long-lost drake by paying four dollars for him. He was then brought back to the aviary in one of the usual cane cages.

As soon as the bird recognized the aviary, he expressed his joy by quacking vehemently and flapping his wings. An interval of three weeks had elapsed since he was taken away by force; but when the forlorn duck heard the note of her lost husband, she quacked, even to screaming, with ecstacy, and flew as far as she could in the aviary to greet him on his restoration. Being let out from the cage, the drake immediately entered the aviary—the unfortunate couple were again united; they quacked, crossed necks, bathed together, and then are supposed to have related all their mutual hopes and fears during the long separation.

One word more on the unfortunate widower, who kindly offered consolation to the duck when overwhelmed with grief: she in a most ungrateful manner informed her drake of the impudent and gallant proposals he made to her during his absence;—it is merely supposition that she did so; but at all events the result was, that the recovered drake attacked the other, the day subsequent to his return, pecked his eyes out, and inflicted on him so many other injuries, as to occasion his death in a few days. Thus did this unfortunate drake meet with a premature and violent death for his kindness and attention to a disconsolate lady. It may perhaps be correctly written on a tablet over his grave—'*A victim to conjugal fidelity*'.

26

A MILLIONAIRE'S COURTSHIP

ALICIA HELEN N. LITTLE

Camões' Garden is a natural setting for a romantic meeting. Or so it struck Alicia Helen N. Little, who set amongst its boulders this first encounter between two future but improbable lovers, from her novel, A Millionaire's Courtship*. The author, who used the pen name Mrs Archibald Little, wrote prolifically during the many years she and her businessman husband lived in China.*

*I*f Hong Kong had delighted Lady Morten, Macao delighted her brother, with its unexpected old-world picturesqueness and associations, its large crucifixes, little Portuguese soldiers, priests, duennas, and shall we add half-castes? Girls with magnificent hair, fine eyes, and an expression of utter irresponsibility, these in European clothes; women with Chinese features, but a sweetness of expression unknown in China, these last in Chinese clothes. He did not speculate about them or consider their future—there was a Portuguese governor and staff charged with this care—he just enjoyed looking at them passing by, listening to the lapping of the waves upon the shore, wandering along the lovely crescent curve of the bay, or among the gardens by the sea, with their innumerable suggestions for vignettes, and spending long hours in the romantic melancholy of Camoens' grove, gazing out to sea, from the marble seat, where the poet is said to have composed a great part of his world-fascinating epic.

'I think the Portuguese have thrown away all their opportunities here.'

Mr Lawrence looked round, startled at these words spoken in a clear, ringing voice. Yes! it was the long-legged child who had spoken them, and she had spoken them to him. She had been standing beside him for half an hour, he believed now, but he had been unconscious of her presence. He remembered only he had seen her there some time before, a rather untidy child, with very short skirts, which hung crookedly.

'So that is the outcome of your meditations,' he said now good-humouredly.

'It isn't only mine. Father says so too. He always says the Portuguese had such glorious opportunities and threw them away completely. You see vice is always nonproductive.'

'Is it indeed?' a trifle of astonishment in his tone, yet mixed with a feeling of *ennui*, as he prepared himself to listen to a mangled réchauffé of the unknown father's views.

'I didn't know what you might be thinking about, you come here so often, don't you? And it seemed it might be that, so I thought I had better speak first.'

'Very sensible,' said he, smiling a little outwardly, and more inwardly. 'I am afraid I was only dreaming.'

'I sometimes do that too,' said the apparently irrepressible child, 'but father says no one should until after forty.'

'Why so?'

'Youth is the time for action,' said she, evidently unconsciously assuming a dry offhand manner that Trevor presumed was that of the absent father. 'On the other hand, possibly the Portuguese have raised and influenced the Chinese more by intermarriage than they could have in any other way. I have noticed whenever one comes across any very progressive Chinese it is generally from the neighbourhood of Macao.'

'Oh! you have noticed that?' asked he, at once interested.

'Yes, but this is me, not father. I don't know what he would say about it. Of course, he says I am not very accurate, and jump too soon at generalisms.'

'No one can observe without theory, even Comte admitted that. But won't you sit down? you must be tired of standing.'

'Thank you, but are you sure I shan't bother you?' Then as she settled herself with a sigh of relief—she had evidently been very tired of standing—'You see it was your expression made me so tremendously interested, and then you are awfully rich, are you not?'

'Oh, good heavens! here it was again.' He nearly swore under his breath, but—'I have got about as much as I know what to do with,' was all he said, assuming at once his most languid tone. 'I don't know that it is particularly awful.'

'Oh no! I beg your pardon. That is what father calls one of my misuses of words,' but going on with what evidently interested her much more than a verbal correction of herself, though she tried to take this meekly, 'I don't at all know whether it is nice to have so much money. You see I have never tried it, and I think it must be so puzzling to decide how it is best to spend it; what do you think?'

'You see, like you, I have never tried anything else,' he said humbly.

'Were you always—at school, were you the richest boy in your class?'

'I suppose I was, I never thought about it then.'

'Had the biggest cakes, and the best watch, and the most pocket-money?'

'I never had any cakes but what I bought for myself, and I don't recollect choosing the biggest. I had the best watch, I know, because that was the reason another boy gave for breaking it; and then I was punished for carelessness, and my father said he would give me a better one. He had it made on purpose for me. I remember being so ashamed of it; the watchmaker said there wasn't another as good in all England. I seem to have been always ashamed, for I recollect now, I thought it such a disgrace never having a hamper sent me, that I used to do everything short of absolutely telling a story to make the others think the cakes I bought had been sent. I recollect the horrid tone in which a little wretch said, "I saw him buying it himself!" Of course I had the most pocket-money.'

'And when you went home everything was very splendid.'

'No! it wasn't. My father knew how to make money, I daresay, but he never knew how to spend it, and he was afraid I did not either. I recollect my last letter from him was asking why I had not drawn a cheque for such a long time, and then—he died.'

The girl actually slid her hand into his and pressed it. 'Were you very sorry?'

'I don't know that I was,' said Trevor, honestly. There was something about the girl that made it impossible to lie to her. 'He had never enjoyed life, as far as I could see, or at least, not in nice ways. I don't recollect ever feeling any love for my father, but you see it was the first time I had been brought in contact with death, and then I became so disgustingly—no, I beg your pardon—so awfully rich, I think was what you said.'

'How dreadful it must have been for you! Just a boy too! But your mother?'

'My mother died when I was very little!' He was fiddling with his watch-chain and presently produced a miniature. 'I have always loved her.'

'I should think so,' said the girl, enthusiastically, gazing at the miniature. 'My mother died when I was eight years old. She was beautiful, too, but not so beautiful as this, and she was always ill, as long as I can remember. Father says he can remember her before that,' she added wistfully.

'Yes, I suppose so,' said the man, taking back his locket and looking longingly at the beautiful young face within before he shut it up with a snap and put it away.

'But you know our mothers, if they were alive, wouldn't know what to do with the world. It is so different now from what it was in their days,' persisted the girl, who was evidently not given to vain regrets. 'What I want to know is what you dream of, as you sit on this seat, day after day, and look out over the sea with that strange expression.'

'I'm afraid I was thinking of nothing better than Vasco da Gama, when you spoke to me, and what his boats must have looked like, and how they controlled them and manoeuvred them, and of all I have learnt of the discovery of China by the rest of the uncivilized world, for there is no doubt but that the Chinese were the most civilized then, whether they are so or not now. And then I often sit and think how Camoens must have felt. How must it feel to do more than any man to render your country illustrious, and to meet with no recognition, to see that no one is capable of even recognizing your genius, and to live and die in poverty and hardship?' He turned around and was looking full into the girl's face, his own eyes softened, as few people had seen them.

But she was looking out to sea, and she shook her head sternly now. 'That would all mean nothing to him, he would know they could not help it. Why, look what blind stupids people are! There's father! there never was a man like him!'

'I'm sure there never was.'

'Why, how do you know?' very quickly, looking full at him.

'I do not, but you tell me so, and I am sure you would not say it if it were not true.'

'It is true. He should have been made Governor of a Province—Viceroy—oh! there have been such openings, such opportunities, if you only knew! England has thrown them all away. And father just makes little jokes, and is pleasant all round, while people say: "What a dear man he is, I do love him so!" and they have not the least idea—not the least idea—what a great man he is under all that little pleasantness—what a burning soul, what clearness of vision, what a grasp of detail, what a burning desire to help—all that makes a leader among men. Greater than Warren Hastings he might have been, and he is a Consul-General in China! Waiting here now, because the Minister cannot think what in the world to do with him. Do you think he is bitter? No! He says, "Do you think, Pet"—father always calls me so. I am not that sort, of course, but he likes to make-believe with me since he has not got mother—"Do you think people would ever choose to be stupid if they weren't born so? And being born so, how can they know who are the people who would serve them best?" But you—you should not sit here dreaming of the days of long ago. You, who have got the power to make the wheels go round, you should be doing great things, not thinking of those who did.'

'May I ask how old you are, young woman, you, who lecture me thus wisely.'

'I am fifteen now,' said she, but only as in passing. 'If I were you—'

'Yes, come now, if you were me—I am used to people trying to put their hands into my pockets, and seeing what they can pull out. I thought you were different from the others, but let me hear what you would pull out.'

'It is not for myself, but for the world,' said she, stoutly and unabashed.

'Apparently the world is your passion. England even is not big enough for you.'

'No! it is not,' she said very decidedly. 'To my mind England is a very small part of the world, and the people in it altogether too comfortable. Too rich, and quite too comfortable.'

'Well, here am I, another of them! Too rich, too rich altogether, and apparently with nothing else remarkable about me. At least, no one else ever seems able to see anything but my money to differentiate me from all the other Snooks, Browns, etc.'

'Now you are angry,' said the girl. 'I must have hurt you very much for that. I am so sorry. Oh, father would be vexed with me,' and half crying she patted his hand, and looked imploringly into his face. 'You don't get angry easily.'

'How do you know that, little woman?'

'Oh, I see it,' she said; 'I notice things, though father says I am always so full of my own ideas, I don't consider other people. But don't you see—don't you see? it was your expression, just—just your own character looking out of your face, made me interested, and ask about you. And it was only after that I heard you were rich. And then I thought, he has the longing to make the world quite different, and he has the power. And it was that made me so interested in you, not just your money. I haven't been so very horrid, have I?'

'Oh! it is all right,' said he with his singularly bright smile, that only had an unhappy trick of vanishing almost as quickly as it came. 'I am not so extraordinarily touchy. But come on now, what would you do in my place?'

'Well, that of course, I can't say off-hand. But some Euphrates Valley scheme, I suppose. I know I should not give my money away in little bits—any man with a moderated income can do that, a little here and a little there. And I should not endow some magnificent scheme of national education, because even if it were the best possible, the mere fact of some one man endowing it, and dictating to the others, as it were, would set them all against it, just as the Dissenters are against the Church now. And I certainly would not endow all the hospitals—because the only thing that keeps them decent, and prevents them from entirely sacrificing their patients to purposes of research, is their being dependent upon the general public. And, besides, they ought all to move out of London at once, get better air for their patients, and not contaminate the cities—spreading disease is what they are doing now, I think, rather than curing it. I have no patience with the hospitals begging—begging, when if they sold their city sites they'd be set up for ever so long, as it is. But what I would do, I think, would be to bring some new market into communication with the rest of the world. Why not run a line of steamers on the upper Yangtse and build this railway through from Burmah?'

'But would it pay? that's the question. Could it possibly be made to pay?'

'And you a millionaire! and you ask that! Yah! I am ashamed of you.'

The strange child had got up and looked him full in the face, a world of reproach on her flushed features. Now she fairly turned and ran away from him.

Trevor Lawrence sat looking after her, astonished at her, and at himself. Was he really so degraded, so sunken in that most disgusting love, the love of money, that this—the most instructive young lady he had ever met—found him absolutely impossible to go on talking with. He recalled her expression of absolute disgust and contempt, shuddering under it, and with the ugly sound of that 'Yah!' still tingling in his ears, he walked forward to meet Lady Morten.

'Who was that long-legged child you were talking to?'

'I have not the very least idea.'

'Well, she seems to be a fairly free-and-easy young woman. First, I see her in such animated conversation with you that I daren't come near for fear of interrupting the *tête-à-tête*, then she rushes up to some man from behind, and flings her arms round his neck.'

'Oh, her father, I suppose. A middle-aged man, was it not?'

'He did not look particularly middle-aged. But even if it were her father, it was before everyone, and she nearly knocked the poor gentleman down, for he was not prepared for such an onrush from behind.'

'I should think her father must be prepared for anything,' was Mr Lawrence's somewhat enigmatic reply. . . .

Who was the girl, he wondered. All he knew of her was that she was the daughter of a Consul-General, who called her 'Pet'. She had certainly succeeded in deeply mortifying Trevor Lawrence.

The *Swiftsure* steamed away that very evening. Macao had no further charm for him after that little scene in Camoens' grove, and as for Lady Morten, she had always regretted the delay there.

PART VI

PIRATES

'I have seen the heads of pirates exposed in cages, attached to the tops of long poles, by the sea-shore at Macao.'

JOHN HENRY GRAY, 1878

Some say that Macao would not exist were it not for pirates. According to legends of the enclave's origins, it was Portuguese victories over swarms of these seaborne raiders based in the islands at the mouth of the Pearl River that first convinced the emperor to permit the foreign barbarian settlement on Chinese soil. Not since the voyages of Cheng Ho during the early Ming dynasty had China truly exerted control along its own southern coast, and piracy was a constant hazard to commerce and to coastal village life. Chronicles of the daring and cruelty of these marauders are an especially bloody chapter in the lore of Macao.

27

FOR SERVICES RENDERED

PIERRE SONNERAT

Macao's earliest history is poorly recorded and therefore much disputed. Whatever the true origins of Macao, bloody and horrific pirate attacks in the waters around the city were recorded into the latter half of the twentieth century. Nevertheless, the idea that the Portuguese earned their tenure in Macao doing battle against pirates had much currency as recorded in this account by a French royal official, scientist, and traveller in the late 1700s.

Before the Canton river was known, and before European vessels had arrived in China, caravans went in search of agricultural and industrial goods, to then distribute throughout all of Europe. They reaped considerable profit and continued to do so until the Portuguese, masters of India, saw the need to establish a maritime commerce to China. It was in 1518 that their first ships anchored in Canton. At that time, that province was infested by brigands who, posted at the entrance of the river in what are now called the Ladrone Islands, left their retreat to pillage ships. The weak and cowardly did not dare to leave their ports, nor do battle with a group of men that a hard life had rendered ready for anything. They contented themselves to call them savages and it was necessary that a European nation teach them that these savages were by no means invincible.

Interested in their destruction for their own sake, the Portuguese also wanted to earn credit with the Chinese. They offered their services which were eagerly accepted. The Chinese armed a fleet together with the Portuguese force but simply remained spectators. The Portuguese won battle upon battle, and finally purged the area of the fearsome pirates. As a reward for their victories, they obtained a small island, dry and barren, at the mouth of the Canton River, where they built Macao. They also obtained privileges of which they were later deprived.

28

THE PIRATE FLEET

RICHARD GLASSPOOLE

If chopping people up and throwing their pieces into the sea is the kind of thing you would expect pirates to do, the following excerpt will not disappoint. The intensity of pirate activity around Macao has fluctuated considerably over the years. One of the more serious outbreaks occurred just after 1800, peaking violently around 1810. It was at this time that Richard Glasspoole was captured by a pirate band, which he calls by the Portuguese term 'Ladrones', meaning thieves. This is his first-hand account of the atrocities he witnessed while sailing with the pirate fleet. Glasspoole's encounter began after being separated from his ship, the East India Company's Marquis of Ely, about twelve miles from Macao. Landing with a ship's boat and a crew of seven men, Glasspoole was doing little more than dropping off the mail and picking up a native pilot when the boat was lost in a storm.

O ur situation was now truly distressing, night closing fast, with a threatening appearance, blowing fresh, with hard rain and a heavy sea; our boat very leaky, without a compass, anchor or provisions, and drifting fast on a lee-shore, surrounded with dangerous rocks, and inhabited by the most barbarous pirates. . . .

Thursday the 21st, at day-light, the flood making, weighed and pulled along shore in great spirits, expecting to be at Macao in two or three hours, as by the Chinese account it was not above six or seven miles distant. After pulling a mile or two perceived several people on shore, standing close to the beach; they were armed with pikes and lances. I ordered the interpreter to hail them, and ask the most direct passage to Macao. They said if we came on shore they would inform us; not liking their hostile appearance I did not think proper to comply with the request. Saw a large fleet of boats at anchor close under the opposite shore. Our interpreter said they were fishing-boats, and that by going there we should not only get provisions, but a pilot also to take us to Macao.

I bore up, and on nearing them perceived there were some large vessels, very full of men, and mounted with several guns. I hesitated to approach nearer; but the Chinese assuring me they were Mandarine junks and salt-boats, we stood close to one of them, and asked the way to Macao. They gave no answer but made some signs to us to go in shore. We passed on, and a large row-boat pulled after us; she soon came along-side, when about twenty savage-looking villains, who were stowed at the bottom of the boat, leaped on board us. They were armed with a short sword in each hand, one of which they laid on our necks, and the other pointed to our breasts, keeping their eyes fixed on their officer, waiting his signal to cut or desist. Seeing we were incapable of making any resistance, he sheathed his sword, and the others immediately followed his example. They then dragged us into their boat, and carried us on board one of their junks, with the most savage demonstrations of joy, and as we supposed, to torture and put us to a cruel death. When on board the junk, they searched all our pockets, took the handkerchiefs from our necks, and brought heavy chains to chain us to the guns.

At this time a boat came, and took me, with one of my men and the interpreter, on board the chief's vessel. I was then taken before the chief. He was seated on deck, in a large chair, dressed in purple silk, with a black turban on. He appeared to be about thirty years of age, a stout commanding-looking man. He took me by the coat, and drew me close to him; then questioned the interpreter very strictly, asking who we were, and what was our business in that part of the country. I told him to say we were Englishmen in distress, having been four days at sea without provisions. This he would not credit, but said we were bad men, and that he would put us all to death; and then ordered some men to put the interpreter to the torture until he confessed the truth.

Upon this occasion, a Ladrone, who had been once to England and spoke a few words of English, came to the chief, and told him we were really Englishmen, and that we had plenty of money, adding, that the buttons on my coat were gold. The chief then ordered us some coarse brown rice, of which we made a tolerable meal, having eat nothing for nearly four days, except a few green oranges. During our repast, a number of Ladrones crowded round us, examining our clothes and hair, and giving us every possible annoyance. Several of them brought swords, and laid them on our necks, making signs that they would soon take us on shore, and cut us in pieces, which I am sorry to say was the fate of some hundreds during my captivity.

I was now summoned before the chief, who had been conversing with the interpreter; he said I must write to my captain, and tell him, if he did not send an hundred thousand dollars for our ransom, in ten days he would put us all to death. In vain did I assure him it was useless writing unless he would agree to take a much smaller sum; saying we were all poor men, and the most we could possibly raise would not exceed two thousand dollars. Finding that he was much exasperated at my expostulations, I embraced the offer of writing to inform my commander of our unfortunate situation, though there appeared not the least probability of relieving us. They said the letter should be conveyed to Macao in a fishing-boat, which would bring an answer in the morning. A small boat accordingly came alongside, and took the letter. . . .

On the first of November, the fleet sailed up a narrow river, and anchored at night within two miles of a town called Little Whampoa. In front of it was a small fort, and several mandarine vessels lying in the harbour. The chief sent the interpreter to me, saying, I must order my men to make cartridges and clean their muskets, ready to go on shore in the morning. I assured the interpreter I should give the men no such orders, that they must please themselves. Soon after the chief came on board, threatening to put us all to a cruel death if we refused to obey his orders. For my own part I remained determined, and advised the men not to comply, as I thought by making ourselves useful we should be accounted too valuable.

A few hours afterwards he sent to me again, saying that if myself and quarter-master would assist them at the great guns, that if also the rest of the men went on shore and succeeded in taking the place, he would then take the money offered for our ransom, and give them twenty dollars for every Chinaman's head they cut off. To these proposals we cheerfully acceded, in hopes of facilitating our deliverance.

Early in the morning the forces intended for landing were assembled in row-boats, amounting in the whole to three or four thousand men. The largest vessels weighed, and hauled in shore, to cover the landing of the forces, and attack the fort and mandarine-vessels. About nine o'clock the action commenced, and continued with great spirit for nearly an hour, when the walls of the fort gave way, and the men retreated in the greatest confusion.

The mandarine vessels still continued firing, having blocked up the entrance of the harbour to prevent the Ladrone boats entering. At this the Ladrones were much exasperated, and about three hundred of them swam on shore, with a short sword lashed close under each arm; they then ran along the banks of the river 'till they came a-breast of the vessels, and then swam off again and boarded them. The Chinese thus attacked, leaped over-board, and endeavoured to reach the other shore; the Ladrones followed, and cut the greater number of them to pieces in the water. They next towed the vessels out of the harbour, and attacked the town with increased fury. The inhabitants fought about a quarter of an hour, and then retreated to an adjacent hill, from which they were soon driven with great slaughter.

After this the Ladrones returned, and plundered the town, every boat leaving it when laden. The Chinese on the hills perceiving most of the boats were off, rallied, and retook the town, after killing near two hundred Ladrones. One of my men was unfortunately lost in this dreadful massacre! The Ladrones landed a second time, drove the Chinese out of the town, then reduced it to ashes, and put all their prisoners to death, without regarding either age or sex!

I must not omit to mention a most horrid (though ludicrous) circumstance which happened at this place. The Ladrones were paid by their chief ten dollars for every Chinaman's head they produced. One of my men turning a corner of a street was met by a Ladrone running furiously after a Chinese; he had a drawn sword in his hand, and two Chinaman's heads which he had cut off, tied by their tails, and slung round his neck. I was witness myself to some of them producing five or six to obtain payment!!!

On the 4th of November an order arrived from the admiral for the fleet to proceed immediately to Lantow, where he was lying with only two vessels, and three Portuguese ships and a brig constantly annoying him; several sail of mandarine vessels were daily expected. The fleet weighed and proceeded toward Lantow. On passing the island of Lintin, three ships and a brig gave chase to us. The Ladrones prepared to board; but night closing we lost sight of them: I am convinced they altered their course and stood from us. These vessels were in the pay of the Chinese government, and style themselves the Invincible Squadron, cruizing in the river Tigris to annihilate the Ladrones!

On the fifth, in the morning, the red squadron anchored in a bay under Lantow; the black squadron stood to the eastward. In this bay they hauled several of their vessels on shore to bream their bottoms and repair them.

In the afternoon of the 8th of November, four ships, a brig, and a schooner came off the mouth of the bay. At first the pirates were much alarmed, supposing them to be English vessels come to rescue us. Some of them threatened to hang us to the mast-head for them to fire at; and with much difficulty we persuaded them that they were Portuguese. The Ladrones had only seven junks in a fit state for action; these they hauled outside, and moored them head and stern across the bay; and manned all the boats belonging to the repairing vessels ready for boarding.

The Portuguese observing these manoeuvres hove to, and communicated by boats. Soon afterwards they made sail, each ship firing her broadside as she passed, but without effect, the shot falling far short. The Ladrones did not return a single shot, but waved their colours, and threw up rockets, to induce them to come further in, which they might easily have done, the outside junks lying in four fathoms water which I sounded myself: though the Portuguese in their letters to Macao, lamented there was not sufficient water for them to engage closer, but that they would certainly prevent their escaping before the mandarine fleet arrived!

On the 20th of November, early in the morning, an immense fleet of mandarine vessels standing for the bay. On nearing us, they formed a line, and stood close in; each vessel as she discharged her guns tacked to join the rear and reload. They kept up a constant fire for about two hours, when one of their largest vessels was blown up by a firebrand thrown from a Ladrone junk; after which they kept at a more respectful distance, but continued firing without intermission 'till the 21st at night, when it fell calm.

The Ladrones towed out seven large vessels, with about two hundred row-boats to board them; but a breeze springing up, they made sail and escaped. The Ladrones returned into the bay, and anchored. The Portuguese and mandarines followed, and continued a heavy cannonading during that night and the next day. The vessel I was in had her foremast shot away, which they supplied very expeditiously by taking a mainmast from a smaller vessel.

On the 23rd, in the evening, it again fell calm; the Ladrones towed out fifteen junks in two divisions, with the intention of surrounding them, which was nearly effected, having come up with and boarded one, when a breeze suddenly sprung up. The captured vessel mounted twenty-two guns. Most of her crew leaped overboard; sixty or seventy were taken immediately, cut to pieces and thrown into the river. Early in the morning the Ladrones returned into the bay, and anchored in the same situation as before. The Portuguese and mandarines followed, keeping up a constant fire. The Ladrones never returned a single shot, but always kept in readiness to board, and the Portuguese were careful never to allow them an opportunity.

On the 28th, at night, they sent eight fire-vessels, which if properly constructed must have done great execution, having every advantage they could wish for to effect their purpose; a strong breeze and tide directly into the bay and the vessels lying so close together that it was impossible to miss them. On their first appearance the Ladrones gave a general shout, supposing them to be mandarine vessels on fire, but were very soon convinced of their mistake. They came very regularly into the centre of the fleet, two and two, burning furiously; one of them came alongside of the vessel I was in, but they succeeded in booming her off. She appeared to be a vessel of about thirty tons; her hold was filled with straw and wood, and there were a few small boxes of combustibles on her deck, which exploded alongside of us without doing any damage. The Ladrones, however, towed them all on shore, extinguished the fire, and broke them up for fire-wood. The Portuguese claim the credit of constructing these destructive machines, and actually sent a dispatch to the Governor of Macao, saying they had destroyed at least one-third of the Ladrones' fleet, and hoped soon to effect their purpose by totally annihilating them.

On the 29th of November, the Ladrones being all ready for sea, they weighed and stood boldly out, bidding defiance to the invincible squadron and imperial fleet, consisting of ninety-three war-junks, six Portuguese ships, a brig, and a schooner. Immediately the Ladrones weighed, they made sail. The Ladrones chased them two or three hours, keeping up a constant fire; finding they did not come up with them, they hauled their wind and stood to the eastward.

Thus terminated the boasted blockade, which lasted nine days, during which time the Ladrones completed all their repairs. In this action not a single Ladrone vessel was destroyed, and their loss about thirty or forty men. An American was also killed, one of three that remained out of eight taken in a schooner. I had two very narrow escapes: the first, a twelve-pounder shot fell within three or four feet of me; another took a piece out of a small brass-swivel on which I was standing. The chief's wife frequently sprinkled me with garlic-water, which they consider an effectual charm against shot. The fleet continued under sail all night, steering towards the eastward. In the morning they anchored in a large bay surrounded by lofty and barren mountains.

On the 2nd of December I received a letter from Lieutenant Maughn, commander of the Honourable Company's cruizer *Antelope*, saying that he had the ransom on board, and had been three days cruizing after us, and wished me to settle with the chief on the securest method of delivering it. The chief agreed to send us in a small gun-boat, 'till we came within sight of the *Antelope*; then the Compradore's boat was to bring the ransom and receive us.

I was so agitated at receiving this joyful news, that it was with considerable difficulty I could scrawl about two or three lines to inform Lieutenant Maughn of the arrangements I had made. We were all so deeply affected by the gratifying tidings, that we seldom closed our eyes, but continued watching day and night for the boat. On the 6th she returned with Lieutenant Maughn's answer, saying, he would respect any single boat; but would not allow the fleet to approach him. The chief then, according to his first proposal, ordered a gun-boat to take us, and with no small degree of pleasure we left the Ladrone fleet about four o'clock in the morning.

At one p.m. saw the *Antelope* under all sail, standing toward us. The Ladrone boat immediately anchored, and dispatched the Compradore's boat for the ransom, saying, that if she approach nearer, they would return to the fleet; and they were just weighing when she shortened sail, and anchored about two miles from us. The boat did not reach her 'till late in the afternoon, owing to the tide's being strong against her. She received the ransom and left the *Antelope* just before dark. A mandarine boat that had been lying concealed under the land, and watching their manoeuvres, gave chase to her, and was within a few fathoms of taking her, when she saw a light, which the Ladrones answered, and the Mandarine hauled off.

Our situation was now a most critical one; the ransom was in the hands of the Ladrones, and the Compradore dare not return with us for fear of the a second attack from the mandarine boat. The Ladrones would not remain 'till morning, so we were obliged to return with them to the fleet.

In the morning the chief inspected the ransom, which consisted of the following articles: two bails of superfine scarlet cloth; two chests of opium, two casks of gunpowder; and a telescope; the rest in dollars. He objected to the telescope not being new; and said he should detain one of us 'till another was sent or a hundred dollars in lieu of it. The Compradore however agreed with him for the hundred dollars.

Everything being at length settled, the chief ordered two gun-boats to convey us near the *Antelope*; we saw her just before dusk, when the Ladrone boats left us. We had the inexpressible pleasure of arriving on board the *Antelope* at 7 p.m., where we were most cordially received, and heartily congratulated on our safe and happy deliverance from a miserable captivity, which we had endured for eleven weeks and three days.

29

THE LADY AND THE PIRATES

FANNY LOVIOT

Sailing for California in October 1854 as one of the few passengers aboard the Chilean cargo ship Caldera, *a French traveller by the name of Fanny Loviot was taken prisoner by pirates after the ship was disabled by a typhoon about twenty miles off Macao. Although the crew managed to escape, the other passenger, a well-off Canton merchant with connections in America, Than-Sing, was also captured. Fanny Loviot survived to tell her tale in a popular adventure book of the time,* A Lady's Captivity Among Chinese Pirates. *The following excerpt begins after the pirates have taken the* Caldera's *Captain Rooney to Macao to raise a ransom for their release.*

To-day, again, the pirates came to watch and mock at us. One of them, more insulting than the rest, pointed first at me and then at the Chinese merchant, and represented the action of two persons embracing. This cowardly insult pained me more than all their previous cruelties. I felt myself become scarlet with shame and anger, and gave way to a passion of tears. In the midst of my distress the pirate-captain happened to pass by, and, as if moved by my affliction, ordered the trap to be closed above our heads.

This chief, unlike his men, had something not wholly disagreeable in the expression of his countenance. He alone inspired me with neither disgust nor terror. His ugliness was, so to say, individual. His face was long and thin; he had high cheek-bones, a wide mouth, a short flat nose with open nostrils, dark eyebrows, and very large black eyes. His head was closely

shaved, excepting on the crown, whence grew a long thick tress, which he wore sometimes clubbed on the nape of the neck; sometimes plaited, and bound round his head like a coronet; and sometimes hanging down his back, a yard or more in length. Transformed as he was by these various styles, his face always preserved a certain pleasant character. His consideration on the present occasion inspired me now with some hope for the future.

Than-Sing, partly to amuse me, partly to set my mind at rest, repeated to me the questions and observations which the pirates had addressed to him. They had asked him the number of his wives, which, in China, is a standard of wealth; and then added that if our ransoms were not sufficiently heavy, they would make a pirate of him, and give me in marriage to one of their companions. Seeing me now look more distressed than ever, the good merchant explained that the men of his country were not permitted to intermarry with aliens, and that these threats were only feints to draw him into conversation. 'Be careful, however,' said he, 'never to lay your hand upon me in their presence. It is contrary to our custom, and they might repeat it to my disadvantage.' To all their other questions he had replied that he was only a poor man, about to seek his fortune in California, and gave them to understand that he was working out a cheap passage on board the *Caldera*. He was therefore, careful to avoid any allusion which might lead them to conjecture the extent of his means. Had they supposed him wealthy, they would not only have quadrupled his ransom, but might even have put him to the torture. He then spoke to me of his family. He had but one wife, he said, and his home was in Canton. He was the father of three daughters, of eight, eighteen, and twenty-five years of age, the eldest of whom was married. He seemed to love them tenderly, and wept when he spoke of them. He scarcely hoped ever to see them again, and had but little belief in our ultimate deliverance. I often enquired of him, at this time, respecting the manners and customs of the pirates; to which he always replied, shudderingly, that they were not to be depended upon, and were dangerously fond of decapitating their prisoners. . . .

That night I strove in vain to sleep. The insects which infested our dungeon tormented me incessantly, and my feet were blistered all over from their bites. The rats, also, which at first had fled before the sound of our voices, were now grown but too friendly, and ran over us in broad daylight, as we were lying on the floor. . . .

On the morning of the 15th, we came up with several other pirate-junks, and joined them in giving chase to a merchant-junk, plying between Hong-Kong and Canton with goods and passengers. All was now excitement on board. The hours of rest were passed by, and Than-Sing overheard the robbers concerting their plans of attack, and calculating the probable extent of the booty. When the evening came, we were fastened down in our dungeon more closely than ever.

It might have been about ten o'clock at night when we once more heard the frightful war-cries which startled us from our sleep that fatal night on board the *Caldera*. These cries were followed by a dropping cannonade. Two shots were then fired from our own junk, the vibrations of which seemed to rend every timber around us. More dead than alive, I vainly strove to still the beating of my heart, and dreaded every instant lest a ball should burst in upon us. Four junks then surrounded the merchant-vessel, which, taken by surprise, offered but a feeble resistance. . . .

Having boarded and pillaged the merchant-junk, the pirates, it seemed, proceeded to interrogate the passengers. Several of these unfortunates unluckily confessed that they came from California, which was alone sufficient to expose them to every kind of ill-usage. In order to wring from them a full avowal of their riches, the pirates had put their victims to the torture. Bound by only one thumb and one toe, these wretched captives were suspended from the masts, and swung violently backwards and forwards. As if this were not sufficient suffering, their agonies were, from time to time, augmented by heavy blows and their shrieks were inconceivably distressing.

Day broke, and the dreary silence which succeeded to the horrors of the night was only disturbed by the slow splashing of the waves, and the dipping oars of the rowers, who were transporting the booty in small boats from junk to junk. . . .

We had hoped that the day would, as usual, bring us some little liberty and fresh air; but the pirates were too busy to heed us. Absorbed in the pursuit of gain, they were all day occupied in negotiating the sale of their plunder, and for that purpose received on board those traders whose special line it was to buy up stolen goods. Bathed in perspiration, racked with acute cramps, and half stifled by the long-confined air, I suffered horribly. My skin, too, was covered with a painful eruption, and I had become so weak that, although my companion strove to amuse and cheer me, I was no longer able to reply. By and bye, we heard the pirates counting their gold, and then the splashing oars that bore the purchasers away. This done, our jailers at length remembered our captivity, and opened the trap. It was time they did so; for we had lain there upwards of four-and-twenty hours! The delight which it was once more to breathe that fresh night-air, I shall remember to my dying day.

30

EUROPEAN PIRATES

GEORGE WINGROVE COOKE

Most pirates were Chinese but there were exceptions. Outcast Europeans, 'Manilla-men' from the Philippines, and escaped African slaves occasionally joined the sea robbers, while captives were sometimes pressed into service. One group of pirates consisted of 'Macao ruffians', policemen-turned-bad who sailed in lorchas—fast Portuguese boats with Chinese sails, usually armed, and constructed at a great profit at the shipyards in Macao. Even in the late 1800s, a lorcha could out-sail and outgun most other craft made on the China coast. In 1858 George Wingrove Cooke, correspondent for The Times, *published this account of their final battle at the trade port of Ningpo.*

We must recollect, which it is so difficult for people in England to believe, that the whole coast of China is so infested with pirates that even a fleet of fishing-boats cannot venture out without armed vessels as a convoy.

The fishing boats which ply off the mouth of the river Yung pay convoy duties to the extent of 50,000 dollars a year; and the wood-junks that ply between Ningpo and Foochow and the other native craft, raise the annual payment for protections to 200,000 dollars (70,000 Pounds) annually. These figures are startling, but I have taken pains to ascertain their correctness.

The vessels employed in this convoy service were Portuguese lorchas. These vessels were well armed and equipped. There were no mandarin junks and no Portuguese ships of war to cope with them or control them, and they became masters of this part of the coast. It is in the nature of things that these privateers should abuse their power. They are accused of the most frightful atrocities. It is alleged that they made descents upon villages, carried off the women, murdered the men, and burnt the habitations. They became infinitely greater scourges than the pirates they were paid to repel. It is alleged, also, that complaints to the Portuguese consul were vain; that Portuguese sailors taken red-handed and handed over to this consul were suffered to escape from the consular prison. Rightly or wrongly, the Chinese thought that the consul was in complicity with the ruffians who were acting both as convoy and as pirates. The convictions of the English and French residents at Ningpo do not differ from those of the Chinese; and although, having no means of guarding my inquiries with the securities of a judicial investigation, I am unwilling to make any strong assertion, I think I may reasonably say that the honour of the Government of Portugal is so compromised that European nations, for common character's sake, should require it to institute a searching examination into the conduct of this official.

The leader of the pirate fleet was—I am going back now to a time three years ago—a Cantonese named A'Pak. The authorities at Ningpo, in their weakness, determined to make terms with him, rather than submit to the tyranny of the Portuguese.

A'Pak was made a mandarin of the third class; and his fleet—not altogether taken into Government pay, for that the Chinese could not afford—was nominally made over to A'Pak's brother, a gentleman with a long name, which I cannot remember.

This fleet, now turned nominally honest, began to compete with the Portuguese for the convoy business, and, their business being now tolerably respectable, they were joined by several English, American, and French deserters from ships-of-war and merchant vessels.

This has been the position of the two parties for the last three years. The fishermen and carrying junks, glad to be rid of the Portuguese yoke, gradually transferred their custom to the Cantonese fleet, and the Portuguese, hungry and furious, became more active in their piracies, and attacked the Cantonese ships when they could get them at an advantage, and murdered their crews with circumstances of great atrocity.

140

The Cantonese do not look upon the Portuguese as Europeans. They have not the same fear of them. They can fight them man to man. Macao would have been taken by the Chinese long since, had they not dreaded the interference of the other Western powers. After a few of these very sanguinary provocations, A'Pak—not, it is believed, without the concurrence of the Toutai of Ningpo— determined to destroy this Portuguese convoy fleet.

For this purpose A'Pak's brother collected snake-boats and convoy junks from along the whole coast, and assembled about twenty of them, and perhaps 500 men. The Portuguese were not long hearing of these preparations, but they seem to have been struck with panic. Some of their vessels went south, some were taken at the mouth of the river. Seven lorchas took refuge up the river, opposite the Portuguese consulate. The sailors on board these lorchas landed some of their big guns, and put the consulate in a state of defence, and perhaps hoped that the neighbourhood of the European houses and the character of the consulate would prevent an attack. Not so. On the day I have above mentioned the Canton fleet came up the river. The Portuguese consul immediately fled. The lorchas fired one broadside at them as they approached, and then the crews deserted their vessels, and made for the shore. About 200 Cantonese, accompanied by a few Europeans, followed these 140 Portuguese and Manilla-men ashore. A fight took place in the streets. It was of very short duration, for the Portuguese behaved in the most dastardly manner. The Manilla-men showed some spirit, but the Portuguese could not even persuade themselves to fight for their lives behind the walls of their consulate. The fortified house was taken and sacked by these Chinamen, the Portuguese were pursued among the tombs, where they sought refuge, and forty of them were shot down, or hunted and butchered with spears.

The *Capricieuse*, French frigate, now came up the river, fired upon the Cantonese who were sacking the consul's house, and put an end to the conflict. The French captain received on board the Portuguese consul, not, I am told, with great cordiality, and also the fugitives who had escaped the massacre. The latter he conveyed as prisoners to Macao, to be tried as pirates.

Merciless as this massacre was, and little as is the choice between the two sets of combatants, it must be owned that the Cantonese acted with purpose and discipline. Three trading Portuguese lorchas which lay in the river with their flags flying were not molested; and no European, not a Portuguese, was even insulted by the infuriated butchers. The stories current of Souero and his Portuguese followers rivalled the worst of the tales of the buccaneers, and public opinion in Ningpo and the foreign settlement was strongly in favour of the Cantonese.

The Chinamen lost only two Chinese. One vagabond Englishman fighting on their side was shot by a Manilla-man.

After the departure of the *Capricieuse*, the Portuguese brig of war, the *Mondego*, came up the river, accompanied by about twelve Portuguese lorchas, and made formal demands of the Toutai, that the captured lorchas should be restored and other restitution made. The Toutai replied that the two convoy fleets must settle their own quarrels, for he had nothing to do with them. The Portuguese and the Cantonese then made ready for a fight, and the general opinion was that the Cantonese would have again been victorious. Meanwhile, however, Commander Dew, in the *Nimrod*, had steamed up the river. He sent a message to the Portuguese commander to say that his instructions were to remain entirely neutral, and if the brig was about to attack, he would move his ship out of the line of fire; but that if the *Nimrod* or the houses of British residents on the river were struck by shot, it would be his duty to interfere. The *Mondego* and her consort lorchas immediately departed for Shanghai. The Canton fleet is still either engaged in convoying or at anchor in the river; and, to the great comfort of the merchants and the missionaries, so also is the *Nimrod*.

I do not for a moment seek to implicate the Portuguese nation in the crimes of the Macao ruffians, except so far that it was the duty of Portugal to prevent such deeds. But these circumstances suggest serious considerations in connection with our next treaty with China. They show how important and how difficult is the question of policing the coast and exterminating piracy; they show also how important it is that the great European powers should exercise a strong control over such lawless vagabonds as those who acted with the Cantonese; they also suggest very grave considerations as to how far it may be right to extend to small and not very conscientious Governments like that of Portugal the treaty privileges which England is about to ask, not only for herself, but for all other civilized nations.

31

A VERY BLACK JOKE

MARK MOSS

One of the most horrific pirate atrocities, and one where the victim survived to record the ghastly tale, was the assault on the schooner, the Black Joke. In the mounting conflicts of the undeclared opium war, the Chinese authorities ordered the expulsion of the English from Macao. The Black Joke's English passenger, Mr Moss, tried to comply, with a ghastly result. His story was recorded in the Chinese Repository.

Deposition of Mr Moss:— Mr Mark Moss, a British subject, born in London, deposeth as follows, before Mr Van Basel, Dutch consul, Mr Paiva, late procurador of Macao, and Messrs Kerr and Leslie, British merchants, in Macao on the 25th day of August, 1839:

'I left Macao on board the *Black Joke*, containing personal and household property, on Friday night last, the 23rd instant, to proceed to Hongkong; having got as far as the point of Lantao, anchored there yesterday evening at about 5 o'clock; supped, and went to lie down. At about nine o'clock; I heard the crew consisting of Lascars [East Indian sailors] cry out, "Wy-lo! Wy-lo!" ran to the skylight, and saw three guns fired at us loaded with charcoal; when I reached the deck, I saw three lascars cut down, and received myself a cut on the left side of the face, on which I went below, when I heard the Chinese crying out, "ta, ta!" and on putting my head out of the companion, got a most severe wound on the top of my head from a pike. The Chinese then laid hold of me, stripped me of my clothes, and cut my arm in three places as I put it up to save my head. They then proceeded to plunder and break up the boat, and coming down with lights into the cabin, one of them, seeing I had a ring on my finger, attempted to cut the finger off, but I took off the ring, and gave it him; another, seeing my watch, took it out of my pocket, and, laying hold of my ear, called to a man who came with a sharp instrument, cut it off with a large portion of the scalp on the left side of my head, as you now see, and put it in my mouth, attempting to push it down my throat. I was then knocked about on all sides by the Chinamen, and saw them bring a barrel of gunpowder, with which they attempted to blow up the boat but did not succeed. I was rendered insensible from the smoke caused by the explosion, and was nearly suffocated, when making a last effort, I reached the deck but found no one there. I called out the names of some of the Lascars, and seeing a rope moving astern, found that the tindal alone of the whole native crew had saved himself by hanging on to the rudder under water. He came up and gave me some water, of which I drunk five basons full, and felt refreshed. A short time after this, the *Harriet*, Capt. Hall, came up, and I suppose, from the Chinese leaving so suddenly, that they had seen the vessel. From Capt. Hall, I met with the tenderest treatment; he took me on board, dressed my wounds, and taking charge of my boat, brought me to Macao this morning at about 5 o'clock.'

32

THE BEST DEFENCE

CROSBIE GARSTIN

The attack on the Black Joke *coincided with the end of the British period in Macao; increasingly the city would be overshadowed by Hong Kong. However, it was not the end of piracy. Long after Macao had been transformed into an exotic weekend destination for bored Hong Kong bureaucrats—served by a scheduled ferry from Victoria—pirates remained a serious threat. Writing in the 1920s, the British writer, Crosbie Garstin, was astounded by the precautions taken by the steamers that plied the waters of the Pearl River estuary to Macao.*

I went to Macao on a neat, flat-bottomed little steamer, divided not into water-tight but bomb-proof compartments. The engines were fenced off with substantial steel grilles. The second-class deck was cut off from the first by a padlocked steel door, and the navigating officers shut away in a bullet-proof wheelhouse and further protected by armed Sikh guards. The trip was as uneventful as a launch ride from Richmond to Hampton Court; but it is not always so; the Ladrone Islands remain faithful to their name. Not once or twice have the Macao boats been cut off, their officers shot and every foreign passenger butchered. There is a little steamer running to this day that has been twice taken; on the second occasion two hundred people perished and she herself was burnt down to the water-line.

For three hours we dodged in and out between islands and fishing-junks and at length Macao came into view: Fort Guia, with its lighthouse—the first in China Seas—the black walls of Fort Monte up on the hill, the bishops' palace, the brightly painted houses of the wealthy along the Praia. Round Fort de Barra we swung and into the Porto Interior, past packed masses of junks, all armed to the teeth. The co-operative guard-junk carried no less than seven guns, two a-side on her main deck, two on her poop, and another forward. The decks were museums of ancient cannon. There were guns mounted for action that must have come East with the first European vessel. Sakers, falcons, falconets and patereroes [light canons] embossed with Portuguese and Spanish royal arms. Dutch and English swivel-guns, and stock-fowlers with arched dolphins for handles; worn out signal-guns; Chinese guns, dragon-mouthed—any old thing that would throw a charge. Most of them looked rusted through and horribly insecure on their mountings. I presumed that they were only for show, that nobody would have the temerity to fire them, but I was assured by a resident that did a pirate show up the aged pieces came merrily into play. A junk lost meant starvation for several families, so the fisher people fought to the bitter end, risking a blow-out at the breach; women ramming and sponging, toddling brats acting as powder-monkeys. The favourite charge was a bottle or two, and I can imagine it would be most effective. Half a dozen old smooth-bores vomiting mouthfuls of splintered glass at short range should be enough to discourage the most enthusiastic pirate.

33

THE QUEEN OF THE MACAO PIRATES

ALEKO E. LILIUS

In the late 1920s, the American journalist Aleko Lilius was commissioned by a group of magazines to write about the pirates who terrorized the Pearl River delta. After weeks of research, Lilius finally met a real pirate—moreover, one willing to take him on one of her voyages of plunder. The go-betweens in the arrangement were a Macao Portuguese sea captain who had played with the children of pirates as a child, and another Macao resident referred to only as 'this Chinaman'.

I had engaged Moon, a young Chinese, as an interpreter, house-boy, and cook, and together we went to Macao to have a last chat with 'this Chinaman', and to tell him exactly what I thought of him and all Chinese pirates.

'This Chinaman' greeted me with a smile.

'Velly good you come to-day. Number One Master she here.'

Then I noticed the presence of a Chinese women in the room. I bowed. Hardly acknowledging my greeting, she began a severe cross-examination with Moon translating her rapid questions. Judging from her questions, she was the Number One Master 'this Chinaman' had spoken of, and he himself was only a subordinate. . . .

What a woman she was! Rather slender and short, her hair jet black, with jade pins gleaming in the knot at the neck, her ear-rings and bracelets of the same precious apple-green stone. She was exquisitely dressed in a white satin robe fastened with green jade buttons, and green silk slippers. She wore a few plain gold rings on her left hand; her right hand was unadorned. Her face

and dark eyes were intelligent—not too Chinese, although purely Mongolian, of course—and rather hard. She was probably not yet forty.

Every move she made and every word she spoke told plainly that she expected to be obeyed, and as I had occasion to learn later, she *was* obeyed.

What a character she must be! What a wealth of material for a novelist or journalist! Merely to write her biography would be to produce a tale of adventure such as few people dream of.

That evening I heard from an American who had sailed the waters around Macao for fifteen years the following story about this remarkable woman:—

'Her name is Lai Choi San. So many stories centre about her that it is almost impossible to tell where truth ends and legend begins. As a matter of fact, she might be described as a female Chinese version of Robin Hood. They have much in common. Undoubtedly she is the Queen of the Macao pirates. I have never seen her. I have almost doubted her existence until you told me of meeting her. She is said to have inherited the business and the ships from her father, after the old man had gone to his ancestors "with his slippers on" during a glorious fight between his men and

148

a rival gang. The authorities had given him some sort of refuge here in Macao, with the secret understanding that he and his gang should protect the colony's enormous fishing fleets and do general police duty on the high seas. He even obtained the title of "inspector" from somebody in authority, and that, of course, placed him morally far above the other pirate gangs.

'He owned seven fully armoured junks when he died. Today Lai Choi San owns twelve junks; nobody seems to know how or when she acquired the additional five, but it is certain that she has them. She has barrels of money, and her will is law.

'You may ask', he continued, 'why I call them pirates, since their job is only to "guard" the numerous fishing craft. However, the other gangs want the same privileges as the present "inspectors" have, therefore they harass and plunder any ship or village they can lay their hands upon. They kidnap men, women and children, hold them for ransom, ransack their homes, and burn their junks and sampans. It is up to the protectors to undo the work of these others and to avenge any wrong done them. Naturally, there is bitter and continuous warfare between the gangs.

'This avenging business is where the piratical characteristics of the "protectors" come in. There is frequent and profitable avenging going on wherever the various gangs meet. Lai Choi San is supposed to be the worst of them all; she is said to be both ruthless and cruel. When her ships are merely doing patrol duty she does not bother to accompany them, but when she goes out "on business" she attends to it personally. When she climbs aboard any of her ships there is an ill-wind blowing for someone.'

PART VII

THE AMERICAN SPINSTER

*'You may laugh at the idea of seeing anything of the
world in Macao, but, I assure you, we see an infinite variety
of characters.'*

HARRIET LOW, 1831

One of the liveliest personal glimpses of European life in
Macao comes from the pen of Harriet Low, who lived in the
enclave from 1829 to 1834. A New Englander of puritanical
upbringing, Low found in Macao an expatriate community
dominated by the East India Company and accustomed to the
luxury and formality of British society. Much of the time the only
spinster amongst the expatriate women, she enjoyed the attentions
of numerous bachelor China traders. They were young men
with considerable leisure time and money on their hands. Yet
Harriet soon tired of a life so far from her native Salem and
offering so little independence for women, especially if they were
unmarried.

Harriet Low kept a journal of her experiences for the benefit of
her elder sister in the United States. Typical of her time and
background, Low's life was sheltered from much of the Chinese
and Portuguese community around her; she is often harshly
critical of the poor, the Chinese, her Roman Catholic neighbours
and the impious of all Protestant sects. And yet there is much
insight in her spirited observations of Macao's cultural
hodgepodge and its frequently frivolous and insular European
community. Her daughter, Katherine Hillard, annotated and
published a selection of Low's journals years later, from which the
following excerpts are taken.

34

LIVING AMONG STRANGERS

HARRIET LOW

The journal entries begin as Harriet Low neared the anchorage known as Macao Roads aboard the Sumatra. *She was travelling as companion to her aunt, Abigail Knapp, whose husband William Henry Low was about to take up the important directorship of the great American trading firm Russell & Co.. Like other traders, William Low would spend the winter trading season in Canton. However, since the Chinese authorities prohibited Western women from living in that city, Harriet and her aunt were to make their home in the Portuguese settlement downriver.*

[September] 26th, 1829

We calculate we shall be in Macao in three days. I long, yet dread to see this place. I have heard so many different opinions about it; but I am determined to take no one's opinion but my own.

Monday, September 28.—Sick all day. Squally, rainy, uncomfortable weather, and a heavy, irregular sea, which made us all sick. I was stretched on the floor all day, or in my trough, until four o'clock, when I heard the cry of 'Land!' and never was it more welcome. To our great joy, we are now within a few hours of our destined port, and glad shall I be to tread again upon terra firma. We anchored off the Lima Isles. It blew very hard all night, and must have been very uncomfortable outside.

September 29.—A delightful morning. It seemed like one of our May mornings at home. We set sail at 6 a.m., and anchored off

Macao Roads at 10. Uncle and Mr A. went on shore soon after and returned about dark. Mr Russell has a house and everything necessary prepared for us.

Wednesday, September 30.—This morning all busy enough getting our things out of the ship. There was a heavy sea, which made it very difficult for a boat to come alongside. Indeed, we were obliged to lower everything over the stern; and you would have been amused to see us tied into a chair and swinging over the stern of the ship. But we got along very comfortably, and saw many very amusing things on our way to shore. There is an immense quantity of boats all about, in which whole families live,—indeed, two or three generations. The women steer the boats, and frequently have an infant slung to their backs,—the common mode of carrying children among the poor,—and the poor little thing only has a shaking if it cries. They sometimes use their children very cruelly.

One idea of the Chinese amuses me exceedingly; that is, that a vessel cannot go without eyes. They therefore have a large eye painted on each side of the bow, which looks very singular; and, if you ask them why, they say, 'Hi yah, how can see without eye?'

Macao from the sea looks beautiful, with some most romantic spots. We arrived there about ten o'clock, took sedan chairs and went to our house, which we liked the looks of very much. The streets of Macao are narrow and irregular, but we have a garden in which I anticipate much pleasure. In fact, there are two, one above the other. All the paths are of flat stones, and are as smooth as a floor. You ascend five flights of steps and come to an observatory, from which we have a fine view of the bay and harbor, and can see all over the town. Round the observatory there is a terrace, and there are many pretty plants. With this little spot and a few birds I shall get along very comfortably. I had no idea there was so pretty a place here, but want some one to enjoy it with me. . . .

152

Friday, 9th.—No one called to-day, but I have been very busy. I find quite enough to occupy my time. I long to go to walk, but cannot until we have our chairs (which are being made in Canton), or some one to wait upon us. However, I have had a fine walk upon the terrace, which is a delightful place. . . .

Sunday, October 11.—Not having our chairs, we were obliged to stay at home to-day. I endeavored to spend the day as it should be spent, but you have no idea how difficult it is to keep alive one's religious feelings here or to pass Sunday in a proper manner. I read aloud one of Buckminster's excellent sermons, but had no sooner finished it, and was feeling somewhat disposed to be serious, than four or five people called. They make calls here on their return from church. You see there is no country like ours for religious principles. The Chinese pay no sort of regard to the Sabbath, but go on with their work just as usual. You hear their gongs every little while, chin-chining joss. This is a feast-day with the Catholics. Apew, our comprador (steward), came in this afternoon to ask if we wanted to see a walky. We could not divine what he wanted, but we followed him up to a terrace that looks into the street. After waiting some time, we at last saw a Catholic procession, and it was worth waiting for, though I cannot tell you what it meant or anything about it, except that the men were dressed in loose white satin trousers, with a sort of loose blue satin gown that came down to their knees, and they carried lighted candles. There were several little girls, rigged up with wings to resemble angels, and a fine band of music. The cannons all round the fort were fired, and the bells were ringing. It seemed, as you may judge, more like a festival than a Sabbath.

12th, 13th.—Very busy preparing our dresses for the ball. There are none but men tailors here, and we are obliged to cut and fit our own dresses, thinking the men would be more trouble than good to us, as it is so difficult to make them understand. . . .

Sunday, October 18.—We attended public worship at Dr Morrison's house to-day. Were quite delighted once more to hear something good, and to pass our day more as we used to. . . . On our return we found several cards, as Sunday is a famous day here for calling, but we intend to discourage it by making none ourselves.

I forgot to tell you of the walk we had yesterday afternoon. We went out with the coolie, and he took us all round the Praya Grande, over a great hill, and back through the town,—a monstrous walk and for the first one it was terrible. It is so long since we have walked that it overcame us all. The streets here are intolerable,—hilly, irregular, and horribly paved. We met no one but Portuguese and Chinamen, who annoyed us very much by their intent gaze. . . .

My dear sister, it is now over a week since I wrote last in my journal. I have had so much to do with company and visiting that my journal has been sadly neglected. . . . I cannot conceive of people calling this a dull place. . . . On Thursday we went to Mrs Fearon's, and I enjoyed myself very much. You would be astonished if you were to see your once diffident sis dancing the first quadrille, not without much urging. However, you must know that I am the only spinster in the place, and I am pulled about in every direction.

Nov. 18.—. . . I suppose father will think that his daughter is in a fair way to be ruined; but tell him it would be considered very ill-natured in this place for the only young lady here to stay way (from a ball), and I must say it's the only amusement we have.

November 21, Saturday.—This evening we proposed walking in Mrs Fearon's garden and taking tea with her. We walked up, and were overtaken by the charming Mr Harard and Mr Clarke. They left us at the gate, and we had a beautiful walk in that paradise of a place. It is large, wild, and romantic. It is a work of art, it is true, but it resembles nature so perfectly that you would think it originally formed in this way. The rocks and trees are immense, and there are several banana-trees growing with their roots almost out of the ground. . . . We then went into the house, where we were soon joined by many other people. Cards were introduced in the evening, which did not suit our Yankee notions. [The New England custom was then to begin the observance of Sunday at sunset on Saturday.] We had a little supper, and returned in our chairs about ten, not altogether pleased with the evening; we have resolved to avoid Saturday evening visits in future, not knowing what will take place among people who think but little of Sundays. . . .

154

May 25. [1831]—Went to call on the new arrivals,—Mrs Malden, a widow, and two Miss Williams, one considerably advanced, may be decidedly called an old maid, and ugly enough, the other about twenty. They are half-caste, and quite dark. I hear the young one is to be married to Mr Mendez, whom we should call black; but he is a pure-blooded Portuguese, and, if ever so black, is considered above a half-caste. . . .

July 19.—Mr Sultan called this morning, introduced by Mr Bull; quite an interesting youth and a good muster of an American. He is one of the Boston aristocrats, and perhaps would not speak to us at home. However, they are very gracious here, and very polite. He and Mr Beadle dined with us. . . .

[September] 20th.—I shall have a summons to breakfast in a minute and a half. The coolies and Nancy are dancing about our rooms now, clearing up. I dare say it would seem very odd to you to see two men coming to clear up and sweep your room, and such sweeping! 'A lick and a promise.' They cannot imagine the use of doing the same thing every day. They say: 'Suppose make clean to-day, all same dirty to-morrow. What for so fashion clean?' They think it a great waste of labor. However, they are pretty well drilled now, and know what they must do. It has become a habit.

September 23.—A typhoon threatens this morning. The wind is blowing a gale. Oh, dead suds! what a stormy day! The wind increased till about two, when the tide coming in made the sea quite tremendous. We could see it from our windows washing over the tops of the houses on the quay. It has completely destroyed the Praya Grande, rooted up two-foot pieces of granite, and thrown them into the halls of the houses. A little boat was anchored out in front of us. At last, they cut their cables, thinking it was their only chance, and let her drive. It was a dreadful sight. It seemed impossible that she could live in such a sea. We watched her till it seemed as though with the next wave she must dash on to the Point. I have since heard that with the assistance of captain W. the men were all saved. The boat was completely dashed to pieces.

September 24.—Nothing but a scene of destruction this morning. Our veranda is quite unroofed, our mats all gone. Where is the quay? Gone, completely demolished! Houses without roofs, a large piece taken quite out of the Company's, from the roof to the ground, and immense masses of granite thrown up. Several Chinese houses at the end of the quay quite levelled, the Peña church much damaged. On the other side, on the point near the Franciscan church, lies a large fishing boat, a complete wreck. Out in the roads is the hull of a large ship that only a few days since I saw coming in with her towering masts filled with canvas. Now they are levelled to the hull, not a stick left standing. This is what meets our eye; but, alas! I fear that is not all. I hear that during the gale masts of ships with numbers of men clinging to them were floating about, the men calling for assistance, but the ships could give them none. I am afraid we shall hear of much more damage.

September 30.—A dreadfully rainy day. The rain ceased about dark, but the wind began to blow, and we feared another typhoon. The Chinese call it 'the Typhoon's wife.' However, we went to Mr L.'s this evening, and danced till after twelve. . . .

[April] 11th. [1832]—Busy as a bee all day, making preparations for our party. . . . At eight we were all adorned and ready. Aunt Low wore a China gauze over white satin, C. pink aerophane over white, and my ladyship blue crepe over white satin. Our hair was dressed with natural flowers that some youths sent us for that purpose. Ibar was master of ceremonies. He said he was not well, but for the honor of Spain he must do his best, and he made everything very agreeable. We had Mrs Daniell's piano, and Mr and Mrs P. played and sang beautifully at intervals. Had the guitar, too, and four Portuguese musicians, to the grinding of whose fiddles we danced. I danced every dance, and when the party broke up, about half-past one, I could have danced as much more. I had got just enough excited to forget my fatigue. We had a handsome supper, and everything in style, I assure you. We mustered about forty,—four American ladies, English, Spanish, Portuguese, French, Swedes, Scotch, and I'm sure I don't know what others. We made the Scotch-man dance a reel, and I joined in myself. . . .

October 6. [1832]—Had a pleasant trip to the Lappa this afternoon, and only one adventure. In crossing a ridge, my foot slipped, and I went half-way up to one knee in thick mud. With an effort I pulled it out, but in such a condition! There was no sign of my silk stocking or my purple silk shoe. I thought I had better dip it in the brook, and the coolie who was carrying our provisions seemed to be of the same mind, for he put down his baskets and jugs, came down to the stream, and with the greatest nonchalance possible took up my foot and washed all the mud nicely off with a cloth. He brought the shoe and stocking to light, but left me in a dripping state, I assure you. This was a piece of gallantry I should never have suspected a Chinese to be guilty of. We have come to the conclusion this evening that he was some lover in disguise, for gallantry and kindness are not understood by Chinese in general. . . .

October 17.—This morning I finished a dress, and spent an hour with Mrs Macondray, who says there is an order issued to take away all Chinese women-servants from the foreigners. As they are generally wet-nurses, this is a very cruel thing. Oh, these mandarins are too barbarous! The moment they see a fellow-creature making money, they begin to 'squeeze' him, as it is called. No doubt this order is to extort money from the nurses. . . .

December 8.—A rainy, drizzly, cold, gloomy day, spent as usual. . . . I have kept my resolution this year, and have hardly become acquainted with any of the strangers. If you do get interested in them, the pain of parting probably forever overbalances the pleasure you receive from their society. . . .

December 26.—. . . Terribly cold! I do not like cold weather in this country; great barns of rooms, great cracks under the doors, and floors that you can see through; the carpet does not seem to do much good. It is so rainy now that we cannot get a walk, and our limbs are almost stiff with the cold. It makes me shudder at the thought of encountering our winters, though I know you have more comforts at home. The Chinamen all look as thick as they are long now, they have so many clothes on. The Portuguese, many of them, go to bed and lie there. . . .

February 7. [1833]—. . . Do you know, my dear sis, what it is to feel alone? It is to be in a far-off land, separated from your kin, in a

157

place where the society is too small, the interest clashing, petty feuds existing, where the voice of friendship is seldom heard,—in a word, where all are strangers to each other. . . .

I must still be what I am, the receptacle of cold and unmeaning compliments . . . a girl who is the object of speculation and criticism, a girl who is expected to walk in the steps of a chaperon, and because she does not happen to be married has no right to give her opinion, and, indeed, is of no consequence. Yes, my dear, this is to be alone. . . .

February 17.—Walked along the quay after service, and into the Franciscan church, a very neat, pretty place, beautifully situated, as is also the monastery attached to it. They were in the act of filling up the grave of a person just consigned to the dust. They always bury their dead in the churches, and the manner seems to us very shocking. The body is carried through the streets exposed in the coffin, it is taken into the church and put into the grave without the coffin, it is first covered in quicklime, and then the earth is beaten down hard upon it by the black boys. When the flesh has decayed, the bones are sometimes taken up and burned. No female friends ever follow the funeral. The padres chant and read prayers in the church, and the bells ring most furiously from the time the person dies till he is buried, which is generally a very short time. The priests, as in all Catholic countries, exact large dues from those who are able to pay for their prayers, and are very extortionate to the poor, I am told. Mr Colledge, who knows more of them than any one else, told me the other day that he was called to visit a woman who was very ill, in fact had quite lost her reason, owing to her father confessor, who thought it necessary to punish her for the heinous sin of saying the English were very good people, when some of her friends attacked them. He told her she must confess to him all her sins from the time she was seven years old. She being then forty, the poor woman thought it impossible, I suppose, and it preyed so upon her mind that she actually went mad, and Mr Colledge says it will no doubt be the death of her. (She has since died.) Is it not horrible? Many such instances of oppression occur, and it seems dreadful that the priests should have such power. I wonder when this Catholic religion will be done away with. By degrees I think it will be; the mild spirit of Christian charity is growing in America, and it cannot fail to spread. I should like to look upon this planet two thousand years hence, and see what mind will be then, see if people will not think for themselves, and consider themselves the keepers of their own consciences, and God their only master, their best judge. How different the world is now from what it was in the fifteenth century, and shall it not go on toward perfection? I prophesy it will! We, or others, shall see these Chinese exalted in the scale, their turn must come, I think; the barriers must be broken down, ignorance must give place to knowledge, and slavery to freedom. Women will then be exalted; what a state they are in now, poor degraded beings! Mere toys for the idle hours of their masters, crippled and tortured merely to please them. As I was walking this morning, I saw a poor creature toddling along on her feet. I am told that the agony they have to endure is beyond conception; they commence swathing the feet at the age of two, and for years they suffer excessively, all to gratify the mother's pride. I am told the men do not like it, although they think it necessary for their first wife to have small feet. I was one day talking with a very intelligent compradore upon the subject, who seemed to think our custom of nipping in the waist was quite as barbarous and cruel as to pinch the feet. In fact, it seems to be a matter of astonishment to them how we can 'catchy chow-chow' (or eat), which would certainly be a greater grievance to them than not being able to walk. . . .

August 17.—We intended to have made some calls this morning, but, alas! we were made to feel our dependence. We called for chair-bearers, but they were not forthcoming, 'no could catch.' You might fancy from such an expression that they were wild beasts or birds, but no, poor creatures, they are far from that, but under bodily fear of every petty mandarin who has the honor of wearing a button. It seems the mandarins have come short in meeting their expenses, and so they have put an extra 'squeeze' upon the poor bearers, and, until that is paid they forbid their carrying the chairs, and their poor backs would suffer sadly did they disobey the order. We cannot help pitying the poor wretches who are subject to such tyranny, but also feel annoyed that we are so dependent upon them, for we lost not only our calls in the morning, but our opera in the evening. . . .

August 20.—That good-for-nothing personage, the Sotow, has

not yet recalled his order respecting the chair-bearers, but not choosing 'to trust our charms to the perilous keeping of Caffre-men's arms,' we made ourselves independent, and with the aid of Mr Gordon got to the opera very comfortably on foot. It was a fine evening, but the pavements of the streets are horrible, they remind me often of 'Old Paved Street' in Salem, in days of yore, but perhaps worse. The whole width of the street is very little wider than the sidewalk there, and paved in the same way. We had some fine music, and I enjoyed the opera much. Messrs Hunter and Gordon walked home with us. How you would stare to see the exhibitions that we see in the streets! They are literally lined with sleeping Chinese and Caffres. They make 'the cold flinty rock' their pillow, and lie there at the mercy of cockroaches and mosquitoes, though I much doubt whether the latter could make any impression upon their well-tanned hides. . . .

[November] 12th. [1833]—This morning we sallied forth 'to see the world, and falter out Adieu.' Saying adieu in this place is not like saying it in most others; it is true that people do not care much about each other, and do not pretend to, and in saying good-bye there is more envy than any thing else in the feelings of those who stay, so they all congratulate you, and hope their turn will come next. Still, say what you will, it is not pleasant to leave the most indifferent with the thought that it is the last time we may ever meet.

November 16.—I am nearly all packed up, and think to-morrow my book must be. . . . I shall have no time to write any more letters till I get on board our Castle. Think, my dear, of a ship of thirteen hundred tons! You never saw such a one. The accommodations are fine, and I think of it with pleasure. . . . Tuesday we shall probably go on board, there to remain till we reach St Helena, which will find us much nearer home than we are now. The one prime object is to restore uncle's health; for that, as well as for everything else, we must rely solely on the One Being who orders all things. My daily prayer is that we may all live to meet once more in our own land, where we can dwell with those whom we call our own. I am tired of living among strangers, as I have often told you before, and I sigh to be again at home.

PART VIII

WAR AND WARRIORS

'This Citty of Macao hath many Castles, Forts, plattfformes, etts., well stored with Ordnance and people, the Cittizens well Furnished with armes For themselves and Negroes, of whom there are Many.'

PETER MUNDY, 1637

'The greatest enemy to be dreaded by the Portuguese would be famine, in the event of a war with the Chinese; for ... the principal supplies come from the mainland.'

HENRY CHARLES SIRR, 1849

When Macao was founded by soldier-adventurers in the 1500s, the Portuguese military men who held the city were some of the world's most fierce and capable. Despite the decline of Portuguese power, Macao has always managed to escape military invasion. But it has often been a close thing.

35

CONQUERING MACAO

RICHARD COCKS

The other European seafaring nations who followed the Lusitanians to Asia were envious of Portuguese possessions. By the early 1600s, the English had established a trading factory in Japan, and by 1605 the Dutch had already defeated the Portuguese in the Spice Islands. Both nations covetously eyed Macao and its commercial riches. In 1621 the head of the English factory in Japan, Richard Cocks, sent a letter home to his superiors in the East India Company wistfully assessing Macao's lack of fortification. Considering its early origin (written only five years after the death of Shakespeare), this letter is surprisingly comprehensible despite its unfamiliar spellings. Exceptions might include 'seale', which is sail, and 'noes', which is noise. 'Amacon' is, of course, Macao.

[30th of September, 1621.]

To the Honorble. Sr. Thomas Smith, Knight, Governor of the East India Company, and to the Right Worll. the Comittys deliver in London, Per way of Jaccatra, in shipp *Swan.*

Yt is very certen that with little danger our fleet of defence may take and sack Amacon in China, which is inhabeted by Portingales. For the towne is not fortefied with walls; nether will the King of

162

China suffer them to doe it, nor to make any fortifecations, nor mount noe ordinance upon any plotforme; and 3/4 partes of the inhabetantes are Chinas. And we are credably enformed that, these 2 last yeares, when they did see but 2 or 3 of our shipp within sight of the place, they weare all ready to run out of the towne, as I have advized the Precedent and Councell of Defence at Jaccatra; and, had but 2 small shipps, as the *Bull* and the *Pepercorne*, entred this yeare, they might easely have burnt and taken 17 seale of galliotas which weare at an ancor, amongst which weare the 6 galliotas which came into Japon, being then full laden; and, had they taken this fleet, the Portingales hadd byn utterly undon, as they them selves confesse, and, that towne being taken, all the Portingalles trade in these partes of the world is quite spoiled, both for Manillias, Malacca, Goa, and else wheare. And the King of China would gladly be ridd of their neighbourhood, as our frendes which procure our entry for trade into China tell me, and doe say that he wished that we could drive them from thence. But this yeare there is 3 kings of China dead, the father and his two sonns, the wives of the two bretheren procuring the poisoning of them both. Soe that now a yong man of 14 or 15 yeares ould is com to be king, being the sonne of one of the deceased brothers; which is a stay unto our proceadinges to get trade into China, for that new petision must be made, and our joyning with the Hollanders to take China juncks is ill thought of. But the barbarousnesse of the Hollanders at Manillias the last yeare is much; for, after they had taken the China junkes and that the pore men had rendred them selves, the Hollandars did cut many of them in peeces and cast many others into the sea; wherof our men saved and took many of them up into our shipps; and much more distrucktion had byn made of them, had not Capt. Adames, the admerall, prevented it.

36

THE DUTCH ATTACK

C. R. BOXER

In 1622, only one year after Richard Cocks' appraisal of Macao's defences, the Dutch, apparently in agreement about the ease with which the city could be taken, decided to invade. For the Netherlanders it was a worthwhile target. Capturing it would allow them to knock out the richest pillar of the Portuguese South-East Asian empire, while taking the city as their own commercial base, and replacing the Portuguese as suppliers of Chinese silk to the Japanese market. Professor Charles Boxer's dramatic account of the unexpected Dutch defeat is based on Portuguese, Dutch, and other contemporary sources.

On the 22nd June [1622], the Dutch Commander sent ashore three men with a Chinese guide, to reconnoitre the Chinese suburb and to find out whether its inhabitants would stay neutral. They could not find anyone and returned aboard without any information. The Portuguese accounts make no mention of this scouting party, so they must have disembarked by night. On the 23rd, Vigil of Saint John the Baptist, Reijersen accompanied by his senior officers, reconnoitred the place from a launch, and it was decided to disembark the landing party on Cacilhas beach the next day. Meanwhile, to distract attention from the intended landing-place, three of the ships—*Groeningen, Gallias* and *Engelsche Beer,* anchored off the São Francisco battery which they heavily bombarded during the afternoon. They received however more hurt than they inflicted, for although their shot caused some damage to houses and much consternation to the inmates, none

164

of these were actually killed if the Portuguese accounts are to be trusted. During this artillery duel, the Dutch crews shouted to the battery's defenders that next day they would be masters of Macao and would rape the women after killing all the men over twenty years old. The ships drew off at sunset, but celebrated the expected victory by blowing trumpets and beating drums all night. Not to be outdone by this bravado, Lopo Sarmento de Carvalho ordered similar martial rejoicings to be made on the city's bulwarks 'so that the enemy should understand that we had greater reason to rejoice, by the manifold mercies which our Lord God had shown us'. Since it was obvious that the enemy would land next day, Lopo Sarmento spent the night in visiting all the fortified posts and exhorting that they could expect no mercy from their heretic foes, nor seek refuge with the Chinese, the majority of whom had abandoned the town.

At daybreak on the Feast-day of Saint John the Baptist [24 June] the Dutch ships *Groeningen* and *Gallias* resumed and intensified their bombardment of the São Francisco bulwark. The Portuguese gunners replied with equal determination and better success, as the *Gallias* was so badly crippled that she had to be abandoned and scuttled a few weeks later. Meantime, about two hours after sunrise, the landing force of 800 men, embarked in 32 launches (equipped with a swivel-gun in the prow) and 5 barges, steered for Cacilhas beach to the north-east of the town, protected by fire from the guns of two of the ships. Further protection was afforded by the drifting smoke from a barrel of damp gunpowder which had been fired to windward,—perhaps one of the earliest instances of the tactical use of a smoke-screen. About 150 Portuguese and Eurasian musketeers under the command of Antonio Rodriguez Cavalhino opposed the landing from a shallow trench dug on the beach. A lucky musket-shot fired at random into the smoke-screen struck the Dutch Admiral in the belly, so that he had to be taken back to his flagship at the beginning of the action. The Hollanders were nothing dismayed at his loss, and the senior military officer, Captain Hans Ruffijn, speedily formed up his men on the shore and drove the Macaonese from their entrenchment, after losing about 40 men in the landing. Antonio Rodriguez and his party did not await the onset of the Hollanders, but withdrew towards the town, fighting a rear-guard skirmish as they went.

The Dutch now disembarked their three field-pieces and the rest of their men without further opposition. Ruffijn then organized two rear-guard companies to stay on Cacilhas beach, with a view to covering the withdrawal of the main body if the attack on the town should prove unsuccessful. This done, he resumed the advance with 600 men, 'boldly marching in orderly array and with even steps along the field which borders the foot of the hill of Nossa Senhora da Guia, firing their muskets with such precision and dexterity that they aroused great admiration amongst our people in this respect', as a Jesuit eye-witness reported.

In this way the Hollanders continued their advance, skirmishing with Cavalhino's musketeers, until they reached a small spring called Fontinha where the local women were accustomed to wash their laundry. This place was within artillery range of the city, and they now came under fire from a large bombard which the Jesuits had planted on a bulwark of the half-finished citadel of São Paulo. A lucky cannon-ball from this gun, which was served by the Italian Jesuit and mathematician Padre Jeronimo Rho, struck a barrel of gunpowder which exploded in the midst of the Dutch formation with devastating results. Disheartened by this unexpected disaster, or else suspicious of an ambush awaiting them in a neighbouring bamboo grove, the Dutch halted their advance on the city, and after some consultation amongst their senior officers, wheeled towards the Guia hill, on whose commanding height a small hermitage was situated. Their advance up this hill was checked by a party of thirty Macaonese and negro skirmishers, to whose harrassing fire from behind the large rocks strewn on its rugged slope, the serried ranks of the Hollanders could make no effective reply.

With all or most of their powder supply lost in the explosion resulting from Father Rho's lucky shot, harassed by the fire of the Macaonese from the Guia hill on the one side and from Cavalinho's party on the other, and hot and tired from the three hour's marching and skirmishing in the heat of a summer day, the Hollanders now halted a second time, whilst their captains deliberated on the next move. After a brief discussion, they decided to occupy a favourable tactical position on rising ground near the Guia Hill which likewise covered the Cacilhas beachhead. In view of the unexpected strength of the defence and the unforeseen loss of their ammunition, they had evidently decided to break off the attack and withdraw to their ships while there was yet time.

Whilst this battle or rather skirmish was in progress, the defenders of the town had not been idle. The commander of the garrison of São Thiago at the entrance to the inner harbour, realizing that the main attack was coming from the landward and that the naval bombardment of São Francisco was a feint, detached a party of 50 men under Captain João Soares Vivas, to reinforce the main body of the defenders who were being concentrated for a decisive counter-attack by the Captain-Major Lopo Sarmento de Carvalho. Vivas arrived with his welcome reinforcement just at the critical moment when the Hollanders had begun their retreat. The Portuguese Captains, seeing what was happening, hurriedly occupied the rising ground towards which the Dutch were moving, before the latter could reach their objective.

Seizing his opportunity Lopo Sarmento gave the signal for the attack by shouting the Iberian battle-cry of Santiago—'Saint James and at them!' His eager followers needed no second bidding and the whole motley throng of Portuguese soldiers, Macaonese citizens and negro slaves—to say nothing of armed Friars and Jesuits to boot—took up the cry and hurled themselves at the Hollanders. A few scattered musket shots had no effect on their ardour, and the death of Captain Hans Ruffijn, who was encouraging his men to stand fast at this critical moment, settled the issue of the day. Discouraged by the fall of their leader and demoralized by the furious onset of the drunken negro slaves, the Hollanders turned and fled after a trifling resistance. To make matters worse, the two rearguard companies at Cacilhas, on seeing the approach of these disordered fugitives, were seized with panic and fled precipitately to the boats without firing a shot. The finishing touch to this demoralisation was supplied by the sailors manning the boats, who, fearful of having their vessels overturned by a mass of fugitives, pushed off into deeper water, so that many of those who escaped the cold steel of the Portuguese were drowned or shot down in the sea. So complete was the panic, that the entire force would probably have been exterminated, save for the fact that many of the negro slaves abandoned the pursuit of the flying foe in order to strip and plunder the bodies of the dead.

37

A WALL TO KEEP OUT THIEVES

GEORGE NEWENHAM WRIGHT

The heroic defeat of the Dutch did not mean that Portuguese city was safe against foreign intervention. According to George Newenham Wright writing in the 1840s, Macao's defensive strength remained very much at the whim of the Chinese authorities. Although his founding date for the enclave is too early, he records an unexpected and interesting local story about the construction of the barrier that marks Macao's northern boundary.

Macao occupies a position rather of beauty than strength; for the rocky summits that surround its peninsular site also command it, and the waters that lave its winding base are navigable by vessels of considerable burden. Its political circumstances have always presented an historic anomaly. Portuguese adventurers having long wandered in the Eastern seas, made occasional descents upon the Chinese coast, and, by bribery, barter, and sometimes brutality, established a species of recognition. About the year 1537—at all events, subsequently to the death of St Francis Xavier at Shan-shan—the Portuguese obtained permission to settle at Macao; not as an independent community, but in conjunction with the native population, and during their good behaviour, or the emperor's pleasure. For this commercial residence they probably consented, at first, to pay a large remuneration, their expectations of prosperity being proportionately high; but their illiberality, in endeavouring to secure for themselves and the Spaniards a monopoly of Chinese trade, operated so ruinously to their speculation, that the emperor is now content to receive from them the miserable ground-rent of £150 sterling, per annum.

The city stands upon a peninsula, three miles in length by one in breadth, one side of which is curved into a beautiful bay, the opposite being somewhat convex towards the sea; the ridge of this rocky eminence, as well as its sloping sides, being covered with churches, and convents, and turrets, and tall houses, such as are seen in Europe. A narrow sandy isthmus  joins the peninsula to the heights of Heang-shan, which are crowned with forts, to awe the humbled settlers; and an embattled wall, after the jealous fashion of the Chinese, crosses the isthmus, and forms an entire separation between the Christians and idolaters. It is said that this barrier was first erected to check the incursions of Romish priests, who were much addicted to the practice of stealing Chinese children, from a desire to convert them to a saving faith. The end was certainly laudable, but not the means. The rigidity with which the Portuguese are ruled, and the well-known character of the Chinese as separatists, would rather induce a belief that the charge of kidnapping was a forgery, invented as a pretext for building up this rampart. A presiding mandarin (Tso-tang) constantly resides in Macao, and gives evidence of the slight nature of Portuguese tenure there, by occasionally stopping the supply of provisions intended for the Christians—by enforcing strictly the conditions of their occupancy, such as prohibiting the erection of new houses, or repairs of old ones—and by inspecting the Portuguese forts, to see that no additional strength has been given to them, nor any increase made to the garrison of four hundred men. Without a licence (for which a stipend is expected) none of these conditions may be violated with impunity; nor can the Portuguese accomplish such objects secretly, all handicraft employments being exercised exclusively by Chinese residents.

38

THE GOVERNOR'S LAST RIDE

THE TIMES

Governor João Maria Ferreira do Amaral was a naval hero who originally made his name by continuing a charge even after his right arm had been struck off by cannon shot. ('Forward my brave comrades. I have another arm left. . . .') After China's defeat in the first Opium War, the Portuguese government was anxious to put their tenuous hold on Macao on to a more secure footing. Governor Amaral's reputation for military heroics made him seem the perfect man for the job, but his new hard-line policy in dealing with the Chinese government won him mortal enemies. His murder and mutilation in 1849 was reported in The Times *of London.*

Saturday, October 27, 1849

Our correspondence from Hong Kong is to the 30th of August. A most atrocious act of barbarity had been committed at Macao on the 22nd of that month in the assassination of his Excellency the Governor, Signor do Amaral. While taking his customary ride in the evening, accompanied by his aide-de-camp, about half a mile from the fort, and 300 yards from the barrier-gate, he was suddenly attacked by eight Chinamen, and dragged from his horse, when the murderers hacked off his head and hand, and disappeared through the gate.

The aide-de-camp was also thrown from his horse, and severely wounded. It was well known that rewards had been offered at Canton and elsewhere for the Governor's head, and no doubt is entertained that the murder has been instigated or connived at by the Chinese authorities to whom the late Governor has made himself obnoxious. The Portuguese soldiers, impatient to avenge the death of the Governor, had taken possession of the barrier-gate, and beyond the gate had destroyed a small fort, the fire from which molested them. In effecting this seven Portuguese soldiers were wounded, and, it is said, 74 Chinese killed. So soon as the intelligence of the assassination of the Governor reached Hong Kong, Her Majesty's ship *Amazon* and steamer *Medea* left for Macao, for the protection of British subjects, and by their presence to give countenance and support to the Portuguese authorities. A French and two American vessels of war were at Macao for similar purposes. About 60 British marines were stationed on shore and a party had charge of the Francisco fort. Marines from the American and French vessels also landed. It is to be feared, however, that on their removal further outrages will be committed by the Chinese, unless conciliatory measures are adopted by the Portuguese.

Senhor Amaral's death had caused universal regret among the foreign community. His vigour, courage, and firmness in dealing with the Chinese nation secured him the respect and admiration of all, but his very eminence in this respect marked him out for assassination.

Wednesday, November 21, 1849

The accounts from Hong Kong are to the 29th of September. The Murder of the Governor of Macao still occupied attention. On this subject the *Friends of China* of the 28th of September writes as follows:—

Last monthly paper contained a lengthened account of the murder of the Governor of Macao by the Chinese on the 22nd of August, the consequent excitement among the Portuguese, and the position of the colony when the overland despatches were closed. . . . Since the Portuguese soldiers captured a small Chinese fort outside the barrier, three days after the murder, there have been no acts of hostility on either side. The number of Chinese killed and wounded on that occasion was not far from 70; in

Canton exaggeration has swollen that number to over a hundred. The Chinese within the walls of Macao are quiet; there has been neither riot nor plunder, and the presence in the town of marines belonging to the French and American ships of war will have an excellent effect. The French Minister to China resides in Macao; and the American Government occupies naval stores there for the supply of the squadron in the east. At these places respectively there is a French and an American guard. The Chinese Commissioner's reply to the despatch from the Macao Government informing him of the crime that had been committed was not received when the last packet closed. It came a few days later and is marked by the cool insolence of its tone. It is said that the answer sent to Mr Bonham's communication was much in the same strain. The Macao Government answered seriously, but it had little if any effect. About the 20th, the Government received another communication (we rather think not written by Seu himself) offering to deliver up the head and hand of the late Governor, also a head said to be that of one of the murderers, provided the Portuguese would release the three Chinese soldiers captured at the barrier gate on the 25th ult. To this the Portuguese could not consent; much value being put on the evidence of the soldiers. It is said they were on guard when the murder was committed, witnessed the whole affair, and feasted in the guardhouse with the murderers, the head and hand being there until near midnight, when they embarked for Canton. They reached Canton the following evening, when there was much rejoicing within the city. At Wampoa—in sight of the foreign shipping—there was a public procession a few days later. Many Chinese soldiers were present, carrying with them the figure of a European on horseback which they placed in the temple of one of their idols. Rumours are current of rewards and even rank having been conferred on the murderers; but of this foreigners have no certain knowledge. The authorities at Macao will spare no exertion to get at the truth. No sane man for a moment can believe that this was the act of mere desperate ruffians. Plunder was not their object; before they committed their deed a retreat was secured in Canton, and the very hour of their arrival at the city timed. It now appears that some days previous to the murder a Mandarin vessel moored in the bay near the barrier. She anchored off the Praya on the evening the deed was done, and left some time during the night. It is probable that after marking the state of excitement this boat put off and embarked the murderers according to previous arrangement. An express boat despatched for Canton that evening returned, saying they had been fired at by pirates and compelled to return. The crew of their express assert that the boat which prevented their going further was the identical Mandarin boat we have referred to. The Chinese continue repairing their fortifications at Caza Branca; but whether they meditate hostilities is mere conjecture. The officials take the capture of their fort by the Portuguese and the slaughter of part of their garrison very quietly. The Mandarins merely demanded back the fort, the barrier guard-house, and the three prisoners; they made no comment on the number killed and wounded. Knowing how very difficult it is to deal with them in an ordinary accidental homicide, when a foreigner happens to take the life of a Chinese, it is difficult to believe that they will refrain from demanding satisfaction.

39

THE ARRIVAL OF THE NEMESIS

WILLIAM DALLAS BERNARD

When Sino-British hostilities exploded into the Opium War in 1839, the British Royal Navy's innovative steam-driven, paddle-wheel iron ship with retractable keels proved marvellously effective for waging battle on the rivers and coasts of China. The first and most famous of these was the Nemesis, *which caused something of a stir by appearing in Macao harbour in November 1841, as described by an eyewitness on board.*

At daylight on the following morning, the 25th November, the Nemesis steamed through the Typa anchorage, which lies opposite Macao, and ran close in to the town, where the water is so shallow that none but trading-boats can venture so far. The sudden appearance of so large and mysterious-looking a vessel naturally excited the greatest astonishment among all classes both of the Portuguese and Chinese residents. The saluting of the Portuguese flag, as she passed, sufficed to announce that something unusual had happened; and crowds of people came down to the Praya Grande, or Esplanade, to look at the first iron steamer which had ever anchored in their quiet little bay. Her very light draught of water seemed to them quite incompatible with her size; and even the Portuguese governor was so much taken by surprise, that he sent off a messenger expressly to the vessel, to warn her captain of the supposed danger which he ran by venturing so close in shore. It is probable, however, that his Excellency was not quite satisfied with the near approach of an armed steamer, within shot range of his own palace; and, moreover, the firing of a salute, almost close under his windows, had speedily frightened away the fair ladies who had been observed crowding at all the windows with eager curiosity.

As soon as the first excitement had passed, Captain Hall waited upon the governor, to assure him that he had come with the most peaceable intentions, and to thank his Excellency for the friendly warning he had given, with respect to the safety of the vessel. At the same time, he begged to inform his Excellency that he was already thoroughly acquainted with the harbour and anchorage of Macao, from early recollection of all those localities; as he had served as midshipman on board the *Lyra*, during Lord Amherst's embassy to China, in 1816.

PART IX

POETS AND ARTISTS

'I agree with the American poet, who has pencilled upon the tomb,–

"I can't admire Camoens with ease,
Because I can't speak Portuguese."'

GEORGE WINGROVE COOKE, 1858

ertilized by the exotic cultures of the Far East, Macao would seem an attractive oasis for poets and artists seeking inspiration. Some did come to Macao in search of their muse, but others who practised their art on the tiny peninsula came for much less noble reasons. The brightest star of Macao's artistic constellation was a classical poet regarded as one of Europe's most important Renaissance writers. The bard, Luís de Camões, was reputedly exiled to Macao as a colonial officer in Portugal's conquering army as a punishment after a sword fighting, womanizing, and otherwise rumbustious life. The painter George Chinnery came to escape large debts accumulated in India and to hide from his wife, whom he claimed was even uglier than he was. Camilo Pessanha, one of Portugal's most important twentieth-century poets, was lured by cheap and legal opium. The following pages collect together poetry and prose written by or about a few of the artists and painters who have passed through the Portuguese enclave, or made it their home.

40

A CURSE UPON DOUBTERS

OSMOND TIFFANY, JR.

The celebrated Portuguese poet, Luís de Camões (c.1524–80), or 'Camoens' in English, is said to have written part of his immortal epic 'The Lusiads' on a rocky outcropping overlooking Macao's inner harbour in the 1550s. The grotto and its surrounding garden now honour the poet, though his sojourn there cannot be proved. As the American Osmond Tiffany discovered in the 1840s, travellers to Macao were unwise to admit such doubts publicly.

The cave of Camoens is a shrine for all who ever heard the name of the first, I might almost say the only, poet that Portugal can claim. Here in sight of the rolling wave it is said he wrote his Lusiad, and the old residents would utter a curse on him who dared to doubt the story. Be that as it may, he was banished to this spot, and if it bore its present look in his time, his feeling might have flowed in poetry.

41

THE IMPORTUNATE 'ROMEO'

R. C. HURLEY

Whether fiction or fact, the stories of the life of the poet Luís de Camões and of the tiny settlement on the fringes of Portugal's empire are now inextricably entwined. Here is an 1898 narrative of the volatile warrior-poet's chaotic and adventurous life from an early guidebook for tourists to the South China coast. It portrays Camões in the style of the European romantics, the epitome of an incautious genius who suffers in love and dies penniless and rejected by society.

L uiz de Camoes, the epic Portuguese poet, was born in Lisbon in 1524, where he spent most of his childhood's days receiving his earlier training at Coimbra. After completing his studies in the Coimbra University he returned, in the year 1545, to his birthplace and it is narrated that whilst domiciled there, he fell deeply in love with one of the ladies of honour of Queen Catherine's court, Senhora Donna Catherina de Athayde. This romantic escapade appears to have caused a general displeasure in aristocratic circles and the importunate 'Romeo' was temporarily banished by King John III to Santarem a small fishing port at the mouth of the river Tagus.

Some two years later Royal permission was sought and granted for the completion of the term of his banishment at Ceuta in Africa, there to serve as a soldier. On his way thither in an attack by pirates off the coast of Morocco he was unfortunate enough to lose the use of his right eye. In the year 1550 he returned again to Lisbon, but was much disappointed when he discovered that his valour as a soldier received scant recognition as compared with the appreciation and honour paid to his genius as a poet. Having giving up all hopes of obtaining the hand of the lady of his

178

endearment, he decided to leave his native land to risk his future fortunes in the Indes, with which object he joined an expedition to the East that same year. Whilst at Goa on the coast of Hindustan he received the sad news of the death of Dona Catherina, and his great affection for the departed lady became suddenly changed into an ardent and patriotic love for his country, which passion inspired him to write that celebrated poem 'Os Lusiadas.'

A man possessing a very romantic temperament, and at the same time imbued with a high estimate of true moral principle, Camoes became horribly disgusted with the vile practices permitted by the Portuguese Authorities at Goa during some of the great festivals in 1556, and as an effort to correct these abuses he wrote a satire boldly exposing them and treating even the Viceroy with contemptuous ridicule. For this praiseworthy offence he was again banished,—this time to the Moluccas in the Pacific, where he remained for about a year, when it was arranged for his transfer to Macao to the Government appointment of Administrator of the Estates of Absentees and of the Dead. During his voyage to Macao when off the coast of Cambodia near the mouth of the Mekong River he suffered shipwreck being washed ashore completely destitute and saving only the M.S. of his epic poem. After many painful experiences in strange lands, he finally reached the Holy City where, in a quiet and secluded life, he completed the closing stanzas of 'Os Lusiadas' in the gardens now bearing his name. Some years later, he returned to his country to find its Capital stricken with black-plague, and to end in extreme poverty a life overburdened with anguish.

Camoes wrote also a number of odes, sonnets, &c., and for masterly simplicity of diction he is spoken of as the Virgil of Portugal, whilst the versification of 'Os Lusiadas' is undeniably charming.

In the possession of Mr Lourenço Marques at Macao is an old autograph album in which is inscribed many a beautiful line to the soldier poet. In this album will also be found the autographs of Prince Alfred, General Grant, the Duke of Alençon, the Grand Duke Alexis of Russia and many other celebrities who have visited Macao during the past century.

The gardens within recent years have undergone certain changes and repairs which have unfortunately not enhanced the beauty of their primeval simplicity.

A translation of 'Os Lusiadas,' procurable in Hongkong, will greatly add to the interest of the visit to Macao.

42

THE LUSIADS

LUÍS DE CAMÕES

'The Lusiads'–'Os Lusiadas' in Portuguese, from the Roman name for Portugal–is a roaring tale of the Portuguese adventurers who first secured their piece of the Iberian peninsula, then set out to conquer the world. The Portuguese nation is embodied in the valiant explorer Vasco da Gama and his conquests. With its rich and fantastic allegory, the poem also established the reputation of Luís de Camões among the first of the Renaissance poets to return to classical styles.

Camões does not mention Macao in his epic, perhaps because he was never there or, perhaps as C. A. Montalto de Jesus reasons, because he doubted 'the colony's stability, after so many disasters in China'. The poem first appeared in 1572 and ran to more than 1,000 stanzas. Included here are the first three, from the 1655 translation by Sir Richard Fanshawe, the first in the English language.

1
Arms, and the Men above the vulgar File,
Who from the Western Lusitanian shore
Past ev'n beyond the Trapobanian-Isle,
Through Seas which never Ship has sayld before;
Who (brave in action, patient in long Toyle,
Beyond what strength of humane nature bore)
'Mongst Nations, under other Stars, acquir'd
A modern Scepter which to Heaven aspir'd.

2

Likewise those Kings of glorious memory,
Who sow'd and propagated where they past
The Faith with the new Empire (making dry
The Breasts of ASIA, and laying waste
Black AFFRICK'S vitious Glebe) And Those who by
Their deeds at home left not their names defac't,
My Song shall spread where ever there are Men,
If Wit and Art will so much guide my Pen.

3

Cease man of Troy, and cease thou Sage of Greece,
To boast the Navigations great ye made;
Let the high Fame of ALEXANDER cease,
And TRAIAN'S Banners in the EAST display'd:
For to a Man recorded in this Peece
NEPTUNE his Trident yielded, MARS his Blade.
Cease All, whose Actions ancient Bards exprest:
A brighter Valour rises in the West.

43

THE ROCKY CLEFT

LUÍS DE CAMÕES

Above all, it is the grotto in Camões Garden that has come to symbolize the immortal bard and his reputed association with Macao. C. A. Montalto de Jesus believed that one of Luís de Camões' sonnets describes the Macao garden and rock cluster. The 'poor rendering' below is his translation of the poem. Its spirit evokes the atmosphere in Camões Garden whether or not the bard ever visited its grotto.

Where shall I find a more secluded spot,
Of all the delightful traits so sadly bare,
That need I say no man betakes him here,
When e'en by beast it rests uncared, unsought.
Some frowning woods with awful darkness fraught,
Or sylvan solitude of dismal air,
Without a sprightly brook or meadow fair,
In fine a place adapted to my lot.
For there, embosomed in the rocky cleft,
In life entombed, there freely may I mourn
O're plaintive, death-like life of all bereft,
Save tears and woes to which there is no bourn.
In cheerful days there shall I feel less sad,
Contended too when all in gloom is clad.

44

SO ODD HE SEEMED DERANGED

WILLIAM HICKEY

The Irish artist George Chinnery escaped to Macao in 1825 because of pressing debts in Calcutta, where he had previously lived. He was to reside in the enclave, and periodically in Canton, until his death in 1852. Many of Chinnery's paintings and sketches, such as the drawings below, on page 186, and on the cover of this book, depict scenes of these two cities. However, he is most renowned for his portraits, for which he earned hefty fees. As his Macao contemporary William Hickey recorded, Chinnery was notable for other reasons as well.

Mr Chinnery, like many other men of extraordinary talent, was extremely odd and eccentric, so much so as at times to make me think him deranged. His health certainly was not good; and he had a strong tendency to hypochondria which frequently made him ridiculously fanciful, yet in spite of his mental and bodily infirmities, personal vanity shewed itself in various ways. When not under the influence of low spirits, he was a cheerful pleasant companion, but if hypochondriacal was melancholy and dejected to the greatest degree.

45

THE OPEN MOUTH

HARRIET LOW

Despite his legendary ugliness, carelessness over debts, and other foibles, George Chinnery had endearing eccentricities. In Macao his contemporaries record him as one might remember a beloved family pet that had a tendency to dig up the garden and track mud into the house. Harriet Low, the niece of the head of the American trading house Russell & Co. who resided in Macao between 1829 and 1833, took sketching lessons from Chinnery and endured sitting for him while he painted her portrait.

[1833] April 2.

This morning called on Caroline, and then went to that amusing man, Chinnery, and stayed till after two sketching. There is a good deal to be gathered from his conversation, and some of his similes are most amusing. He has been a great observer of human nature, for which he has had every opportunity, his profession having brought him in contact with people of high and low degree. He has been in Calcutta for twenty years, and has seen a great variety of characters, as you may suppose, in that changing place. He has excellent sense, and plumes himself upon being, 'though not handsome, excessively genteel'; his personal appearance, I think, however, is rather against him, for he is what I call fascinatingly ugly, and what with a habit he has of distorting his features in a most un-Christian manner, and with taking snuff, smoking and snorting, I think, were he not so agreeable, he would be intolerable. But, to give him his due, he is really polite, and speaks well of every one. Being one of his especial favorites, I must say something for him; to use his own expression, he 'buckles' to me. We were asking him if Afun (in Mr Colledge's picture) could keep still enough to be painted. 'Ma'am,' he said, 'the Rock of Gibraltar is calves'-foot jelly to him.'

April 9.—Spent part of the morning translating English into French. About twelve, Caroline came in with Chinnery. . . . I am to have my phiz painted, great presumption on my part, I think, but it was the request of Uncle and Aunt, and the thought of the pleasure it would give you all that induced me. I sat for an hour, looking at one of the ugliest men in existence, but he makes himself so agreeable that you quite forget how ugly he is. He requested me to have the mouth open, a thing which I abominate in a picture, but he says it will never do to have it shut, as I generally keep it a little open.

46

A WONDERFUL STOMACH

WILLIAM C. HUNTER

The China trader William Hunter's experience of the great painter George Chinnery was entirely in Macao and Canton, where the two knew each other well. Although fond, the descriptions do not spare Chinnery's reputation for physical ugliness and gourmandism, nor do they spare the reputation of his wife who, despite her absence, became a figure of fun throughout the European community on the China coast.

To the subject of the following lines justice cannot be done but by a much more nimble pen than mine. . . .

This gentleman was George Chinnery, by birth an Irishman, by profession an artist, whose works in portraits, crayon sketches, and paintings in oil may yet have a universal Eastern renown. As a 'story-teller' his words and manner equalled his skill with the brush, while to one of the ugliest of faces were added deep-set eyes with heavy brows, beaming with expression and good-nature. . . .

After an uneventful life at Madras. . . . Chinnery lived at Calcutta until 1825, when, after 'serious troubles,' and being tied, as he would say, 'to the ugliest woman he ever saw in the whole course of his life,' he disappeared and came to Macao. Threatened by his wife, however, that she would join him there, he packed up and came to Canton, and there I first made his acquaintance. 'Now,' I heard him say, 'I am all right; what a kind providence is this Chinese Government, that it forbids the softer sex from coming and bothering us here. What an admirable arrangement, is it not?' he asked. 'Yes, Mr Chinnery,' I replied, 'it is indeed;' he rolled up his eyes and exclaimed 'Laus Deo.'

At Canton he became a general favourite, his anecdotes of Indian life, his powers of description, his eccentricities, made him a much sought for guest. Mr B. C. Wilcox, of Philadelphia, then an old resident, and like Chinnery always wearing the high white cravat and corresponding coat collar then so much in vogue, took to him immensely, and they became the best of friends. 'You'll dine with us this evening at half-past seven,' he would say. 'Much obliged,' answered Chinnery, 'I would do so with indescribable pleasure, but at the moment I have not such a thing as a suitable coat.' 'Come then,' replied Wilcox, 'in your shirt; it will be a novelty; but come. Suy-pee will find something for us to eat, and you some one to chat with.' I happened to sit near Mr Chinnery the same evening. When rice and curry were served he transferred to his plate nearly all the rice. Observing it from the head of the table, 'Chinnery,' called out Wilcox, 'you are taking all the rice; twice as much as you can manage.' 'I always do so,' replied Chinnery, 'that while I am eating one half, the other half will keep it warm. . . .'

After two years' residence in the Imperial Hong, during which Mr Chinnery made remittances to his wife ('there goes another thousand rupees,' he would say), and having arranged for a yearly sum 'to keep her quiet,' he took up his quarters at Macao, but for some time after kept a trunk ready packed with which to fly to the provincial city, if, as he would say, 'my Thalia should try to surprise me;' and on one or two occasions he did fly to the haven of safety, and returned when the scare was over. What fun all this created! He would join heartily in it himself, merely saying, 'Was any man ever so tortured as I am?' or, 'Another false alarm; may it not be followed by fire some day or other? Who was ever so persecuted?' At last came the dreadful news that Mrs C. was positively coming on in a vessel about to sail. Another ship, however, anticipated that one, by which he learnt that the cabin had been secured by a well-known gentleman named Brown, and consequently Thalia was prevented from coming. . . .

When the ship which brought Brown anchored in the roads of Macao, and he had landed, away went Chinnery to call upon him. 'Brown,' said he, 'I owe you one;' when he was interrupted by the latter, who assuming not to be in family secrets, began to apologise for having secured the cabin, thereby depriving him of the great pleasure of cordially welcoming Mrs Chinnery after so long an absence. 'Excuse me, Chinnery, my business was unusually pressing;' and, 'Excuse you, Brown!' said C. 'Your hand, my good fellow; you have played a card I shall never forget. You'll breakfast with me to-morrow; grateful thanks for the immense and never-to-be-forgotten service you have rendered me. Chin-chin and good luck to you; may your shadow never grow less and your Patna yield you 1,000 per cent. Sharp 12.'. . .

In 1825 arrived at Canton an American gentleman named W. W. Wood. . . . He joined Russell & Co. some time after I did, and we occupied an office in common. The poor fellow was awfully pock-marked; his face resembled a pine cone, but his expression was one of very good humour and full of intelligence. He was besides well educated and a most gentlemanly young fellow. He was the son of the famous tragedian of Philadelphia. . . . Wood was very clever at draughting and sketching; thus on his visits to Macao, as well as in Canton, he met Chinnery constantly, and being brother chips with the pencil, of similar tastes, besides being a most amusing fellow, and a toss up in respect to looks, they became fast friends. Wood was quite equal to Chinnery in wit and metaphor, while over their mutual disfigurement each one insisted that he was the most marked of the two. Meeting one day at Macao, Chinnery assumed an air of displeasure, held up his clenched hand and shaking it at him, exclaimed, 'Oh, you wicked man! I was some one until you came. You are marked, it's true, but I was remarked. Passers-by would say, "There goes old Chinnery; what an ugly fellow." Poco poco, my title became undisputed. What a triumph! now you would carry off the palm. Oh, you ugly piece of wood.' There followed, of course, a deal of fun. . . .

We all came to know that differences between Mr and Mrs Chinnery were not exclusively the cause of his disappearance from Calcutta. There were differences with his creditors too. Certain laws, considered so absurd by debtors, restricted their movements, while if the City of Palaces became too hot to hold them and they could manage it, they would take a change of air.

Macao was then the asylum of the East, open to all, bond or free, and thus it became a proverb, Macao is the paradise of Debtors and of Tan-Kas. Wood, looking in one morning, just from Canton, found his friend lying on the sofa in apparently a towering rage. 'Come here,' exclaimed the latter, and taking up a late number of the 'Bengal Hurkaru,' which was lying on the floor by his side, he pointed out an advertisement in it. 'Read that,' he said. 'Was there ever such an insult? It is insufferable.' Wood read, 'Notice! Whereas George Chinnery, an absconding debtor, is hereby required,' &c. 'Well, you know, Chinnery, these things will happen. What with bad luck and losses, you know, debts are hard to avoid, but—' 'What's hard? What do you mean?' roared C.; 'is *that* all you see there? Debts, what on earth are debts? Fiddlesticks for your debts!' (with emphasis). 'Think of George Chinnery, neither Mr nor Esquire; of George Chinnery, without head or tail; that is too much to bear!'. . . .

In 1834 Wood left China for Manila. . . . Years passed, eighteen more years from the departure of Wood, when our old friend became seriously ill, and it was too evident that his days were drawing to a close. . . . He died at half-past four a.m. of May 30, 1852. After seeing his effects placed in his studio we sealed the doors, left his servant Augustine and several Chinese in charge, and I came home to bed at five o'clock. During the whole time that Mr Chinnery had passed amongst us, twenty-seven years, he had been remarked for two characteristics, one of being an enormous eater, the other of never drinking either wine, beer, or spirits. His sole beverage was tea, oftener cold than hot. Everyone supposed therefore, from his wonderful eating powers, that his stomach would be found in a most deranged state. An autopsy was made by Doctor Watson, our Macao medico, who attended Chinnery in his last illness, the morning of his death, about ten o'clock, at which Stewart and myself were present. On examining the brain it was evident that he had died of serious apoplexy, while the stomach was wonderfully healthy.

A few days after his death Doctor Watson and I were requested by Judge Cavalho, chief judicial officer at Macao, to look through his books, papers, trunks, &c., in case a will might have been left, but there was nothing of the kind. Several camphor wood trunks, however, were found, filled with pen-and-ink sketches and very choice oil-paintings. Amongst the latter was one finished with great care, and which no one of us had seen. It represented the bund at Calcutta. . . . At length, there being no claimant for his effects, they were sold by order of the judge, when this painting was purchased by Mr John Dent, then chief of the old Canton and Hong-Kong house of Dent & Co., in whose possession it probably is now.

47

MACAO

MANUEL MARIA BARBOSA DO BOCAGE

The Portuguese poet Manuel Maria Barbosa do Bocage (1765–1805) enlisted as a naval cadet at the age of seventeen. Driven by a love of adventure as much as his occupation, he travelled to Rio de Janeiro, the Indies, and, finally, to China and Macao. Bocage liked to compare his destiny to that of Luís de Camões. However, more than two centuries after Camões immortalized the heady days of Portugal's great overseas expansion, Bocage experienced a Macao that was anything but glorious and golden. His brief stays in the territory in 1789 and 1790 inspired this poem. In the Portuguese original, Bocage skilfully wedded the intricate rhyme and metre of the sonnet form with an ironically prosaic message. This English version is faithful to the poet's feelings about Macao, but not to the sonnet form. The nhons *referred to in the poem are the Eurasian offspring of Portuguese.*

A government without power, a similar bishop,
   a den of virtuous nuns,
      three monasteries of friars, five thousand
nhons and Chinese Christians who behave very badly.

A cathedral that today is exactly the same,
fourteen penniless canons,
many poor people, many base women;
one hundred Portuguese, packed altogether as if in a stable.

Six forts with no soldiers, but one drummer
three parishes ornamented only in wood
a vicar general without assistant
Two colleges, one of them very bad,
a Senate that is above everything
is as much as Portugal has in Macao.

ODE TO MACAO

JOHN BOWRING

The contrast between Bocage's satirical sonnet and Sir John Bowring's flowery poesy could hardly be more stark. Bowring, one of the foremost British intellectuals of his day and a Governor of Hong Kong, wrote this sonnet in 1849 inspired by Camões' great epic and grotto. The Marques family, which then owned the romantic gardens, had Bowring's poem carved in stone into the rocks around the poet's bust along with other verses commemorating the bard.

Gem of the orient earth and open sea,
  Macao! that in thy lap and on thy breast
  Hast gathered beauties all the loveliest,
Which the sun smiles on in his majesty.
The very clouds that top each mountain's crest,
Seem to repose there, lingering lovingly.
How full of grace the green Cathayan tree
Bends to the breeze—and now thy sands are prest
With gentle waves which ever and anon
Break their awakened furies on thy shore.
Were these the scenes that poet looked upon,
Whose lyre though known to fame knew misery more?
That have their glories, and earth's diadems
Have naught so bright as genius' gilded gems.

DESIRES

CAMILO PESSANHA

Macao was more than a place of transit for Camilo Pessanha (1867–1926), who lived in the territory most of his life and was to die there, weakened by opium addiction and disease. Pessanha is best known for Clepsydra, *the book of poetry published in Lisbon in 1920 that established his literary reputation. However, in Macao he variously made his living—and kept his opium pipe filled—as a lawyer, judge, teacher, keeper of the colonial government's estate registry, and journalist. Arriving in Macao in 1894, Pessanha had three Chinese mistresses and fathered several children. One of his grandsons reportedly still made his living pedalling a trishaw through Macao streets in the late 1960s. His poetic and other writings were scarce, and he rarely wrote about Macao explicitly. Still, he sometimes employed Chinese imagery in his poetry, and critics point to Pessanha's oriental attitude of mind.*

When I ponder the delight promised
By her mouth fresh and tiny
and the breast hidden in fine lace,
Below the bodice's light curve;

I desire, in a giant's transport,
To clasp her firmly in my arms,
Until almost crushing in these embraces
Her flesh white and palpitant;

Like, in Asian tropical forests,
The serpent's Herculean muscles
Squeeze, in a golden luminous spiral,
The trunks of colossal palms.

And like, afterwards, when tiredness
buries the serpent in dull lethargy,
Slumbering repose all day,
In the shade of the palm, the body weary;

I also want, falling asleep,
In fever's phantoms to see the sea,
But always under the blueness of her gaze,
Enveloped in the heat of her gown.

Like the delirious Chinese inebriates
inhale, already sleeping, the tranquil smoke
That their long beloved pipe
Dispersed in the atmosphere a little before. . . .

50

CAMILO PESSANHA

SEBASTIÃO DA COSTA

To many onlookers, Camilo Pessanha's life in Macao was far from exemplary. An inveterate opium smoker, he had been attracted to the Portuguese settlement by the drug's legal status and plentiful supply. He lived with a succession of local women in the jumble of books, Chinese art, and bric-à-brac that engulfed his house, as his friend Sebastião da Costa recalls in this essay written on the occasion of the poet's death in 1926. Pessanha never reconciled himself to the plight of the exiled and what he called the 'the material and moral rubbish heap' of Macao. Arminho, who appears in the essay, was Pessanha's much-loved Pekinese. The author occasionally quotes from Pessanha's own poems.

In the afternoons in Macao, when after concentrated work my body would no longer tolerate the muscular strain of tennis, beneficial and refreshing, I used to seek spiritual refuge in the room of the poet.

The city lacked bread for the soul.

The crass materialism that today is Chinese life, the cheap oriental commercialism, the obstinate preoccupation with gain, the unbridled and voracious graft, the overflowing sensuality, are reflected and perfected in our colonial people. One needed two lamps and considerable careful selection to find a pure and stainless soul in that desert. Pessanha was at least a beautiful spirit.

Along the Praia Grande, angular in its Portuguese lack of planning, ostentatious palace-like residences and sad and shabby houses aligned themselves irregularly. In front, the muddy waters of the two rivers mingled, separating the peninsula from the border islands, verdant and distant. Hardly had I taken in the spectacle of the graceful junks, those fantastic birds with big yellow wings tacking to enter the bar at the harbour entrance, when I would find myself at the green railing of that dark and solitary little house where the poet lived. At the fountain beside it, Chinese bawled nasally as they distributed water in vessels of various forms. A gold-coloured sign said in Chinese ideograms that there practised the lawyer Camilo Pessanha.

It was unnecessary to knock. One lifted the latch, and there was the wide patio that could have belonged to a house in Minho, with a staircase to the first floor and the penthouse above. The thousand barks of the guards of the house penetrated inside. Then, three or four small dogs thronged to the veranda, running around my legs. Behind them was the smiling face of the Chinese damsel, lit by the ivory and gold of her teeth.

The poet was always at home at that hour, always in bed; he passed entire afternoons like that, and only went out exceptionally. One opened the door, crossed two museum salons, turned at a right angle to arrive at the room. One lifted the drape and saw across the yellow screens, the still black beard and those small, luminous eyes of the day-dreamer.

How astonishing it would appear to someone suddenly emerged here, coming from afar and unfamiliar with the lack of neatness and confusion of the Chinese. Were it not for the wide European bed of shining metal and so many books badly arranged on a cupboard and on the chairs, we could have been in any local Chinese house. That romantic disarray distressed the classical nature of my spirit. On the floor, on the cupboards, filling a French-imperial console, obstructing the corners, almost impeding our movements, an infinity of toy figures, jars, vases, Chinese porcelains and bronzes of various forms, beauty, and value. Beside the big bed another small one, out of use and badly covered by a low folding screen, an unrefined piece. Behind that, rolls of Chinese paintings were heaped on a tall, tottery rack. Many others, unrolled and hanging on the walls, rotted against the masonry, so humid in an atmosphere saturated much of the year.

On top of the French-imperial furniture piece, a beautiful silk painting of a wicker basket of flowers, full of life, rich in colour.

The poet was there in his rudimentary attire, stretched out length-wise, like an Indian mystic or fakir. He said to me: 'Enter, enter' with his weak voice growing in sharpness. I arrived at the chair near him. The dogs, who had followed me, jumped on and under the bed in enthusiastic clowning. But always Arminho, the preferred, ended up expelling the others and installing himself in his uncontested domain with the owner. He placed himself very near, on the legs, on the reclined head of the poet, licking his hair. He slept like this every night.

Pessanha read and smoked at this hour in a short night shirt that only just covered him and a sheet badly burned by cigarettes. Beside the bed a table, also French-imperial, its iron fittings shining, recently gilded in the office of a friend (who was undeserving of his friendship) in easy and poor gratitude for clearing up some judicial complications. On it a lamp, pipe, and canister of opium. At the foot, a small chair heaped with books. On the canopy of the bed, topped with a ducal crown, hung two fantastic brass fish. At the head of the bed an antique rosary that the poet, with tears in his eyes, told me had belonged to his dead mother and that he always kept with him. It was his best souvenir of his mother's soul who walked errant and 'begging at the doors of couples'. They should have had it enclosed in his coffin if there had been anyone there who understood this.

In this atmosphere Camilo Pessanha received all of his visitors.

We discussed a thousand things: history, Chinese art, universal poetry, our contemporary poetry were favourite themes. Pessanha spoke with vivacity, almost without conceding to his interlocutor an observation or a judgement. He cut his words with innumerable sharp *heim! heim!* and short laughs, displaying the black mouth of an opium smoker, a cavernous and horrible vortex. . . .

As the afternoon began to fade the vital tension of the poet diminished. His expression deadened. He was missing something, the already indispensable exciter of his life. The first few times he still stood on ceremony. After, he excused himself, rang the bell to call the Chinese concubine, and ordered the opium prepared. The honey-coloured ball swelled the flame of the lamp three times— three pipefuls. Each one absorbed the poet for two or three pulls, and not only one like the skilful Chinese smokers.

One watched a chapter of de Quincey or Claude Farrère. Afterwards, no stupor. To the contrary, a recuperation of lucidity and life, an awakening of nerves. More words, more ideas, more fire. Thomas de Quincey is right when he said: 'During the ten years that I took opium, not regularly but intermittently, the day following that in which I gave myself to this pleasure was always a day of uncommonly good disposition. As for the stupor that one supposes follows, or actually (if we give credit to the numerous descriptions of Turkish opium smokers) accompanies this practice, I negate that also.' Every afternoon at the same hour (and once in the morning, they told me) he repeated the three little balls. This represented a still moderate dose if we compare it to oriental smokers, and a monthly outlay of some one hundred patacas. His Chinese friends knew that the best present for him was some little canisters of the stupefacient and did not forget to send him some of 'Macao Opium Farm' once in a while, the most famous and appreciated opium among smokers.

He almost always spoke animatedly in Chinese with his companion during the operation and afterwards continued the thread of the conversation. His thin, eagle-like profile, made parched and wan by the climate and opium, the eyes squinting a little, the strange and crazy look, gave him the semblance of an *aedo* poet returned from the dead to tell us the legends of his time. When he told me some Chinese poem put into his own verse, the illusion almost became reality. He was a phantom declaiming things as deep and old as the earth. . . .

When the shadow of night started enveloping us, I would dismiss myself and once again cross that room where, on the floor in ceramic, clay, and gilt wood, Laozi the philosopher and Guanyin the goddess of mercy and Chinese incarnation of the Virgin Mary, Guandi the god of war, prophets and scholars, demons and gods mingled their hierarchies. In that twilight of the gods, the image of China these days, there were beautiful and great things and worthless junk. There were precious screens on which warriors clad in brilliantly coloured armour made dominating gestures, and pieces of silk of no interest, decomposing and emitting stench. But it was all without harmony, without plan, without order, in an apocalyptic and distressing confusion.

Outside this place the scene was now so different. On the silvered water of the bay, the lorchas and tankas cut themselves out of little black shadows. The erect figures inside and the mast ropes looked like Nanjing brush strokes traced on rice paper by the delicate hand of a Japanese painter. In the distance the two islands, dark in the pallid sky, completed the water-colour.

The poet without doubt felt the beauty of those Macao afternoons. Would he not leave us some pretty verses, written in the impressionist style of the 'complicated tatoo' and 'conches, stones, pieces of bone', verses in which his soul's emotions spoke to us in the face of that 'languishing of nature', that 'vague ache of the day's end'?

It seems to me it is the obligation of his friends to endeavour that the great deal that beautiful spirit could have produced, and the little that indolence granted him, is not lost among his papers.

Sometimes I met him in the China Bazaar, with his steps hesitating to one side and the other, avoiding contact with the disorderly rabble. Arminho accompanied him, not lingering in front of any happy encounter. Both followed the inevitable zigzags between people impervious to the norms of traffic. In one corner some squatting coolies played an extravagant game on the ground, concentrating, outside of everything. From the gilt doors of tea houses people in blue *cabaia* [tunics] came and went. An old women cried out her wares: 'Giant crickets and cockroaches! Dainties for sweet toothes.' Further on a hawker transported his entire kitchen on his shoulders, with a flame burning, offering a complete meal to the public in suggestive bellows. Three rickshaws passed on the swift trot of coolies, transporting painted *pipachás*, the harlots of China. Through the doors and windows of the fantan houses one saw faces creased with attention as they gazed upon mounds of golden *sapecas* [coins]. Behind us came a Chinese bearing the weight of two pots of rice brandy balanced on the extremities of a great bamboo and shouting at passers-by to stay away: 'Here comes boiling water!' 'Look out! I am loaded down.' A pagoda with polychrome frescos rose on the height opposite. Here the multitude widened itself in the square only to squeeze itself together again as the street narrowed further on. In the corner of sky offered by that open space glided hundreds of multicoloured kites, managed by hands hidden in roofs and terraces and fighting to knock one another down. From the windows of a Chinese restaurant came shrill noises of exotic tonality, a protracted and incomprehensible melody accompanied intermittently by loud banging. Some urchins, their mouths dirty with rice, ate their *chau-chau* with grimy chopsticks from ordinary ceramic bowls.

There the poet went along, sleepwalking, eyes fixed in his chimera, looking for a rare piece in some bric-à-brac shop. Like Junqueiro in Spain, he bought a plate there and a little ornament of those thousand species in which Chinese art is unique in prodigious variety. One saw the solitary walker on the zigzagging, endless street leading to the palace of illusions, the 'lost country'. My imagination divested him of the long white shirt that covered his body, and instead envisioned him in the tattered shirt and trousers of the tramp, old and hungry, like the figure in a picture he once showed me. It would have been a prime work were it not for the carelessness of the photographer, who left in one corner his own walking stick with its wrought silver knob.

And Arminho followed him, looking in the darkness of his irrational brain for some explanation of that incoherent sailing and such a great absence of the bed's soft comfort.

'The doctors tell me that I have arteriosclerosis', Camilo Pessanha said to me one day. 'Any day I will fall down dead in the street.' Pointing to the little Pekinese, he said: 'What will Arminho do when he sees me like that and I totally disappear?'

In seeing them walk together, one could not but remember that the eyes of the poet became wet with tears in the foreknowledge of this sad day.

Like a soul, like a spectre, he went there among the village multitude, walking now, soon stopping as if he had encountered a chosen place good for a sepulchre and was going to fall down exactly there, 'to sink into the ground like a worm'. Now that he has already been lowered into the earth and rests 'sleeping, without sighing, without breathing', poor Arminho will walk there, looking in vain for his companion in happiness and sadness who ceased to 'ponder and sound the abyss'. Or he will have died on his tombstone like so many faithful dogs.

PART X

STRANGERS ON THE COAST

'Upon the gate was a Chinese inscription: "Dread our greatness, and respect our virtue".'

C. A. MONTALTO DE JESUS, 1926

'The residents enjoy a perfect freedom from the curiosity or ill will of the natives, and one may live in complete European style.'

OSMOND TIFFANY, JR., 1849

It was in Macao that the Chinese and Western worlds first came face to face on a permanent basis, sometimes with violence, at others with admiration, often with misunderstanding. Writers from both civilizations have recorded their impressions of one anothers' curious customs, incredible inventions, peculiar foods, and presumptuous claims to control the tiny piece of the South China coast. Macao was also a meeting place for Europeans and Americans drawn by the China trade, who often found westerners of other creeds and cultures just as peculiar as the Chinese. Out of Macao's rich melange of oriental and occidental emerged the Macanese. Now largely a diaspora scattered throughout the world, the Macanese are spiritually rooted in Macao, a city that has been a magnet for so many strangers.

51

WHERE FISH RISE UP

ANONYMOUS

Records of the founding of Macao have largely been lost. This storybook version by an unidentified Chinese writer dates from the Qing dynasty (1644–1911) and was recorded by the historian C. A. Montalto de Jesus.

About the middle of the Ming dynasty the Portuguese borrowed the use of Haou-king-gao [Macao], where immense fish rise up and plunge again into the deep; the clouds hover over it, and the prospect is really beautiful. They passed over the ocean myriads of miles in a wonderful manner, and small and great ranged themselves under the renovating influence of the glorious sun of the Celestial Empire.

52

TRYING ON GLASSES

KONG SHANGREN

Macao was the conduit through which such European inventions as clocks, firearms, and certain astronomical instruments entered China, a kingdom convinced of its own technical superiority. The life of the scholar Kong Shangren (1648–1718), author of the popular drama The Peach Blossom Fan, *was transformed because of one such innovation.*

I'm more than forty now.
Both eyes have slowly grown dim.
Addicted to reading since youth,
I dissipated all my energies:
Burning the mid-night oil,
Facing the dawn still clothed.
Grinding on like this, even now,
I'm well-aware, yet in the same rut.
But clear glass from across the Western Seas
Is imported through Macao.
Fashioned into lenses big as coins,
They encompass one's vision in a double frame.
I put them on—things suddenly become clear.
I can see the very tips of things!
And read fine print by the dim-lit window
Just like in my youth.
My eyes borrow the light of the lens
As the lens borrows the light of the sun or lamp.
Each borrows from the other, never ceasing.
The principle of this seems hard to understand.
Ignorance is naturally critical

But why worry over children's taunts.
If Heaven grants me a few more years,
I'll use these to study the Way.

NOTT OFFENSIVE TO THE STOMACKE

PETER MUNDY

Europeans also learned of many Chinese marvels through Macao—new methods of ship construction, curious birds, and foods like dwarf oranges, rhubarb, celery, and tea. In one of the earliest English-language accounts of the city, dating from the 1630s, Mundy, a ship's factor (who also drew the sketch), highly recommends a wondrous fruit served by the priests of the city.

From the Generalls house wee were conducted to the Jesuitts Collidge (having broughtt 2 of them passengers From Mallacca), where they made us a Collation or Banquett off sweet Meats, Fruit, etts. Among the rest a Fruitt Named Leicheea, as bigge as a Wallnutt, ruddy browne and Crusty, the skynne like to that of the Raspis or Mulberry, butt hard, which Doath easily and cleanly come offe, having within a Cleare white (somwhatt) hard palpy substance, in tast like to those Muscadine grapes thatt are in Spaine in some Country houses aboutt their Courtts etts. They are nott offensive to the stomacke, allthough a man eat many of them, and now hard to bee gotte, the season going outt. It is said they are proper only to this Kingdome of China, And to speake my owne Mynde, it is the prettiest and pleasauntest Fruit thatt ever I saw or tasted. There is another sort like them butt they have another Name and may bee compared allmost as Crabbes are to gardein apples.

206

THE BARBARIANS OF MACAO

PAN SIJU

Chinese Imperial officials were perpetually preoccupied with containing Macao's potentially dangerous influence. In this memorial to the Emperor, dating from the early 1700s, the Guangdong surveillance commissioner, Pan Siju, advised a firm, but benevolent hand in dealing with the barbarians at Macao, which he calls by its Chinese name 'Aomen'. The Emperor approved his suggestions.

I verify that, in the prefecture of Guangzhou, and subordinate to the district of Xiangshan, is a place called Aomen extending over more than 10 *li*. It is surrounded by water on three sides and has direct communication with the ocean. There is only one road from Weiqian Shan Fort to the district seat. It is a very important territory for coastal defence and an optimal strategic position for foreign ships.

In the old Ming dynasty, foreign ships from the Western Ocean came to expand their trade and were permitted temporarily to set up huts in the outer islands so that they might have somewhere to rest.

When they had to return, they took down the huts and left. Later, they were charged an annual ground-rent and, from that time, began building houses and residences in Aomen, having been given permission to bring their wives to reside there. In addition, they attracted local people to whom they rented the ground floors of their houses as residences, receiving annual rents. They also built foreign ships for conducting trade, which became the common practice.

The benign and great affection of our Emperor permits the foreigners from the Western Oceans to stay in Aomen. Currently, there are more than 3,500 male and female barbarians and more than 2,000 local people engaged as workers and professionals throughout the settlement. They generally work happily and live in peace.

The benevolence of the sacred Son of Heaven extends the generosity of his government to those from outside. Because of this, in my humble opinion, I think it possible to completely suspend the prohibition against the barbarian foreigners entering the interior of the country, since they only stay there with the aim of encouraging commerce and conducting business so as to take an annual profit.

In his memorial, Pang Shangpeng, censor in the old Ming dynasty, entreated the suspicion that the barbarian residents of Macao came to usurp and spy. He asked that we destroy their dwellings, obliging them to live in their ships anchored in the old bay, and making them establish their residence on the sea so as to deprive them of their dwellings. However, this would not be fitting.

There are, meanwhile, barbarians of an overly greedy and crafty nature, and those who use in their domestic service negro slaves, who are even more fierce and cruel. There also are knaves from the interior of the country who hide amongst the barbarians, frequently teaching, instigating, and inciting them to disrespect the interdictions and scorn the laws. Therefore, tyrannical and proud, the barbarians come to disobey. They insult and maltreat the residents and mock the laws. Furthermore, they seduce the stupid people to join their religion, auction off their sons and daughters as slaves, and clandestinely export prohibited goods overseas.

Although the Governor and Viceroy have dealt rigorously with all of this insubordination, I also strove officially to investigate it. I verify that, because Macao is situated in a maritime corner, there are not yet sufficient reliable functionaries to deal specifically with these matters, so difficult are they to control and investigate completely.

In my humble opinion concerning the barbarians from outside who are associated with this country, although it is not necessary to treat them in the same way as hooligans, which would be harsh and tedious, we must have clear regulations for them to follow. . . .

Therefore, it seems proper to copy, according to the regulations, the laws governing the three aboriginal tribes, the Yao, Wu, and Li, moving one of my deputies to deal with matters concerning the barbarians of Aomen. He will have the additional functions of ensuring the order of sea defences, spreading the high moral virtues of Your Majesty, elucidating the laws and regulations of the country, registering all the population of foreign barbarians who reside in Aomen, and inspecting all ocean-going ships at the regulated time of their coming and going. If on these occasions lawbreakers are found hiding amongst them or inciting the barbarians to fight, steal, or even trade in human beings or clandestinely export prohibited merchandise, etc., then this official will investigate, deal with, and communicate concerning all of these cases.

If all of these reports are thoroughly investigated, then it gradually will be possible to prevent the barbarians living in Aomen from practising all of those irregularities. The celestial dynasty of long prosperity thus will enjoy felicitous joy and, on the coastal border, the joy of tranquillity will last forever.

Whether my humble opinion gains support or not, prostrated I implore Your Majesty to condescend to cast a sagacious glance and order the execution of this exposition. This I reverently submit.

55

AN IDEAL LOCATION FOR STRANGERS

ALEXANDER MICHIE

Despite the vagaries of official Chinese toleration, wars, pirates, and dramatic fluctuations in economic fortune, the tiny settlement endured. In 1900, the English writer Alexander Michie published his views of the secret to Macao's survival.

The three hours' transit from Hongkong to Macao carries one into another world. The incessant scream of steam-launches which plough the harbour in all directions night and day gives place to the drowsy chime of church bells, and instead of the throng of busy men, one meets a solitary black mantilla walking demurely in the middle of a crooked and silent street. Perhaps nowhere is the modern world with its clamour thrown into such immediate contrast with that which belongs to the past.

The settlement of Macao is a monument of Chinese toleration and of Portuguese tenacity. The Portuguese learnt at an early stage of their intercourse the use of the master-key to good relations with the Chinese authorities. It was to minister freely to their cupidity, which the Portuguese could well afford to do out of the profits of their trading. To 'maintain ourselves in this place we must spend much with the Chinese heathen,' as they themselves said in 1593 in a letter to Philip I. Macao is, besides, an interesting relic of that heroic age when a new heaven and a new earth became the dream of European adventurers. The spot was excellently well suited for the purposes, commercial and propagandist, which it was destined to serve; for in spite of the crimes and cruelties of the sixteenth century argonauts, the religious element was strongly represented in all their enterprises. Situated outside the river proper, though within its wide estuary, and open to the sea, the settlement yet communicates by an inner passage or branch of the Pearl river with the city of Canton. It possesses two sheltered harbours adequate to the nautical requirements of the Middle Ages.

The small peninsula of Macao combined business conveniences with salubrity of climate in a degree absolutely unrivalled in the torrid zone. Its picturesque scenery was always found refreshing to the eye wearied by long contemplation of brick walls, malarious swamps, or the monotonous glare of the melancholy ocean. From the Chinese point of view, also, it was an ideal location for strangers, since they could be thus kept out of sight, isolated like a ship in quarantine, and put under effective restraint. The situation lent itself to the traditional Chinese tactics of controlling barbarians by stopping their food-supply, a form of discipline of which the efficacy had been proved at an early period in the history of the colony. The Chinese adopted all the measures they could think of to confine traders to Macao, where certain indulgences were held out to them, subject to good behaviour.

The Portuguese adventurers of the early sixteenth century, to whom the modern world owes so much, did well in pitching on this 'gem of the orient earth and open sea' as a link in their chain of trading stations, which extended from the coasts of Africa to the Japanese islands. To trade as such the Chinese Government  never seem to have had any objection, nor, would it appear, to foreigners as such. So long as there was nought to fear from their presence, the ancient maxim of cherishing men from afar could be followed without reserve, for the Chinese are by nature not an unkindly people. . . .

The influence of Macao on the history of foreign relations with China extended much beyond the sphere of mere commercial interests. For three hundred years it was for foreigners the gate of the Chinese empire, and all influences, good and bad, which came from without were infiltrated through that narrow opening, which also served as the medium through which China was revealed to the Western world. It was in Macao that the first light house was erected, a symbol of the illuminating mission of foreigners in China. It was there also that the first printing-press was set up, employing movable type instead of the stereotype wooden blocks used by the Chinese. From that press was issued Morrison's famous Dictionary, and for a long series of years the *Chinese Repository*, a perfect storehouse of authentic information concerning the Chinese empire, conducted chiefly by English and American missionaries. The first foreign hospital in China was opened at Macao, and there vaccination was first practised. It was from Macao that the father of China missions, Matteo Ricci, started on his adventurous journey through the interior of the country in the sixteenth century, ultimately reaching the capital, where he established an influence over the Imperial Court scarcely less than miraculous, thus laying the foundation-stone of the Catholic propaganda in China. The little Portuguese settlement has therefore played no mean part in the changes which have taken place in the great empire of China.

56

A PATIENT TAKES HIS LEAVE

TAN SHELING

Traditional Chinese medicine has always had its own sophistication, but, by the early nineteenth century, Western doctors were more knowledgeable in areas such as the treatment of eye diseases. The author of this grateful letter and poem, printed by the Chinese Repository, was a patient in a Macao ophthalmic hospital in the 1830s. Mr Colledge, formerly a surgeon to the British East India Company, ran the infirmary using donations from rich Chinese and Westerners.

Your disciple, Tan Sheling of the district of Haeping in Shaouking foo, deeply sensible of your favor and about to return home, bows and takes leave.

It seems to me that of all men in the world, they are the most happy who have all their senses perfect, and they the most unfortunate who have both eyes blind. What infelicitous fate it was that caused such a calamity to befall me, alas, I know not. But fortunately, Sir, I heard that you, a most excellent physician, having arrived in the province of Canton and taken up your residence in Macao, compassionated those who have diseased eyes, gave them medicines, and expended your property for their support; and that by the exertion of your great abilities, with a hand skilful as that of Sun or Hwa [eminent physicians who lived in the third century], you drew together hundreds of those who were dim-sighted, furnished them with houses, took care of them, and supplied them with daily provisions. While thus extending wide your benevolence, your fame spread over the four seas. I heard thereof and came, and was happily taken under your care; and not many months

213

passed, ere my eyes became bright as the moon and stars when the clouds are rolled away. All this because your great nation, cultivating virtue and practising benevolence, extends its favors to the children of neighbouring countries.

Now completely cured and about to return home, I know not when I shall be able to requite your favors and kindness. But, Sir, it is the desire of my heart, that you may enjoy nobility and emoluments of office, with honors and glory; happiness and felicity that shall daily increase; riches that shall multiply and flourish like the shoots of the bamboo in spring time; and like that shall be prolonged to ten thousand years. Deeply sensible of your acts of kindness, I have written a few rustic lines, which I present to you with profound respect.

England's kind-hearted prince and minister
Have shed their favors on the sons of Han:—
Like one divine, disordered eyes you heal,
Kindness so great, I never can forget.

Heaven caused me to find the good physician,
Who, with unearthly skill, to cure my eyes,
Cut off the film, and the green lymph removed:—
Such, Sir, were rarely found in ancient times.

Honorable Sir, thou great arm of the nation, condescend to look upon your disciple,

TAN SHELING,

Who Bows his head a hundred times, and pays you his respects.

57

A VERITABLE MANDARIN

WILLIAM C. HUNTER

With so many writers obsessed by what they imagined were inherent differences between the Westerners and the Chinese, this tale from the American trader William C. Hunter makes an amusing change.

One day at Macao, 1853, the bell announced a visitor. This is a very convenient mode in houses there, when a call is made the sound being heard all over it. The bell is hung at the foot of the stairs, inside the street door, which is furnished with a knocker. Soon made his appearance Monsieur Durran, a French gentleman, an old resident, who on entering said:— 'A Mandarin has just arrived from Pekin. We have always been anxious to hear about that celebrated city, of which we know little or nothing authentic, and if you would like to see him, I'll bring him in. He is stopping with our friends the Padres at the Missions Etrang'res. What do you say; to-morrow?'

'I shall be delighted,' was my reply, and Durran took leave.

The next day he came, and with him the Mandarin. The latter was of middle height, stout, and comfortable-looking, with a pleasant air; his dress was the ordinary robe and black silk boots, with cap as usual, but without button, as being less ceremonious. After chin-chin-ing and inquiries as to his journey, he looked about the room with much curiosity, took a book from a table, opened it, and exclaiming inquisitively, 'This is a foreign book,' asked its title and the subject of it. He seemed struck with the pictures on the walls, asked an explanation of them, and at length sat down, exclaiming, 'Koo-kwae-tih-han; how curious indeed! And these are all foreign objects?' he asked.

Tea and pipes having been offered, the Mandarin spoke of Pekin, 'Pae-Ching' as he called it, in northern dialect. He described its walls and temples, its gates and towers, and the Hwang-Ching, or Imperial city, the residence of the Emperor's family. He had been about six weeks on his journey to Canton, and was availing himself of the opportunity of coming to the southward to see Macao. Thus we passed a couple of hours most agreeably.

When he rose to leave, he closed his hands and brought them together, saying at the same time, 'Kaow-Tsze, I announce my departure.' It was a great treat to see and talk with a veritable Mandarin just from Pekin, nor did I regret an invitation to call on him at the Missions Etrang'res, where he was stopping, and for the members of which (missionaries) he had brought letters from the 'Northern City.'

A day or two after I called accordingly, and while being conducted to his room, after first sending up my card, I saw him on the verandah, coming toward me laughing, and in French apologising for the deception he had put upon me in passing himself off for a Chinaman. I was thunderstruck!

'I was anxious,' said he, 'to see if I could be mistaken for a Chinese. Pray excuse me, I am a Frenchman, I am the Abbé Huc.' I had never been so thoroughly taken in. We met many times after; he became a constant visitor at my house, until he left in the French frigate Sybille for Bombay and Europe.

58

THE OLD CURIOUS CITY

OSMOND TIFFANY, JR.

After the establishment of Hong Kong, Shanghai, and the other treaty ports following the first Opium War, Macao gained a reputation as little more than a curious backwater. Visiting in the 1840s, the American Osmond Tiffany, Jr found a city lacking in dynamism, albeit with romantic inhabitants and charming vistas.

Across the broad sheet of water that forms the mouth of the Pekiang River, lies the old city of Macao. Enter a ship, and spreading sail, dash out of the harbor of Hong Kong, a few hours' run brings you within hailing distance of the old Portuguese city.

There is nothing Chinese in its appearance; it bears a striking resemblance to Naples in its curving beach and hills, and its buildings. Around the beach is a stone pier, wide and level, the resort of the inhabitants at the hour of sunset, when the sea breeze comes gently over the waves. The quiet of the place is also soothing after the close reeking Canton and the upstart Hong Kong. The residents enjoy perfect freedom from the curiosity or ill will of the natives, and one may live in complete European style.

The houses are in many instances large, with vast rooms, palatial staircases, and mysterious verandahs, behind which a great deal of fun is often going on. Along the pier the garden gates of these old residences warily open and disclose the gay parterres, the solitary courts and green lattices. Macao is one of the most romantic looking cities that imagination can picture; probably the illusion is increased after a sojourn among the matter-of-fact Chinese, but its air of loneliness and antiquity is always interesting.

Every thing in China is old, so old as to run back into dim ages, but in Macao the time-worn buildings date only a few centuries prior to our own being.

The inhabitants look as secluded and as singular as the houses; in the broad day few are seen, but in the evening they saunter along the beach, and the women, in the garb of old Portugal, turn a dark eye on the stranger. Few of the residents are of consequence, they are of old decayed families, as proud as Lucifer, the men lazy and the women mischievous, and they doze away the days, and only appear as the night approaches. A man sick of the world, worn out and disgusted with himself and every one else, would find Macao a home more suited to his palled tastes and jaded spirit than any other spot that I could name.

Around the city are good roads, and one may pass the barrier, enjoy a gallop along the sands, wind around by the native fort, and look far over the bay from the green eminence. . . .

The Chinese town, back of the city, is a hole of filth and wretchedness which few persons find worth visiting. Along the brow of the hill are scattered mansions surrounded with high walls, and in the midst of large cultivated inclosures. Pleasure grounds with bright grass and luxuriant trees, houses with vast airy apartments, and the perfect seclusion of these chosen spots make Macao beautiful. It was my good fortune to be domiciled in one of these for the little time I spent in the old city. The house was an ancient family property, with a hall wide and lofty enough for a palace in Lisbon. It was placed on the summit of the hill, and from its deep shaded verandah, the eye could through the waving trees, catch glimpses of the city below, and of the broad blue flashing bay. Above the garden, on a precipitous crag, an old deserted convent rose high into the air. Throughout the day the breeze blew through the halls, and the sun's fierceness was tempered by the leafy shade. And when the luminary sunk in his splendor, and twilight stillness brooded over the scene, the ear drank in the music, that arose where the curving beach bent in pity to the moan of the waters.

59

MACAO UNBOUND

ALICIA HELEN N. LITTLE

*Other writers found Macao anything but backward. Alicia Helen N.
Little, who used the pen name Mrs Archibald Little, visited Macao in
the closing years of the nineteenth century. She was travelling in
support of the campaign against the binding of women's feet.*

I
t is a little sad to have to own that anti-footbinding seems much
farther advanced in languid, sunshiny Macao than in bustling
Hong-Kong. Of course the Portuguese have been established
there for centuries, and they mix with the people and inter-marry
as we do not. It may be that which makes the difference. But some
say a doctor, a leading member of the reform party, has made the
change at Macao. There on the Praya, a miniature Bay of
Naples, with the exceptionally romantic public gardens at
one end and the Governor's palace at the other, the
Portuguese band making music in the
evenings, the waves lapping on the
shore, mothers walking out with their
children round them, as we never seem
to see English mothers in the East, and
young girls with their duennas, there in
Macao several of the best European
houses are occupied by Chinese, and in
one, conspicuous with heavily-gilded
railings, I was delighted to find that all the
children were growing up unbound.
  Mr Ho Sui Tin, the leading Chinese of
Macao, and a Portuguese subject, not
only arranged a Chinese meeting for

me to address, but took me home to his house afterwards and assured me one of his little girls was about shortly to be unbound. But though they had every luxury in the way of costly and artistic furnishing, even to a billiard table, on which they said they played, it was sad to see the elder daughters with their bound feet. He had not however been a member of the Reform Doctor's Society. My interpreter had, and he seemed full of earnestness, when at a little Christian meeting, at which the enthusiasm of everyone impressed me very refreshingly, one of the first to join the society was a bound-foot lady—his wife—who said, smiling, 'If you will take my money, and accept my promise that I am going to unbind.' The secretary of the Portuguese Club, Signor d'Assompcão, was kind enough to organise a meeting there for all people, who understood English. A good many of the members, who did not, came in to listen at first, then gradually went away not quite noiselessly, and it was amusing next day to note the indignation of the Chinese portion of the audience: 'The Portuguese might at least have kept quiet if they could not understand!' because the remark seemed to indicate the very different way in which the Chinese regard the Portuguese at Macao from the way in which the English are regarded at Hong-Kong. I must not however in passing forget to mention the great kindness of their then Governor Galhardo, even hampered as he was by the carnival—a great affair at mediæval Macao!

The exquisite views, the orange trumpet flowers of the bignonia, the merry children in carnival costume, the soft sunshine, the romance that attaches to Camoens garden and everywhere romantic accessories, all transport one to Europe, and make Macao a place quite by itself in China. I cannot help hoping also that it is one of the first places where footbinding will die out. The Roman Catholic Sisters appeared eager to bring this about, though as usual it was impossible even to ask them to combine for the purpose with Protestant missionaries.

60

MACAO IS ROOTS

FREDERIC A. SILVA

Until the last century, very few metropolitan Portuguese served and settled in the colonies. In Macao, so distant from Lisbon, most non-Chinese residents were a mingling of European blood with that of the diverse Asian and African outposts of Portugal's once extensive trading routes. Frederic A. Silva is a descendent of these people, and these reflections on Macanese history and culture date from the late 1970s. Although his family has lived in Hong Kong for five generations, and Silva himself now resides in California, he firmly declares that, 'Hong Kong is home: Macao is roots.'

Racially, most of us are Eurasians. It is an anthropological fact. Some can trace back to a Portuguese ancestor, especially those who are in, or have recently come from, Macao. Some can also trace direct Chinese ancestry. But for the majority it has been a case of mixed blood and subsequently a mixture of mixtures. For most, the percentage of European Portuguese blood and Oriental blood cannot be determined. This has been even further clouded by more intermarrying with other national groups. Though Portuguese and Chinese strains obviously dominate, other forebears appear as well. Goans are a traceable strain. There is Japanese blood too. Malays from Malacca and Filipinos are part of the mix. Siam and the Moluccas were Portuguese trading partners that more likely than not contributed to the racial strain. There was also evidence of Burmese contact through the Arakans, a province of Burma. English and French ancestry is also common. These combinations have to do with

221

Portuguese mariners travelling, settling and intermarrying and also with the diverse national elements that found their way to Hong Kong, Macao and the coast of China.

In time, all who intermarried settled down to become Sons of Macao. A son of Macao is not so much a description of a racial type as a frame of mind. One belongs to the community because one wants to belong, and in turn the community accepts, with no barriers other than a willingness to belong.

It was amusing to see an attempt to make sense out of this hodgepodge. When there was a move towards emigrating to the United States in the post war years there were United States immigration laws that had to be complied with. Before 1965 there were racial restraints against immigrants. These restraints purported to limit entry quotas to the percentages of the national racial mix that prevailed in the United States on a particular year early in this century. This quota was political and racially biased. Among other things, it was weighted in favor of Anglo-Saxon and Nordic entry, and discriminatory against Latin, Asian and South American entry. Chinese immigration was limited to a mere trickle.

It then fell to the Hong Kong Office of the United States Immigration Department to classify racially the Sons of Macao who intended to emigrate. Here you had to deal with persons who were born in Hong Kong, had Portuguese names and whose looks and features ran a gamut which only another practiced Filho Macao eye could recognize as 'one of us'.

The United States Immigration law then required a minimum of 51 per cent European ancestry to process and admit an immigrant and, furthermore, needed proof of this. One can imagine that our tangled roots did not readily accommodate such easy classification. Nevertheless, a solution was found. It was felt at the United States Consulate that if an intending emigrant could produce birth or baptismal certificates of four grandparents, and if at least three of these had Portuguese surnames, this was regarded as proof positive of being patently Portuguese and logically Lusitanian.

Ancestor tracing expeditions were organized to the small old parish churches of Macao to uncover baptismal and marriage certificates to photostat and notarize. Properly armed, one could then proceed to sail legally through the Golden Gate.

PART XI

TEMPLES AND PADRES

'The names of Xavier and Ricci cast a halo over the first century of the existence of Macao.'

ALEXANDER MICHIE, 1900

'What must be the estimate of Christianity, in the minds of the Chinese, who continually witness such scenes as the one described; they may well inquire in what consists the distinctive mark of difference, apparent in the ceremonies ordered, by pagan, and papal idolaters.'

HENRY CHARLES SIRR, 1849

Macao has long been a place where believers of various creeds, both Eastern and Western, met and mingled, if not always comfortably. From the beginning, the Portuguese rationale for the conquest of unknown lands was as much religious as commercial. Macao became the Jesuit base for the evangelization of all of East Asia, and for hundreds of years it remained the principal outpost of Christianity, first Roman then Protestant, on Chinese soil. Macao had its Chinese temples and festivals as well and even took its name from the Chinese pantheon. These tales of Macao's most important churches and temples, its Chinese deities, European saints, and missionaries offer a glimpse of the enclave's rich religious history.

61

TIGERS AND OTHER LABOURS
THE CHINESE REPOSITORY

In 1541, Francis Xavier, an early disciple of Ignatius Loyola and the Jesuit order, departed for the Far East to propagate the faith. Many of the miracles he performed en route to Japan and China—his speaking in tongues, raising of the dead, and healing of the sick—are well known and typical of the activities of saints. Less famous are the marvels attributed to the saint during his 1552 sojourn on Shangchuan (Sancian) Island near Macao. This nineteenth-century account quotes from the chronicles of the Jesuit Father Dominick Bohurs.

Leaving our readers to form their own opinions of Xavier's life, we will, as briefly as possible, recount some of the principal actions of this early disciple of Loyola. 'Nothing can give a greater confirmation of the saint's miracles, than his saint-like life; which was even more wonderful than the miracles themselves: it was'—we quote the words of Bohurs—'in a manner of necessity, that a man of so holy a conversation should work those things which other men could not perform; and that resigning himself to God, with an entire confidence and trust, on the most dangerous occasions, *God should consign over to him some part of his omnipotence, for the benefit of souls.'* . . .

The royal vessel, *Santa Cruz*, being at length upon the point of sailing, Xavier again embarked, and arrived at Sancian, or St John's island, a few miles westward from Macao, in twenty-three days after her departure from Malacca. Here Xavier resumed his usual labours, raising the dead, &c., and also cleared the country of tigers. 'These furious beasts came in herds together out of the forests, and devoured not only the children, but the men also, whom they found scattered in the fields, and out of distance from the intrenchments which are made for their defense. One night the servant of God went out to meet the tigers, and when they came near him, threw holy water upon them, commanding them to go back, and never after to return. The commandment had its full effect, the whole herd betook themselves to flight, and from that time forward, no tigers were ever seen upon the island.'

62

THE APOSTLE OF THE EAST

LOUIS LE COMPTE

Saint Francis Xavier died on Shangchuan (Sancian) Island without setting foot on the Chinese mainland he so much wanted to convert—and never reaching Macao. Yet the Saint is still corporally and spiritually linked with the territory. His humerus sits in a chest in a chapel on Macao's Coloane Island. Inspired by stories of the Saint's zeal and miracles, Macao Christians and others made pilgrimages to Shangchuan Island until the Chinese Communists stopped the journeys. This is the story of the rediscovery of the Saint's original tomb on Shangchuan by the Governor of Macao in 1688, as told by a Jesuit missionary to China shortly after the event.

To Monsieur Rouillé, Counsellor of State in Ordinary. Of the Establishment and Progress of the Christian Religion in China.

Sir, . . . It was in the year 1552 that Saint Xavier went tither in hopes to add this new Conquest to the Kingdom of JESUS CHRIST. It seemed that the great Man had made but an Essay in the Indies, and if I may use the expression, had but served an Apprenticeship to that Zeal, which he would be perfect Master of in China. And surely Moses never had a more ardent desire to enter into the Holy Land, to gather with his People the Temporal Riches of that Country, than this Apostle longed to carry into this new World the Treasures of the Gospel. But one and t'other dyed by the Providence of God, in a time when their long Voyages and infinite Labours seemed answered by a great probability of success.

The Scripture tells us Moses's death was punishment to him for his lack of Faith; Saint Xavier's seems to be a reward for the abundance of his. God had a mind to reward his Zeal, his Labours, and his Charity; and was willing to defer for a time that torrent of Mercy which he designed for the Empire of China, that he might reward his Servant with that Glory, which he had procured for so many Nations. He died in the Isle of San-cham, or as we speak it San-ciam, under the Jurisdiction of the Province of Canton; it is well known that he lay in the ground several months, all which time God preserved him from the usual Corruption, from hence he was carried to Goa, where from that time we hath been honoured as the Protector of that place, and the Apostle of the East.

The touch of his body Consecrated the place of his burial. That Island became not only a famous place, but also an holy Land. Even the Heathens honoured it, and fled thither as to a City of Refuge. In the mean time Pirates haunted those Coasts, that no Vessels dared to go thereabouts, so that the place where this Sacred Tomb lay, was quite unknown to the Europeans; and it is but a little while ago that they discovered it by a particular accident.

In the year 1688, a Portuguese Vessel which coming from Goa, had on Board the Governor of Macao, was seized by a sudden gust of wind, and forced to let the Ship drive towards these Islands do what they could. They cast Anchor between the Isles of San-ciam and Lampacao, which were so near one another as to make a kind of Haven. Contrary Winds continuing eight days, gave Father Caroccio a Jesuite, who was on board, an opportunity of satisfying his devout resolutions. He went on shoar, and was resolved in spite of Danger to go in search of the Saint's Tomb. The Pilot and most part of the Sailors followed him, they searched the whole Island but to no purpose.

At last a Chinese, and Inhabitant of the Place, imagining with himself what it was which they so ardently sought after, undertook to guide them, and led them to a place which all the Inhabitants reverenced, and where he himself began to perform Actions and Gestures of Piety. The Father who could not understand him, began to search about for some sign or mark of the Sepulchre, and found at last a Stone five Cubits long, and three broad, upon which was cut these words in Latin, Portuguese, Chinese, and Japanese, *Here Xavier a Man truly Apostolical was buried.* Then they all fell on their Knees, and did with Devotion kiss that Earth, which the Fears and the last Groans of that Apostle had sanctified. The Inhabitants of the place came in and followed the Example of the Portuguese: even the English, for one of their Vessels came to an Anchor in the same place, came thither to honour the Saint, and prayed great while at his Tomb. Father Caroccio some time after said Mass in his Pontificalibus, while the two Vessels, the English and Portuguese, did several times discharge their Artillery, and gave marks of their common joy.

Lastly, to preserve the memory of that holy place, they resolved to build a good square Wall all around the Tomb, and to dig a Ditch to secure it from all inundations. In the midst between these Walls they raised the Stone which they found overturned, and built an Altar, as a Memorial of the august Sacrifice of the Eucharist which had been offered up there, which might also serve to Celebrate it upon again, if either Accident or Devotion should carry the Ministers of JESUS CHRIST thither any more. The People of the place did themselves assist toward the carrying on this little work, and showed as much Zeal for the honour of the Saint as the Christians did.

This place is of itself very pleasant. You see there a small Plain extended from the bottom of a Hill, on one side of which is a Wood, on the other are Gardens Cultivated; a Rivulet which turns and twines about, renders the Island very Fertile. It is not uninhabited, as some have wrote, there are seventeen Villages in it. The Land is manured, even the very Mountains, and the Inhabitants are so far from wanting the necessities of Life, that the growth of their Island is enough to carry on such Commerce as yields them a moderate plenty.

You will easily pardon me, Sir, for this short digression concerning St Francis Xavier. A Missionary can't speak of him without being naturally inclined to enlarge about every thing that concerns this great Man. It was he who settled upon a solid Foundation all the Missions into the Indies, and who, in the last Year of his Life, encouraged his Brethren to enterprise the great Design of the Conversion of China. His Zeal passed into their minds and hearts; and tho' every body but Xavier thought it impossible that the Design should take effect, the Fathers Roger, Pasio, and Ricci, all three Italians, did resolve to spend all their pains, and if it were necessary, all their blood in this great Work.

63

THE TEMPLE OF MATSOO PO

ANONYMOUS

There are many versions of the legend of Tin Hau, the beloved Chinese goddess of the sea. This particular rendering is from an unidentified Chinese writer, as recorded in the Chinese Repository *in 1840. 'Matsoo' (Mazu), meaning 'mother ancestor', is another name for the goddess, as is 'Ama', meaning 'mother', from which Macao's name—'Ao-men' in Chinese—is thought to be derived.*

The temple of Ama ko is an ancient structure. In the reign of Wanleih, of the Ming dynasty (about AD 1573), there was a ship, from Tseuenchow foo in the province of Fuhkeën [Fujian], in which the goddess Matsoo po was worshipped. Meeting with misfortunes, she was rendered unmanageable and driven about in this state, by the resistless winds and waves. All on board perished, with the exception of one sailor who was a devotee of the godess, and who, embracing her sacred image, with the determination to cling to it, was rewarded by her powerful protection, and preserved from perishing. Afterwards when the tempest subsided, he landed safely at Macao, whither the ship was driven. Taking the image to the hill at Ama ko, he placed it at the base of a large rock—the best situation he could find—the only temple his means could procure.

About fifty years after this period, in the reign of Teënke, there was a famous astronomer, who from some correspondence (unknown to common mortals) between the gems of heaven and the jewels of earth, had discovered that there was a pond in the province of Canton containing many costly and brilliant pearls, upon which he addressed the emperor, respectfully advising him to send and get them. His imperial majesty, availing himself of the important information, dispatched a confidential servant in search of this wonderful pond. On arriving at Macao, and passing the night at the village of Ama ko, the goddess appeared to the imperial messenger in a dream, and informed him, that the place he sought for, was at Hopoo in Keaou chow or the district of Keaou. He went to the place and procured several thousands of the finest pearls. Glowing with gratitude for the secret intimations he had received, he built a temple at Ama ko, and dedicated it to his informant. This temple stood until the 8th year of the present monarch (12 years ago), when it was found that the temporary repairs were not sufficient to supply the wastes of time. The ruined condition of the building aroused the zeal of the Fuhkeën and Taychew merchants, who subscribed more than 10,000 taels of silver to erect something more honorable to their favorite goddess. This was the origin of the present assemblage of buildings. The upper temple they dedicated to Kwanyin, the Goddess of Mercy; the middle one they designated the temple of Universal Benevolence, and the lower one they called after the name of the village in which it stands. At the side of the latter they erected buildings, designed both for a temple and monastic apartments, and in both of these they placed images of Matsoo po. In the last-mentioned residence several priests dwell, who pay the usual morning and evening adoration to the goddess, keep the temple clean, and assist the worshipers to present their offerings and prayers.

The hill of Ama ko is beautified with many venerable and shady fig-trees, the path is circuitous and ornamental, and the water prospect in front is extensive and varied. Those who visit the temple always extol the beauties of the place, and in later times, some of them inspired by the muses have written verses, which have been engraved on the rocks.

64

THE WORM-LIKE BARBARIANS OF MACAO

FUJIWARA TADAZUMI

European evangelization efforts in the Far East, like those in trade, initially focused on Japan, not China. Macao was the staging point for both the economic and religious projects and, thus, a focus of conflict when Japan's feudal rulers resolved to stop the missionaries before the Europeans put the swelling ranks of converts to political use. The Tokugawa shogun, Hideyoshi, issued an edict in 1587 expelling all missionaries. The persecutions culminated in 1638 under Iemitsu, the third shogun, who ordered the brutal suppression of an uprising in the Nagasaki region, with its large number of Christian converts. He then had many Christians cruelly killed, and the Portuguese traders and many Japanese converts fled to Macao. In 1640, fifty-seven members of a Macao delegation charged with restoring peace met a grisly end. A Japanese official sent this letter back with the survivors.

To take the reins of good government and make the people well content is the basis of ruling the state. To civilise people and make the people of far distant countries adore him is the virtue of the Supreme Commander.

In our country, at the beginning of the Keicho period, when the Great Lord Minamoto [Tokugawa Ieyasu] occupied the ruler's seat, civil and military virtues distinguished themselves side by side. The generosity and the strictness of his rule were blended in perfect harmony. Then came the four kinds of Barbarians from the four quarters surrounding our country, asking for the opening of trade and intercourse. The office for supervising foreign shipping was accordingly established at the port of Nagasaki in Hizen. Merchants of all kinds frequented this port, buying and selling, going and coming continuously. The worm-like Barbarians of Macao who had long believed in the doctrine of the Lord of Heaven, wished to propagate their evil religion in our country; and for many years they sent people called 'Bateren' [Padre] on board their own ships, or in hired Chinese ships. They did this with the intention of seducing our ignorant people, thus paving the way for the eventual occupation of our country. On account of this, the Great Lord [Ieyasu] became angry, seized the Bateren and their converts, beheaded or crucified them in great numbers, and promulgated an edict strictly prohibiting that faith. Any converts found were to be punished with the utmost severity, not only themselves, but their parents, children, and relations as well.

From that time onwards, during the reigns of the three Lords [Shoguns], including the late Lord [Hidetata] and the present Lord [Iemitsu], the faith of those miscreants became more hated, and the prohibitions increased in severity. Nevertheless, on the excuse of trading, Macao continued to send more Bateren, sometimes concealing them at the bottom of Chinese merchant-ships hired for that purpose. They also disguised themselves so that they could penetrate into the interior of the provinces of this country, seducing the ignorant people by their evil arts. The Barbarian ships, too, likewise afforded them concealment and protection. Therefore they were ferreted out and caught year after year, some being thrown down the great cliffs, and others being burnt to death.

In addition to this, in the winter of the year of the younger brother of fire and the ox [1637], these evil people gathered together at Shimabara in Hizen. They attacked the villages, burned the houses, and killed the people. They repaired and dug themselves in at the old castle [of Hara], where their stubborn resistance could not be overcome speedily. If we had not destroyed and annihilated them as quickly as possible, their numbers would have greatly increased, and the revolt would have spread like the rebellion of Chang Lu. In the spring of the year of the elder brother of earth and the tiger [1638], the rebels were annihilated, about forty thousand being beheaded; but our own horse and foot soldiers likewise suffered very heavy casualties in killed and wounded. The instigators of this revolt were deserving of the severest punishment, and therefore a government envoy was dispatched to Nagasaki, warning your people that they should never return to this country, and that if they did, everybody on board the ship(s) would be killed infallibly, etc. etc.

But now, in spite of this strict command, your people came again to this land under the pretence of peace negotiations, but the government officials have no proof that this is their real intention. We therefore had no alternative but to obey the existing order and could not spare their lives. We therefore destroyed the ship; arrested those on board; exposed the heads of the several chiefs in the market-place; and killed all the others, young and old, except some sailors and the surgeon whose offence was not so grave in comparison with the several chiefs who were beheaded, and whom we ordered to report the facts to your country. They were therefore spared from execution, and it was arranged that they should be sent back in a small ship in order to bring this letter to Macao.

The elders of Macao and its dependencies when they hear the foregoing facts must needs acknowledge the righteousness of our country and be impressed by the strength of our military virtue.

65

ANCHORING OFF ILHA VERDE:
ARRIVING AT MACAO AFTER THE MORNING RICE

ZHANG RULIN

In composing these lines Zhang Rulin, an Imperial magistrate posted near Macao in the 1730s, was following a well-established Chinese tradition of using poems for political purposes. Comments like 'The excessive spread of a hundred years has been cleared' were meant to ingratiate Zhang to the Qing authorities. The line refers to the Qing emperor banning Christianity in 1724. Similarly, 'No wonder Jesus was born during the declining Han' may be read as a criticism of both Christianity and the Ming rulers, the Han Chinese dynasty that the Manchu Qing had overthrown. Ilha Verde in Macao's inner harbour was the site of the monastery of the Jesuits, who had been influential in the Ming court.

Morning winds hasten on our large turreted boat with its drums and horns
Carry us on to smoke from kitchen fires and a column of emerald mountain mists
The mountain terrain is rootless, floating trees jut out
Sounds of bells are slightly muffled, a ribbon of tidewater comes in
Already with stalks of corn, children from the West arrive
I still see leaning sunflowers, doors open to the north
A bit of morning sea cloud, areas soaked with sunlight
Whitewashed walls, high and low, clusters of lotus terraces

There are fields as wide as sea vessels that fishermen plough with
the wind
Asking the way there over the misty waves, their boats change
course many times
I gaze into the distance over sea and mountains, they still have not
come back
Unmoved, the grass will have overgrown the towers and pavilions
on their return
No wonder Jesus was born during the declining Han
What intentions did Ricci have in paying tribute to the former
Ming
In our sacred age, up till now our prosperity is untouched by rain
The excessive spread of a hundred years has been cleared in a
single moment

(At this time I had received an Imperial decree to prohibit the evil
Catholic faith. Thereupon I wrote these lines.)

66

THE IMPULSE OF CURIOSITY

THE CHINESE REPOSITORY

With Christians and non-Christians living so closely together in Macao, the latter by far outnumbering the former, the Roman Catholic clergy had a full-time job protecting their flock from pagan spiritual contamination, as this story reveals.

P revious to the overthrow of the inquisition at Goa in 1812, delinquents were sent thither for chastisement, and various measures were adopted to free Macao from the Chinese theaters and religious processions. In one instance, a stage on which the Chinese were acting, was, by order of the vicar-general, broken down: the viceroy of Goa, in a letter to the senate, dated 1736, disapproved of this conduct, and gave orders to the chapter to reprehend the vicar-general, and recommend him in future to abstain from similar behavior. 'This salutary admonition (says our author) was set aside by a letter of March 18th, 1758, in which the tribunal of the inquisition prohibits any kind of Chinese theatricals or processions to be suffered. However, several of the governors, recollecting that the Portuguese can exercise no jurisdiction over the Chinese, were prudent enough to connive at their fleeting recreations; but in 1780, at the instigation of a delegate from the holy office, then residing at Macao, the senate gave orders to the procurator to demolish scaffolds, which had been erected on occasion of a solemn festival, which was to wander through the place. His zeal was frustrated. Having permission from the mandarins to raise temporary stands, the insult of throwing them down would be resented; and the Chinese advised the Portuguese not to provoke tumult by an act of intemperate zeal. Convinced that no effort of the civil police could hinder a pagan festival, duly prepared, from showing itself in the town, a bishop resolved to try spiritual influences on the flock. His excellence, dom Fr. Francis de Na. Sra. da Luz Cachim, issued a pastoral admonition, which the curates published in their respective parishes. It was dated 15th of April 1816, and breathes a fatherly exhortation, that all Christians should, for the sake of the salvation of their souls, abstain from having a peep either through the window from behind the Venetian blinds, or in the street, at the pageants the Chinese were going to carry through the city. Disobedience was threatened with the penalty of the great excommunication; a punishment which could not be applied, because out of the whole population there were perhaps not fifty adult Christians, who had resisted the impulse of curiosity; and others gratified it by looking at the gorgeous ceremonies, repeated by the Chinese during three days, and by gazing at night, in the bazar, at ingenious illuminations, theatrical jests, and amusements.'

67

THE PRICE OF SECRECY

W. H. MEDHURST

Much of the training of Chinese Roman Catholic missionaries took place at the Jesuit College of São José (St Joseph) in Macao, which remained the bridgehead for Roman evangelism in China into the 1840s. By then, the College and its complex and costly operations were of great interest to the Protestant churches intent on spreading their version of the Gospel in China. This particular report came from W. H. Medhurst, who visited Macao on behalf of the London Missionary Society.

The college of St. Joseph, in Macao, is intended for the purpose of raising up native teachers, for China. It was founded, by the Jesuits, in 1730; transferred to the Propaganda, in 1784; and, in 1800, provided for by regular allowances from the senate of Macao. The college contains six European priests, of whom, one is the superior. The number of Chinese students is limited to twelve, who are clothed, boarded, and educated, at the expense of the institution; if they desire it, they are trained for the priesthood, and it generally requires ten years before they can attain the first order. Instruction is given in Portuguese, Latin, arithmetic, rhetoric, philosophy, theology, &c. The Chinese language is, also, taught; and the College possesses a Chinese library, moveable types, and conveniences for printing. A Portuguese and Chinese Dictionary has been published by the Superior, besides other works, tending to illustrate the language and opinions of the natives. In 1831, the number of students was: seven young Chinese, two Manilla youths, and thirteen Portuguese; besides those who attended for daily instruction. A large stock of

Christian books, in the Chinese language, is kept on hand, and missionaries are frequently dispatched from thence, to the provinces. The Superior is in correspondence with the agents of the missions, in various parts of China, and can convey and procure intelligence, to and from the interior, with the greatest regularity.

Besides the Lazarites and the agents of the Propaganda, the Spaniards have an establishment, at Macao, for receiving Missionary candidates from Europe, instructing them in the language, and conveying them into the country. Scarcely a month passes, without some new arrivals, or departures; and the vacant posts in the interior, are thus kept constantly supplied with pastors. They all wear the European habit in Macao, but adopt the native dress on entering the field. When Europeans are to be introduced into the provinces, information is previously sent to the places appointed, where adherents are prepared to receive and conceal them. On arriving at the place of destination, the missionaries generally retire to some secret dwelling, known only to the Christians, and seldom appear abroad; while all who desire instruction, or the administration of the sacraments, go to them. Some remain, fifteen or twenty years, in their secluded retreats, and thus keep up the number of their followers, without attracting the notice of government. The allowance to an European missionary, in the interior, is about one hundred and forty dollars a year; considerable sums are, however, required for travelling expenses—for ensuring secrecy—for supporting the poor—and for carrying on the other business of the mission: and a commercial gentleman, connected with Canton, informed the author, that the different superiors of the missions, in Macao, negotiate bills in Europe, to the amount of £40,000 annually.

68

A PILE OF RUINS

THE CHINESE REPOSITORY

The dramatic stone façade of São Paulo (St Paul's) church is Macao's most well-known landmark and emblem. This is an eye-witness report of the 1835 fire that destroyed much of the rest of the building, once described as second in grandeur only to St Peter's in Rome.

At about half past six o'clock p.m., on the 26th ultimo, the discharge of cannon from the fort above St Paul's, (Macao), gave the alarm of fire. The signal was quickly answered by guns from the other forts, by ringing of church bells, and the beating of drums. The principal authorities, with the troops and many of the inhabitants of Macao, were soon in motion. But, except to those who were near the church, it was for some moments doubtful what building was on fire;—the state of the atmosphere at the time being such that the smoke could not ascend, but driven by a light breeze from the north-west, it enveloped the whole eastern part of the town. It was not long, however, before the flames, bursting through the roofs, left no doubt as to the point from whence they issued. All the apartments which constituted the left wing of the church, and which were formerly occupied by priests, but recently by the Portuguese troops, were soon on fire. For a while, some hope was entertained that the main part of the church, the chapel, might be saved. But before eight o'clock, the fire reached the highest part of the building and also the vestry in the rear of the great altar. Dense smoke mixed with flames soon burst from the windows on all sides, and then rising through the roof presented a sight awfully grand. The flames rose very high, and the whole town and inner harbor were illuminated. Just at the moment the clock, (which was presented to the church by Louis XIV) struck eight and a quarter. Hitherto, efforts had been made to check the progress of the flames; but now, when it was quite evident that they would not extend beyond the buildings of the church, every one seemed willing to stop and gaze at the scene. . . .

As early as 1565 the Jesuits had erected a church in Macao, near the site of the late one. The former was burnt by accident; and the latter was built in its stead. This was named '*S. Paulo*', and has remained to the present time, one of the most noble and magnificent buildings in the east. On the corner stone was the following inscription:

VIRGINI MAGNÆ MATRI
CIVITAS MACAENSIS LIBENS,
POSUIT AN. 1602.

The site of the church was well chosen, and the whole edifice was formed of the best and most durable material, and in beautiful style. You approached the building by a broad and lofty flight of stone steps. The front of it consisted entirely of granite, 'where the ingenious artist has contrived to enliven Grecian architecture by devotional objects. In the middle of ten pillars of the Ionian order, are three doors leading into the temple. Above them range ten pillars of the Corinthian order, and constitute five separate niches. In the middle one, directly above the principal door, there is a female figure trampling on a globe, the emblem of human habitation, and underneath it is written Mater Dei. On each side of the queen of heaven are statues of saints. In a superior division, St. Paul is represented; and above him there is a dove, the emblem of the Holy Ghost.' On various parts of the front there were inscriptions, some in Latin, others in Chinese. The interior of the building was every way equal to its exterior. The whole is now a pile of ruins.

241

69

THE CHAPEL IN THE GREAT
TEMPLE OF MACAO

GEORGE NEWENHAM WRIGHT

*Travellers were often struck by similarities between the Roman Catholic
and Chinese religious traditions they observed in such close proximity
at Macao. These commonalties aided early Jesuit missionaries, who
explained Christianity to potential converts in Chinese philosophical
and religious terms. Protestants like George Newenham Wright were
unsympathetic. However, his is still one of the best descriptions of what
may be Macao's oldest institution, the Guanyin Temple (or the Old
Temple of the Lady) in the mid-nineteenth century.*

Many resemblances between the monastic habits of the
Roman Catholic Church and worship, and those of the
priests of Buddha, have been observed. The missionaries
themselves acknowledged the fact; and some of them,
notwithstanding their unquestionable learning and philosophy,
have exhibited an unbecoming weakness in speaking, or rather
writing, on this coincidence. The arrangements of the temple of
Macao may probably present a still closer resemblance to the
modes of Christian conventual life, than those of temples in the
interior, from the accidental circumstance of the presence of
Roman Catholic churches in this particular place: but, wholly
independent of any such adventitious aid in the argument, the
analogy in costume, mode of life, form of worship, and other
essential considerations, is so very striking, that no European can
witness the ceremonies in a Buddhist temple, without being
forcibly reminded of it. Here, at Macao, is an extensive collegiate

242

or monastic establishment, the residence of bonzes, who observe celibacy, dress in the simple vesture . . . and live principally upon the bounty of the benevolent. The walls of their apartments are not as plain and unpretending as their garments: richly ornamented with carved-work, interspersed with bas-reliefs, and occasionally decorated with paintings, their homes present an appearance of wealth and elegance; and, if public report were not too often identical with public calumny, it might be added, that the luxuries and pleasures of life are not excluded from the bonze's board.

Entering by the chief porch, which is decorated in a style of grace, delicacy, and perfection, equal to that of the central building; animals of monstrous conception, but cleverly executed, are placed on pedestals at either side. Escaping from this contemptible specimen of art, the principal apartment of the temple is reached, where all those horrible mummeries that belong to the theory of Buddhism are performed. . . .

At the opposite side of the temple from that by which the visitor enters, a staircase leads down to a second esplanade, more limited in extent, but equally pleasing in all its accompaniments. In the semicircular area before the chief façade, a broad paved terrace, close to the margin of the waves, is enclosed by a stone parapet, profusely sculptured, and on which are graven moral maxims and sentences, extracted from the Book of Fate, or other foolish fictions. Amidst the rocks that rise abruptly, and with a peculiarly picturesque effect, above the later, a small chapel is intruded, containing an image of Buddha, over which a large paper lantern is suspended. Beside this tiny temple, is a second building, with a porcelain roof, something of an Italian cornice and decoration, but having a spacious circular opening in front, that occupies the principal part of the whole elevation. On a rock immediately opposite the window, stands a pedestal, with a recipient vessel, for the offerings of the humane and zealous amongst the visitors. Whether the expectation associated with the little hexagonal pedestal may extend its influence to any portion of the faithful, it is difficult to decide; but certainly the number that visit this secluded and romantic part of the temple is considerably smaller than is constantly to be seen in the principal cells of the building.

This fact is the more remarkable, because the scenery around the little chapel is highly picturesque, and of that mixed and contrasted character that pleases particularly in China. The terrace has been gained from the sea, the site of the temple from the ledge of rock, and the intermixture of the beauties of nature with the works of art is as close and complete as a Chinese artist could desire. Yet hour succeeds to hour, in this sequestered spot, and neither the tread of a footstep, nor the sound of a voice, falls on the ear of the miserable bonze, who sits within view of the place of tribute, and presents a taper to the devotee to light his dedicatory red paper at, which he comes to offer in the adjoining temple.

70

THE PROTESTANT BURIAL GROUND

THE CHINESE REPOSITORY

The Old Protestant Cemetery of Macao is most strikingly a monument to the pirate attacks, disease, wars, and other hardships borne by European traders to the Far East—and the shocking youthfulness of those who fell their victims. It is also known for its famous 'residents'— Henry John Spencer Churchill, captain of the Druid and great-grand-uncle of Sir Winston; artist George Chinnery; and Robert Morrison, the sinologue and Protestant missionary who translated the Bible into Chinese. It was the death in 1821 of Morrison's wife, Mary, that prompted the establishment of the burial ground, as this article from 1842 records.

Previously to 1821, there was no burial place within the walls of Macao for foreigners. The remains of those who died here, were either carried from the settlement, or interred outside of the walls. On the hill-side, between the Campo gate and the Monte fort, several tombstones are still to be seen, some erect, and some thrown down and half buried in the earth; others are visible on Meesenburg hill, directly north of Casilha's bay, and likewise in the Caza, or garden, enclosing the Cave of Camoens. The inscriptions on these sepulchral stones still tell the stranger, who visits them, from what different and distant countries men came hither to traffic—from India, Persia, Arabia, and many of the states of Europe and America.

The English burial ground is situated just beyond the church of St Antonio, eastward from the entrance to the Caza. The circumstances which led to its selection are detailed in a letter describing the first interment. The letter is dated Macao, June 12th, 1821, and was addressed to the parents of Mrs Morrison by the bereaved husband, their son-in-law. After describing the particulars of their child's death, Dr Morrison thus proceeds:

'On Monday I wished to inter Mary out at the hills, where our James was buried; but the Chinese would not let me even open the same grave. I disliked burying under the town walls, but was obliged to resolve on doing so, as the Papists refuse their burying-ground to Protestants. The want of a Protestant burying-ground has long been felt in Macao, and the present case brought it strongly before the committee of the English Factory, who immediately resolved to vote a sum sufficient to purchase a piece of ground, worth between three and four thousand dollars; and personally exerted themselves to remove the legal impediments and local difficulties; in which they finally succeeded. This enabled me to lay the remains of my beloved wife in a place appropriated to the sepulture of Protestant Christians, being denied a place of interment by the Romanists. Mr Livingstone, Mr Pearson, the president and committee of the English factory, Mr Urmston, Sir W. Fraser, &c., bore the pall. All the gentlemen of the factory, also counsellor Pereira, Sir A. Lyungstedt, the Russian consul, and other foreigners in Macao, attended the funeral. Mr Harding, chaplain to the factory, read the funeral service at the grave; and the whole detail of the funeral was conducted with decency and respectability by the English servants of the factory. Rebecca, John, and I attended their dear mamma to the tomb; we were loath to forsake her remains. Our Chinese domestics and teachers also, voluntarily accompanied the funeral. Our Mary was much esteemed by all who ever conversed with her. She had an excellent understanding, and a well-principled heart. Mr and Mrs Molony have to-day joined in a letter of condolence, saying, that in their voyage out, they had an opportunity of ascertaining Mrs Morrison's Christian disposition, and were then much comforted by her society. . . .'

This spot, rendered sacred by the remains of many who were very dear and much loved by those who yet live, was well chosen, being sequestered, and so surrounded by a high wall as to be screened from public view. It is an oblong plot of ground, say fifty yards by thirty, and partly shaded by trees standing close to the wall, which is covered with the cereus and other flowers. Nearly two-thirds of the ground is already occupied; but over most of the graves there is nothing to indicate even the names of their tenants. These are chiefly the graves of seamen, who have died in the hospitals. But the care of friends and relatives has here and there erected mementoes, with inscriptions to perpetuate the memory of those for whom they mourn. The whole number of these inscriptions is perhaps 75; they exhibit a variety of style even greater than what is usual in burial grounds, bearing dates from June 10th, 1821 (the day of Mrs. Morrison's death), down to the present time.

71

TOAD VISITS THE PALACE

GERALD LOCKLIN

The contemporary California poet, Gerald Locklin, takes a gentler, more tolerant, if irreverent view of Macao's religious institutions than most earlier writers. Locklin writes in an autobiographical style, representing himself in the character 'toad' (although 'the identification is not absolute,' he says). These poems are from The Macao/Hong Kong Trip, *a volume of verse published in 1996 following a visit to Macao where his daughter was then a teacher.*

phil lays down his saturday for his new friend

they dine at a spicy thai restaurant
with his daughter's fellow teacher, charlotte,
whose husband, phil, is not only principal
of a private primary school, but who is also a
former world-class high-jumper from
villanova and is still, as time allows,
a jazz saxophonist at the local club
and a force behind the annual macao
jazz festival. there is no way that he
and the toad are not destined to hit
it off immediately. phil even agrees,
for toad's sake, to attend the christening
and reception the next day, at the
cathedral and the military base, to
which the women have committed themselves,
for the grandchild of one of their colleagues.

after the christening everyone is milling about
outside the cathedral doors

when toad suddenly notices all of the group
of which he is a part

milling towards an adjoining mansion. his
daughter is gesturing for him to join them.

they are following a jolly but trim
middle-aged chinese man, bespectacled of course,
and so casually dressed that his attire
could be construed as work clothes.

toad kibitzes on his british english
long enough to conclude that this eager guide
is the caretaker
of what toad now comes to understand
is the official residence of
the bishop of the macao diocese.
no doubt, on this lazy saturday afternoon,
the pucciniesque major domo
is only too proud to spend a few minutes
showing off to this mixed bag of educated
expatriates the portuguese/oriental,
antique/modern palace, currently in the
throes of extensive restoration and conversion
to the most efficient cybernetic technologies,
which has been entrusted to his humble
supervision.

unfortunately, the minutes turn to at least
an hour of chapels and
auditoriums, roofs and fountains,
confessionals and courtyards, cultural
centers and communication centers,
ballrooms and refectories and executive bars,
archives and relics and maps and
contrasting lavatories, primitive and european.

it's a wonder some american billionaire
hasn't bought the joint for cash
and rebuilt it in the middle
of the mojave desert.

toad is a little surprised when even the
threshold of the bishop's private bathroom
is unlocked for them,
and their intrepid guide makes a joke
about the plumbing.

in the corridor is a wall of portraits
of the former bishops,
and phil is gesturing at toad to take
a gander at them,

but toad is badly in need of the
promised free buffet and champagne

and, anyway, you know,

if you've seen a pseudo titian
of one colonial portuguese bishop,
you've pretty much seen them all.

a couple more marble staircases
and, thank god, and his domestic servants,
they are finally being released into
the humidity of the pre-monsoon season.

toad catches up to phil and says,

'hey, it was a bit overly fast for my
limited attention span, but the
guy was a good host—how much
should i tip him?'

phil hurries toad away from
the waving, broadly smiling flunky:

'that was the fucking *bishop* toad; the
first chinese bishop of macao.'

he would've doubled the tip

and a few months later
when toad's daughter wrote him
that she had observed the bishop
dozing off at a stuffy, obligatory

civic ceremony,

toad's affection for him grew by bounds.

PART XII

TIPS FOR VICTORIAN TOURISTS

'Foreign visitors to the ancient Portuguese city of Macao . . . are delighted with its calm quiet life, its brilliant atmosphere, and lovely climate.'

WILLIAM C. HUNTER, 1882

For many years the only permanent European settlement in China, Macao was an obligatory stop on the itinerary of foreign merchants, travellers, and explorers making their way to the Middle Kingdom. By the latter 1800s, Macao had also become a popular destination for a new breed of traveller—the tourist. It additionally had earned a place in the new genre of popular guide books aimed at the growing numbers of Westerners visiting China on an expanding world network of steamships. Often remarkably thin on historical and cultural detail, the guidebooks are replete with advice on the most efficient itineraries; cheapest rickshaw tariffs; most notable institutions and monuments; and most advantageous vistas. If local people and their habits figure at all, particularly if they were poor and Chinese, it was often only as curiosities to amuse the amateur photographer. Some aspects of tourism has not changed much over the years, however quaint the following tips and tales seem today.

72

INTERCEPTED LETTERS

'BETTY'

*By the turn of the century, Macao was well established as a weekend
jaunt for Hong Kong residents, drawn to its reputedly cooler climate,
old world charms, and–of course–games of chance. So much so that
'Betty' included this lively description of 'her' first trip to Macao in a
series of letters satirizing Hong Kong expatriate society and its foibles,
first published in the* China Mail.

The Peak
Hongkong
June 12, 1904.

My Dear Nell,

The thermometer stands at 87° in the shade, and I'm lying
simply panting in a long chair (and very little else) in my
verandah, feeling very unlike keeping my promise of writing
to tell you about Macao. However, a promise is a promise, but if
this letter is deadly uninteresting, put it down to the climate.
Macao you must know is an island or a peninsula, I can't remember
which (and anyhow it is almost the same thing isn't it?) belonging
to the Portuguese, about thirty miles from Hongkong. Boats
run between the two places daily, taking about three hours for the
run.

William and I being heartily sick of Hongkong and wanting to
get away from it and its inhabitants for a while, decided at the
beginning of the month to run down there for a week or so. We
booked rooms beforehand at the Macao Hotel and made up our
minds it should be a sort of second honeymoon. Alas! for our

charming little plan. When we got to our destination, we found that at least half the European inhabitants of Hongkong had arranged to amuse themselves in precisely the same way, so we gave up honey-mooning and took to sight-seeing and gambling instead. The sight-seeing was a little limited,—one lighthouse used also as a prison and a fort, and some public gardens where the band plays once a week and where a great poet named Camoëns once lived in a grotto. The poet's name is never mentioned in polite society in Hongkong, chiefly because the said polite society has not the remotest notion of how to pronounce it. I shall always remember those gardens as harbouring the very finest breed of mosquitoes I have ever seen or felt. I suppose you will be very shocked at the notion that your best friend has taken to gambling, but really in Macao one is driven to it, there is absolutely nothing else to do, and as the gambling houses are run by the monasteries, one feels it must be a good thing to do; indeed on one or two occasions when I came away very poor and having spent some hours in an atmosphere which to say the least of it was distinctly 'niffy,' I almost felt as if I had been doing penance. At the end of one week spent in gazing at the lighthouse and being eaten up by mosquitoes in the day time, and gambling with unsatisfactory results in the evenings, William began to get restless and to long for the comforts of home, to say nothing of his club, so back we came and here we are!

73

FASHIONABLE PROMENADES
AND RINGING ROCKS

R. C. HURLEY

In The Tourists' Guide to Canton, The West River and Macao, first published in 1898, Victorian travellers were tempted with busy itineraries to suit every taste, whether their passion was Macao's religious monuments, industrious silk and tea workers, or infamous gambling parlours and opium factories. For those with more time and plenty of wind, the steep hills of Lappa across the Inner Harbour in China sheltered natural wonders largely inaccessible today. The accompanying map, printed on this book's endpapers, locates the lesser known attractions, many of which no longer exist.

PROGRAMME No. I for a trip occupying the time from the arrival of the steamer in the afternoon until departure (7.30 for Canton or 8 o'clock for Hongkong) the following morning.

Secure one of the guides who generally meet the steamers; take rickshas and proceed to hotel thence to—

No. 1.—THE PRAYA GRANDE is a pretty crescent-shaped esplanade extending along the shore of the bay of that name, about three quarters of a mile in length by some 100 feet wide. On the north side are many fine buildings including Government House, the residences of the different Consuls, Government Offices, Post and Telegraph Offices, several of the merchant hongs and a number of private houses. In front of these, close to the beach, protected by a substantial granite wall and extending nearly the full length of the Praya, are planted banyan and other trees which add a very

255

pleasing effect to the picture. This is the resort of the residents, as a fashionable promenade, especially during the summer months.

No. 2.—THE FACADE OF SAN PAULO, as seen from the harbour or any of the points on the ridge to the southward of the settlement, is the most striking object in the view of Macao. . . .

The flight of granite steps leading up to the entrance is very imposing, and beneath them vaults containing treasures are known to exist:- these subterranean passages are said to connect with the Guia Fort as also with Green Island a mile distant under a considerable expanse of water.

No. 3.—THE GROTTO OF THE POET CAMOENS, naturally formed by a group of granite boulders, situated in the grounds attached to the gardens bearing the poet's name, is perhaps the most interesting of the many sights of Macao. . . .

No. 4.—FLORA, the summer residence of the Governor of Macao, is situated on a very pretty country road about a mile from the town. Standing in its own grounds, which are enclosed with a granite wall surmounted by balustrades in green enamel with a granite coping, the general picturesque appearance of the place is very striking.

No. 5.—'BELLA VISTA', or beautiful view, is situated on the cliff overlooking the Area Preta about half a mile beyond Flora in the same direction. Its position makes it a charming spot where one can enjoy the full benefit of the south sea breeze. It is the fashionable afternoon resort of the residents of Macao.

No. 6.—PORTA CERCO, defining the boundary between Portuguese and Chinese territory, is situated about a mile beyond Bella Vista, and as the road to it is well kept, forms a good terminating point for one's afternoon or evening ricksha ride. It was erected in 1573.

No. 7.—THE PUBLIC GARDENS are situated at the northern end of the Praia Grande and, although small, being well shaded by fine old trees, form a delightful afternoon promenade. The military band plays here nearly every evening.

No. 8.—THE MILITARY CLUB, situated close to the public gardens, is a very pretty structure and contributes to give a pleasing effect to the tout ensemble of the picture.

No. 9.—THE 'FANTAN' GAMBLING SALOONS, the principal of which are situated in the Rua dos Jogos, should be visited after dinner, the effect of the guilded decorations under the brilliant lights is much more impressive than in the day time. The game of 'fantan' is played with cash, a small Chinese coin. . . .

No. 10.—THE PRAYA GRANDE PROMENADE. See No. 1.

*

PROGRAMME No. 2 occupying the second day.

No. 11.—A SEA BATH may be taken on the beach a little beyond Bella Vista or from the grounds of the Boa Vista Hotel at Bishop's Bay. The water is always beautifully clear and before breakfast a dip will prove very refreshing.

No. 12.—ST. JOSEPH'S COLLEGE, situated on one of the elevations about the centre of the town is . . . one of the principal education establishments in the Far East.

No. 13.—The Union Club, a comparatively large building with no architectural pretensions worth the mention, is situated in Rua do Santo Agostinho. It is the social meeting place of all the principal Portuguese residents of Macao. . . .

No. 14.—The Barracoons are places to be found in the basement of some of the older houses of Macao, and were formerly used as receiving depots for coolies awaiting shipment to foreign parts. The question of this coolie traffic and its ultimate suppression in 1874 is one which should interest the world at large both from a humanitarian stand-point, as from that of political economy. The suddenness with which this traffic was abolished in all probability curtailed the issue of many events that might have materially contributed to assist in the opening up of the Chinese Empire.

No. 15.—Government House, the present official residence of the Governors of Macao, is a handsome building with two projecting wings, and occupies a commanding position on the Praya Grande. This mansion was built by the late Baron do Cercal for his family residence and on his demise was purchased from the estate for the Government.

No. 16.—The Opium Farms and Smoking Divans. The former is where the drug is stored, prepared, and finally disposed of wholesale, by special licence from the Macao Government which reaps a considerable revenue in farming out the monopoly to the highest bidder.

Opium smoking can be seen in many of the coolie dens and divans frequented by the unfortunate victims to the fascinating vice. It is indeed a curious pastime, far more absorbing in its narcotic effect than any of our Occidental habits.

No. 17.—The Tea Industry is similar to that in Canton. The fresh picked leaves arrive from the plantations in the country, and in native hongs (houses) are subjected to the various processes of picking, firing, curling and serving, being finally packed to suit the different markets, according to demand. The tea-pickers, native girls, form a very curious if not interesting picture and one which should amuse the amateur photographer.

No. 18.—CHINESE RESTAURANT.—The best one to visit is the Man Sing Lau situated in the Rua de Bazar. In the upper story, where its best patrons are entertained, the appointments are unique, with its number of small apartments, pretty stained-glass windows and verandahs overlooking the inner harbour.

No. 19.—THE ROMAN CATHOLIC CATHEDRAL, situated in the Rua da Sé, is a very plain looking structure without any pretensions to architectural effect. From the outside its appearance is very uninteresting, but as if to make up for external deficiencies, the interior is very pretty not to say beautiful.

It is an imposing spectacle every Sunday morning at 11 o'clock, when High Mass with military music is performed, and at which service the Governor and officials, civil and military, nearly always attend, the congregation mostly ladies, attired in gay colours with black mantillas, being in great contrast with the prettily decorated surroundings.

No. 20.—THE TABACCO FACTORY.—This is indeed a curious indus-try conducted with some pretensions to system. It is very extensive and, although entirely without the aid of steam power, can boast of being one of the largest factories in South China.Every operation is put through in the most primitive manner in all sorts of rambling passages and sheds. Specially curious is the pressing-room where some thirty presses may be seen worked by clumsy looking hand levers. A visit to this factory will prove very interesting.

No. 21.—ST DOMINGO CHURCH is one of the oldest of the many religious institutions in Macao, and will serve to take the visitor back to the early days when the Holy City could rightly claim its name as such. . . .

No. 22.—LEAL SENADO (Municipal Chambers). In former times the Leal Senado was vested with the government of the Colony which was carried on by the Senators in conjunction with the Governor or Captain-General and the Ouvidor (Chief Justice). In 1835 a new colonial *régime* supplanted this mode of government, and with the appointment of a Civil Governor, the Senate was vested solely with the municipal administration of the Colony. At the entrance hall of the Senate may be seen the following historical inscription:—*Cidade do name de Deos näo ha outra mais leal.* (City of the name of God, there is none more loyal.) This inscription was placed by the command of King D. João IV. at the restoration of the Portuguese monarchy, as a recognition of the loyalty of the Macaenses in giving their allegiance to Portugal instead of Spain as then sought for.

No. 23.—SUPREME COURT AND TREASURY, situated on the Praya Grande, is of no particular interest. It was formerly the residence of the Governor.

No. 24.—THE MILITARY HOSPITAL, situated high up on the cliff close to the Lighthouse, is a pretty looking building, and helps to complete the picturesqueness by which the visitor is welcomed in the approach to Macao.

No. 25.—THE GUIA LIGHTHOUSE, the oldest on the coast of China, may be visited by any who are curious to see the workings of such a useful institution.

No. 26.—THE SILK FILATURE FACTORY, worked by natives, is interesting, and to those who are acquainted with modern methods in this particular industry, it will appear a very curious contrast.

No. 27.—THE BISHOP'S SUMMER PALACE is situated on Green Island about half an hour from the Praya Grande. There is not much to see of a palatial description. Whilst on Green Island a visit might be made to the extensive cement works of the Green Island Cement Company.

No. 28.—LECAROS' GARDENS at certain seasons of the year are very pretty and serve to give the visitor some idea of Macao's earlier pretensions to affluence. . . .

*

PROGRAMME No. 3.—for those who can remain longer. Picnic to the 'Ringing Rocks' and the 'Eleven Tables'. Arrange for a cold tiffin to be taken with you. Leave the hotel about 9 o'clock and proceed by boat to Lappa (20 minutes) where on landing you will find a pretty winding pathway by the side of a small watercourse. Follow this and in half an hour, you will arrive at the Ringing Rocks. Having inspected them continue up over the spur of the hill above, and in fifty minutes you should begin to descend, coming suddenly upon the 'Eleven Tables'. Here you can rest and partake of tiffin. Leave about 4 o'clock and proceed to the shore where your boat of the morning will meet you and in a very short time you will be once more in the hotel. . . .

THE RINGING ROCKS comprise a number of massive granite boulders distributed by Nature and grouped over a little watercourse, averaging from fifty to one hundred tons each in weight. On the visitor striking any of them with a stick, or with the heel of his boot, a clear bell-like sound with gradually receding vibrations is heard. The tones vary according to the size of the boulders which is very curious. This strange phenomenon is attributed to some supposed metallic formation.

THE ELEVEN TABLES are situated in a very charming spot and represent a resting place for the pilgrims to the many shrines which are distributed in all sorts of secluded nooks amongst the granite boulders which abound in the immediate neighbourhood. The picture is certainly one of perfect peace and retirement with Nature alone as hostess. A delightful brooklet trickles down a somewhat stony bed and passes under a curious hunchback bridge, which is in itself a full canvas for the artist. There are many winding paths and viaducts leading from one shrine to another amongst the rocks, which latter bear some extraordinary inscriptions cut into the granite in large characters. A short distance from the spot is a simple but pretty waterfall which lends a decided charm to the stillness of the place.

BIBLIOGRAPHY

Auden, W. H. and Christopher Isherwood, *Journey to a War*, London: Faber & Faber, 1939.

Azevedo, Ávila de, *A influência da cultura portuguesa em Macau*, Lisbon: Instituto de Cultura e Lingua Portuguesa, 1984.

Bennett, George, *Wanderings in New South Wales, Batavia, Pedir Coast, Singapore, and China*, Vol. II, London: Richard Bentley, 1834.

Bernard, William Dallas, *Narrative of the Voyages and Services of the Nemesis, from 1840 to 1843*, Vol. I, London, Henry Colburn, 1844.

'Betty', *Intercepted Letters. A Mild Satire on Hongkong Society*, Hong Kong: Kelly and Walsh, 1905.

Boxer, C. R., *Fidalgos in the Far East, 1550–1770*, The Hague: Martinus Nijhoff, 1948, reprinted Oxford University Press, 1968.

Boxer, C. R., *The Great Ship from Amacon: Annals of Macao and the Old Japan Trade, 1555–1640*, Lisbon: Centro de Estudos Históricos Ultramarinos, 1959.

Bridgman, Elijah Coleman and S. Wells Williams, eds., *The Chinese Repository*, Canton: American Board of Commissioners for Foreign Missions, 20 vols., 1832–51.

Caldeira, Carlos José, *Apontamentos de uma Viagem de Lisboa à China e da China a Lisboa*, Lisboa: 1851/2; reprinted as *Macau—1850: Crónica de Viagem*, Lisbon: Quetzal Editores, 1997.

Camões, Luís de, *The Lusiad*, Richard Fanshaw, trans., London: Humphrey Moseley, 1655.

Coates, Austin, *City of Broken Promises*, Hong Kong: Oxford University Press, 1990.

Cocks, Richard, *Diary of Richard Cocks, Cape-merchant in the English Factory in Japan, 1615–1622*, Vol. II, Edward Maunde Thompson, ed., London: The Hakluyt Society, 1883.

Compte, Louis Le, *Memoirs and Observations Made in a Late Journey through the Empire of China*, London: Benj. Tooke and Sam. Buckley, 1697.

Conwell, Russell H., *Why and How. Why the Chinese Emigrated, and the Means They Adopt for the Purpose of Reaching America*, New York: Lee, Shepard and Dillingham, 1871.

Cooke, George Wingrove, *China*, London: Routledge, 1858.

Costa, Sebastião da, 'Camilo Pessanha', *Seara Nova*, No. 85, 29 April 1926.

Crow, Carl, *Handbook for China*, 5th edn., Hong Kong: Kelly & Walsh, 1933, reprinted Oxford University Press, 1982.

Daniell, Thomas and William Daniell, *A Picturesque Voyage to India by the Way of China*, London: Longman, Hurst, Rees, and Orme, 1810.

Davis, Sir John Francis, *China: A General Description of that Empire and its Inhabitants*, Vol. II, London: John Murray, 1857.

Drage, Charles, *Servants of the Dragon Throne, Being the Lives of Edward and Cecil Bowra*, London: Peter Dawnay, 1966.

Faria y Sousa, Manuel de, *Asia Portuguesa*, Tom. III, Lisbon: Antonio Craesbeeck de Mello, 1675.

Fleming, Ian, *Thrilling Cities*, London: Jonathan Cape, 1963.

Garstin, Crosbie, *The Dragon and the Lotus*, London: William Heinemann, 1928.

Glasspoole, Richard, 'A brief Narrative of my captivity and treatment amongst the Ladrones, December 8, 1809', in C. Neumann, *History of the Pirates Who Infested the China Sea, From 1807 to 1810*, London: Oriental Translation Fund, 1831.

Gomes, Luis G., *Lendas Chinesas de Macau*, Macau: Notícias de Macau, Macau-Oriente, 1951.

Gray, John Henry, *China: A History of the Laws, Manners, and Customs of the People*, Vol. I, William Gow Gregor, ed., London: Macmillan and Co., 1878.

Guillén-Nuñez, César, *Macau*, Hong Kong: Oxford University Press, 1984.

Hadley, Leila, *Give Me the World*, London: The Travel Book Club, 1958.

Hamilton, Alexander, *A New Account of the East Indies*, 2 Vols., Edinburgh: John Mosman, 1727.

Hickey, William, *Memoirs of William Hickey*, Vol. IV (1790–1809), Alfred Spencer, ed., London: Hurst & Blackett, 1925.

Hunter, William C., *Bits of Old China*, London: Kegan Paul, Trench & Co., 1885.

Hunter, William C., *The 'Fan Kwae' at Canton Before Treaty Days 1825–1844*, London: Kegan Paul, 1882.

Hurley, R. C., *The Tourists' Guide to Canton, The West River and Macao*, 2nd edn., Hong Kong: Published by the author, 1898.

Itier, Jules, *Journal d'un Voyage en chine en 1843, 1844, 1845, 1846*, Vol. I, Paris: Chez Dauvin et Fontaine, 1848.

Low, Harriet, *Harriet Low: My Mother's Journal*, Katherine Hillard, ed., Boston: George H. Ellis, 1900.

Lilius, Aleko E., *I Sailed with Chinese Pirates*, J. W. Arrowsmith, 1930, reprinted Oxford University Press, 1991.

Linebarger, Paul, *Sun Yat Sen and the Chinese Republic*, New York and London: The Century Co., 1925.

Little, Mrs Archibald, *The Land of the Blue Gown*, 2nd edn., London: T. Fisher Unwin, 1902.

Little, Mrs Archibald, *A Millionaire's Courtship*, London: T. Fisher Unwin, 1906.

Locklin, Gerald I., *The Macao/Hong Kong Trip*, Dorset: Tears in the Fence, 1996.

Loviot, Fanny, *A Lady's Captivity Among Chinese Pirates in the Chinese Seas*, Amelia B. Edwards trans., London: Geo Routledge & Co, 1859.

Medhurst, W. H., *China: Its State and Prospects with special reference to the spread of The Gospel*, London: John Snow, 1838.

Mendoza, Juan Gonzalez de, *The History of the Great and Mighty Kingdom of China and the situation thereof . . .* , Sir George T. Staunton, ed., London: The Hakluyt Society, 1854.

Michie, Alexander, *The Englishman in China during the Victorian Era*, Vol. II, Edinburgh and London: William Blackwood and Sons, 1900.

Milne, William, *Memoirs of the Rev. William Milne, D.D.*, Robert Morrison, ed., Malacca: The Mission Press, 1824.

Montalto de Jesus, C. A., *Historic Macao, International Traits in China Old and New*, Macao: Silesian Printing Press and Tipografia Mercantil, 1926, reprinted Oxford University Press, 1984.

Mundy, Peter, *Itinerarium Mundii—Sundry Relations of certaine Voiages, Journeies ettc*, MS Rawl.A.315, The Bodelian Library, University of Oxford.

Nieuhof, Johannes, *An Embassy from the East India Company of the United Provinces to the Grand Tartar Cham, Emperor of China, 1655*, John Ogilby, trans., White-Friers: John Ogilby, 1673.

Pearson, John, *A Life of Ian Fleming, Creator of James Bond*, Coronet Books: Hodder and Stoughton, 1989.

Penfield, Frederic Courtland, *Wanderings East of Suez in Ceylon, India, China & Japan*, London: George Bell & Sons, 1907.

Pessanha, Camilo, *Clepsidra e Outras Poemas de Camilo Pessanha*, João de Castro Osório, ed., Lisbon: Ediçoes Ática, 1969.

Pires, Daniel, ed., *Homenagem a Camilo Pessanha*, Macau: Instituto Português do Oriente, Instituto Cultural de Macau, 1990.

Shaplen, Robert, *A Corner of the World*, London: Cresset Press, 1950.

Silva, Frederic A., *All Our Yesterdays, The Sons of Macao, Their History and Heritage*, California: Uniao Macanese Americana, 1979, reprinted with revisions, Macau: Livros do Oriente, 1996.

Sirr, Henry Charles, *China and the Chinese*, Vol. I, London: Wm. S. Orr & Co., 1849.

Sonnerat, Pierre, *Voyage aux Indes Orientales et à la Chine, faite au ordre du roi depuis 1774 jusqu'à 1781*, Vol. II, Paris: n.p., 1782.

Strassberg, Richard, *The World of K'ung Shang-jen: A Man of Letters in Early Ch'ing China*, New York: Columbia University Press, 1983.

Teixeira, Manuel, *Macau Durante a Guerra*, Macau: n.p., n.d.

Tiffany, Osmond, Jr., *The Canton Chinese or The American's Sojourn in the Celestial Empire*, Boston and Cambridge: James Munroe and Company, 1849.

Thomson, John, *The Straits of Malacca Indo-China and China or Ten Years' Travels, Adventures and Residence Abroad*, London: Sampson Low, Marston, Low, & Searle, 1875, reprinted as *Thomson's China: Travels and Adventures of a Nineteenth-century Photographer*, Oxford University Press, 1993.

Turner, J. A., *Kwang Tung or Five Years in South China*, London: S. W. Partridge & Co., 1894, reprinted Oxford University Press, 1982.

Wright, George Newenham, *China in a series of views drawn by T. Allom, with historical and descriptive notices by G. N. Wright*, London: Fisher, Son & Co., 1843.

Zhang Rulin and Yin Guangren, eds., *Aomen jilue*, Guangzhou: Guangdong Gaodeng Jiaoyu Chuban She, 1988 (originally published 1751).

From *The Tourists' Guide to Canton, The West R*

The streets named on this plan are the principal thorough-fares from one point of interest to another and tourists are recommended to keep, as much as possible, to them.

No. 1   Barrier

No. 2   Lui Fong Miu, Monument to Governor Amaral

No. 3   Sea Bathing Place

No. 4   Bella Vista, evening resort for cool sea breeze

No. 5   Flora, Governor's Summer Palace

No. 6   Lighthouse

No. 7   Military Hospital

No. 8   Public Gardens

No. 9   Military Club

No. 10   French Consulate

No. 11   Consul for Italy and Siam

No. 12   Roman Catholic Cathedral

No. 13   Chinese Tobacco Manufactory

No. 14   Ruin, Façade of San Paulo

No. 15   Camoens Gardens

No. 16   Camoens Gardens: The Poet's Grotto and Bust

No. 17   'Fantan' Gambling Saloon

No. 18   'Fantan' Gambling Saloon

No. 19   San Domingo Church

No. 20 } Hing Kee's Family Hotel —
No. 21 } front entrance

No. 22   Post Office

No. 23   Telegraph Office

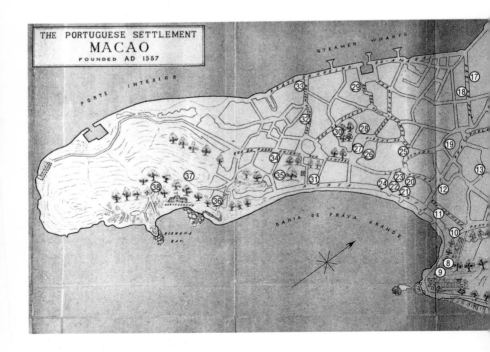